Industrial Strength Bluegrass

MUSIC IN AMERICAN LIFE

A list of books in the series appears at the end of this book.

Industrial Strength Bluegrass

Southwestern Ohio's Musical Legacy

Edited by
FRED BARTENSTEIN
and CURTIS W. ELLISON

Foreword by
NEIL V. ROSENBERG

UNIVERSITY OF ILLINOIS PRESS
Urbana, Chicago, and Springfield

Foreword

NEIL V. ROSENBERG

TODAY BLUEGRASS MUSIC is internationally recognized as one of America's vital musical arts.[1] Southwestern Ohio's bluegrass scene was central to the development of this art. The region is still one of the wellsprings of bluegrass activity. If there are fewer full-time professionals than in previous years, a far larger number of people in the area now play and listen to bluegrass for their own enjoyment than ever before. Ohio furnishes one of the highest numbers of subscribers to *Bluegrass Unlimited*, the leading national monthly for followers of this music, and also has one of the highest numbers of annual bluegrass festivals. What was at first a new music, built on old traditions by a few key figures in the Appalachian migrant community, is now itself a widespread tradition whose words and sounds evoke for many people images of an old home and of friends and relations who brought a way of life from the hills and coalfields.

Bluegrass music originated with Kentucky-born mandolinist and singer Bill Monroe and His Blue Grass Boys. A featured artist on Nashville's WSM Grand Ole Opry since 1939, who recorded on major labels Victor, Columbia, and Decca (MCA), Monroe oversaw the development of what folk music pundit Alan Lomax called in 1959 with characteristic hyperbole "the first true orchestral form in five hundred years of Anglo-American music."[2] Based on traditional styles and repertoires, it offered innovative vocal harmonies and newly composed songs by musicians who accompanied themselves in distinctive styles on guitar, mandolin, fiddle, bass, and five-string banjo. Monroe assembled his definitive band in 1946–1948, with guitarist Lester Flatt, banjo picker Earl Scruggs, fiddler Chubby Wise, and bassist-comedian "Cedric Rainwater" (Howard Watts). In cities of southwestern Ohio—such as Cincinnati, Dayton, Hamilton, Middletown, Springfield, and their surrounding areas—the radio broadcasts of this influential group were especially popular with the many people who had recently moved in from the upland South.

This new music, which almost everyone at that time identified simply as "hillbilly music," came in person to Dayton in February 1947, when Bill Monroe (then thirty-five years old) played before an audience of over four thousand. For several members of the crowd, the concert had a life-altering impact, leading to careers as professional bluegrass musicians. Pike County, Kentucky, native Scotty Jackson, just six months old, had recently moved to Dayton with his parents:

> My mother told me that my aunt, my dad, and herself took me . . . to see Bill Monroe and His Blue Grass Boys. Playing with him that night were Lester Flatt and Earl Scruggs: bluegrass as we know it today. Although I was too young to remember that show, which had to be the ultimate, I think that must have had something to do with the way I grew to love bluegrass. Maybe it was embedded in my subconscious mind or something, at least I would like to think so. . . . I was the only one of us kids that cared anything about bluegrass music—I still say it was from the Bill Monroe thing in Dayton.[3]

Also in the audience was a somewhat older Hyden, Kentucky, native living in Dayton, fifteen-year-old Bobby Osborne. A fan of Ernest Tubb, he'd emulated the singing of the Texas Troubadour until recently when his voice changed. He then began learning to sing Monroe's songs and listening closely to Monroe on the Opry. After seeing the band in person, he got thumb and finger picks so he could play the guitar like Lester Flatt.

Appalachian migrants listening to Kentuckian Monroe and playing for other Appalachian natives—this was how bluegrass came to southwestern Ohio. The region is a corridor extending roughly fifty miles northward from the Kentucky/Ohio/Indiana border, with one end marked by Cincinnati and the other by Dayton and Springfield. Into this urbanized and industrialized region, during the 1940s and '50s, moved hundreds of thousands of people whom the Ohioans called hillbillies, or Kentuckians, or briarhoppers, or briars. Originally terms of contempt spoken by others, these words, particularly "briar," were ultimately adopted with cultural pride by the working-class folk from rural Kentucky, Tennessee, and neighboring areas who came to southwestern Ohio seeking a better life.

Some Kentuckians—like Robert Osborne of Hyden, father of Bobby, Louise, and Sonny, or like Bob Lilly of Harlan County, father of Mike and Keith—were adults leaving the subsistence of the farm or the dangers of the coal mine for safer and more lucrative factory work. Others were youths like Harley "Red" Allen, from Pigeon Roost, near Harlan, who "wanted to get out of that place soon as I turned nine or ten years old."[4] He believed there were better places and left the holler to see what the rest of the world was like. Others were just small children who came because the family was moving. Many headed to Ohio because a sister, cousin, or uncle was already there. Those who were old enough when they left to remember the old home are likely to still think of it as home, but they also created a new home and a new way of life in southwestern Ohio—changing its culture and their own in many ways. With a new way of life came new musical traditions.

The first generation of Ohio bluegrass musicians grew up "down home" with traditional Southern music and early country music. It was heard in the home from older relatives, parents, and older siblings who sang, played the guitar, fiddle, or banjo. It was in the church. The old-time topics and musical styles came in modern shapes from the radio, in programs of hillbilly music broadcast out of Southern urban centers like Knoxville, Bristol, Raleigh, and Nashville; listening to the radio was a family or community experience. Occasionally someone owned a few records, but these and the machines needed to play them were a luxury that relatively few could afford.

When the young people arrived in southwestern Ohio, they found the music they were familiar with on local radio stations like WPFB in Middletown, hosted by Smokey Ward; or WCKY in Cincinnati, hosted by Nelson King. Gradually they met others like them, maybe not from *their* down home but from another, similar down home—fellow "briars" who shared their enthusiasm for country music. In the early 1950s the country music they liked was just beginning to receive the label "bluegrass." For them it was a vital new music. But many bluegrass songs were about the old home. Bluegrass instruments, particularly the banjo and the fiddle, were familiar reminders of the music played by earlier generations from back home, yet they were played in new ways.

This combination of old and new was a perfect metaphor for the lives of people who sought to preserve the old ways from home while creating a new life. The assembly-line discipline that their new jobs demanded was reflected in the tightly organized structure of the bluegrass band, in which each musician had a special part to sing and a special job to do on their instrument. Down home the most popular early bluegrass vocal format was the duet, which gave plenty of room for individual harmonic variation and freedom. In Ohio the bluegrass musicians gravitated toward the vocal trio, a more complex harmonic form that required careful planning and skill in execution.

The pace and intensity of factory work was echoed in the pace and intensity of bluegrass; as Alan Lomax—always ready with a handy metaphor—said, it was "folk music with overdrive."[5] While the old-time banjo of their fathers had a soft and plunky sound, the young Appalachian migrants made their bluegrass banjos sound loud and metallic. When bar owners would pay for only three musicians, the instruments abandoned were the bass, its rhythm taken by the guitar's bass strings, and the fiddle, its lead voice taken by the mandolin, which could also provide the percussive "chop" that delineated the rhythmic structure of the music.

In the early 1950s the young musicians of southwestern Ohio were working to master the intricacies of bluegrass, shaping the music to their needs and tastes. They entered talent contests and appeared as guests on local radio shows. For some it was a passing fancy—recreation—but for talented others a musical life unfolded. Playing on radio and in local taverns and bars, they worked to move up and out, to place their music on records, to build a career. Bob Osborne went south to apprentice with the Lonesome Pine Fiddlers and the Stanley Brothers. Sonny Osborne, Carlos Brock, and Noah Crase worked with Bill Monroe on Nashville's Grand Ole Opry. Frank Wakefield went north to play in the bars of Detroit and work with the new bands springing up among the Appalachian migrants there.

For young men whose relatives and friends were punching the clock at local factories, the prospect of playing music—getting paid to do something you enjoyed and were creative at—could be very appealing. With it came the excitement of travel, the attention of women, and the possibility of stardom. But beneath the glamour lay a hard and risky business. For most it meant weeks, months, or years in rough-and-tumble bars. Reminiscing about the dues they paid, bluegrass veterans offer a colorful catalog of venues: Ruby's White Sands, Aunt Maudie's Country Garden, the Hilltop Inn/Tavern, Keg #1, Keg #2, Otto's Café, the Mecca Bar, the Ken-Mill Café, the Mermaid, Johnnie's, the Blazing Stump, Dick's Tavern, Charlie's Nite Club, Little Mickey's, the Ring Bar, Babe's Place, the Horseshoe Bar, Tom's Tavern, the Friendly Inn, the Circle Bar, the Family Room, the Golden Fly.

New friendships were made and down-home connections reinforced in these crowded bars. But they could also be as alienating to the musicians as the industrial labor they replaced. They were places where people came and went noisily, often not caring about the music or the musicians; where fickle owners offered minimal wages and abysmal working conditions; where fights were constantly erupting. As Suzanne Thomas of the Hotmud Family put it, "People in Dayton work hard, live hard—need to let their hair down quick."[6] Mike Lilly was seventeen and picking banjo for the Powell Brothers in one such Dayton bar:

> One night, just a mess of truckers and cops got into it in this one Dayton bar we had been picking at regular. We were picking on stage and looking down at them boys. They were going at it like cats and dogs. Before it was over, some cop got mad and fired his gun. His bullet grazed me in the leg and went right through Jack's new bass. Lord, I cut my teeth on some good ones that night![7]

There was the fatigue of the road, the threat of failed marriage, the pitfall of drink, and the unfortunate reality of untrustworthy promoters. Just keeping a band together in the face of all these problems was a challenge. But the southwestern Ohio bluegrassers were committed, ambitious, and innovative. By the mid-1950s they were exporting their music. Between 1956 and 1958 the Osborne Brothers and Red Allen, recording in Nashville and performing out of Wheeling, West Virginia, set new standards for vocal trios and hot instrumental styles with classics like "Ruby, Are You Mad?" and "Once More." In Detroit Frank Wakefield recorded his acclaimed composition "New Camptown Races," turning the world of bluegrass mandolin upside down. In Cincinnati Noah Crase planted the seeds of melodic-style banjo with his recording of "Noah's Breakdown."

As their reputations grew, they became recognized leaders in the music that by the early 1960s pickers in the area were affectionately calling "grass." Now there was a flourishing local bluegrass scene involving people whose parents and relatives were from down home or who had neighbors and friends with down-home connections. Growing up in sections of town known as "little Kentucky," they heard this music on the local radio shows and at local bars.

And there were others listening to it as well. In March 1960 the Osborne Brothers were invited to play at Antioch College in nearby Yellow Springs and were amazed to find that not only were there college students who wanted to hear bluegrass, but a few of them were even trying to play the music. Bluegrass was moving into the folk revival, with the Osbornes being the first to play a college concert. Within a few years Red Allen and Frank Wakefield would be heard on a New York City folk music label, Folkways, in an album produced by a young New Jersey bluegrass acolyte named David Grisman. The music moved in other ways too, as in 1964 the Osborne Brothers joined the cast of the Grand Ole Opry and began working to integrate the bluegrass and Nashville sounds with a string of hits that won vocalist of the year awards for them into the early seventies.

By the late 1960s a new younger generation of southwestern Ohio bluegrass musicians was coming up. Larry Sparks, born to Kentucky migrants in Lebanon, Ohio, in 1947, followed Bobby Osborne's example by working briefly with the Stanley Brothers before Carter Stanley's death in 1966. In 1967 Sparks became Ralph Stanley's first lead singer and guitarist, setting a high standard for vocal and instrumental artistry, and by 1969 he was leading his own band, developing a unique soulful sound. When two Appalachian migrants from Dayton, Mike Lilly and Wendy Miller, joined Sparks's band in 1971, it quickly became recognized as another classic group.

Others continued to move into the area. In 1964 another Stanley Brothers veteran, Paul "Moon" Mullins, came to WPFB. Telling his listeners that WPFB stood for "We Play For Briars," he soon became the most popular bluegrass DJ in the area. One of his early honors was being asked to share master of ceremonies duties at Bill Monroe's second annual Bean Blossom bluegrass festival with WSM's Grant Turner. In the late 1960s Mullins and Monroe alumnus Noah Crase formed the Valley Ramblers, featured on a weekly TV program over WKEF, channel 22, out of Dayton. In 1974 he helped form another classic group in the region that also included Noah Crase, called the Boys from Indiana.

Other newcomers to the musical scene sought new patterns. The Hotmud Family, which began life in the early seventies on Dayton Street in Yellow Springs, mixed country, folk, and old-time music at first. Relocating to Spring Valley, they played bluegrass and folk festivals as well as the bars; they thought of themselves as a working band for a down-home country audience. They moved closer to mainstream bluegrass when Toronto's Mariposa Folk Festival told them they already had an old-time band and asked if they could play bluegrass. They not only played the festivals and bars, but in the mid-1970s they also did a series of concerts at Dayton Public Schools aimed at making those from Appalachia and their children aware of their own heritage.

Another new band trying new ways was the Dry Branch Fire Squad. They were led by Virginia native Ron Thomason, who grew up listening to bluegrass on the radio on auto trips back home from Ohio with his dad, who was stationed in the army there. Only after going through a round of folk revival music did he come to really appreciate bluegrass. In this he was something like Mike Lilly, who played in a family bluegrass band when he was ten and eleven and then spent seven years in rock and roll before returning to pick banjo with Larry Sparks. Thomason, who also spent some time working with Ralph Stanley, set out to make solid music that preserved the purity that comes with being an amateur in the first sense: playing for the love of it. By keeping day jobs, he argued, his band did not have to "sell out" in order to succeed. Other new bands appeared in the 1970s and '80s. Among them were Red Allen's sons, who bridged the generation gap with a new repertoire built on the bluegrass fundamentals instilled by their expert father.

Bluegrass in southwestern Ohio evolved in many different musical directions, shaped by strains of gospel, traditional, progressive, folk, "newgrass," new acoustic, Nashville, and other sounds. What ties it all together is the sense of down-home appropriateness, the nurturing of skills in the rough but enthusiastic environment of working-class bars, and the belief that it is an appropriate art form in which to make a personal statement about life in Northern cities. A new urban folk music, nurtured and shaped by a folk community in an industrial setting, has made the world familiar with southwestern Ohio's bluegrass. Many facets of the region's rich musical heritage are explored and celebrated in this book, a welcome addition to the literature on bluegrass.

Notes

1. An earlier version of this essay appeared in the program booklet for "The Dayton Bluegrass Reunion: An All-Star Salute to Dayton's 40-year Bluegrass Legacy," presented

by Cityfolk, a nonprofit organization designed to support the active awareness of and appreciation of folk traditions in the Dayton metropolitan area at Montgomery County Memorial Hall on April 22, 1989. Performers included the Allen Brothers, Red Allen, Porter Church, Noah Crase, the Dry Branch Fire Squad, David Harvey, the Hotmud Family, Paul "Moon" Mullins and the Traditional Grass, the Osborne Brothers, Larry Sparks, Red Spurlock, and Frank Wakefield.

2. Alan Lomax, "Bluegrass Underground: Folk Music with Overdrive," *Esquire*, October 1959, 108.

3. Donald G. Dallich, "Scotty Jackson and the New Frontier," *Bluegrass Unlimited*, August 1982, 23–24.

4. Melissa Green, "That Old Lonesome High Hollerin' Tenor," *Ohio*, July 1988, 54.

5. Lomax, "Bluegrass Underground."

6. Charles Wolfe, "The Hotmud Family: An Interview," *Pickin'*, November 1976, 7.

7. Robert Leach, "Mike Lilly," *Bluegrass Unlimited*, November 1986, 36–39.

Preface

I STARTED VISITING southwestern Ohio in 1971 and moved here from the East Coast in 1975. At that time the region still boasted one of the world's densest populations of bluegrass virtuosos; their recordings and appearances had gained national and even international attention. It was a remarkable scene, analogous to New Orleans' jazz heyday of the 1920s or Chicago's blues heyday of the 1950s.

My earlier exposure to bluegrass had been in southwestern Virginia, Piedmont North Carolina, metro New York, and New England. As editor of *Muleskinner News* (1969–1974), a festival director and emcee, a record collector, and an amateur scholar of music history, I had learned that the Cincinnati/Dayton corridor was one of the richest producers of bluegrass talent, product, and innovation. Before I got here, I had already met Red Allen, the Osborne Brothers, Larry Sparks, and Earl Taylor, and had played in a band with Joe Isaacs and Frank Wakefield.

The very first week that I arrived for a job in Dayton city government, I found myself playing guitar with Jack Lynch at Otto's Paradise Inn on heavily Appalachian Wayne Avenue. My girlfriend, Joy—now my wife—had been taught by Ruby and Opal, two elderly regulars, to dive under the table at the first sign of trouble in such joints, as drunks tend to throw or shoot high. I listened to Paul "Moon" Mullins on Middletown's WPFB and shopped for records at Lake Jewelry in Franklin. Later in 1975 I sat in regularly with the Katie Laur Band at Aunt Maudie's Country Garden in the Over-the-Rhine district of Cincinnati and produced three vinyl albums at Rusty York's Jewel Studio in the city's Mt. Healthy neighborhood. By 1979 I was hosting a weekly bluegrass show on WONE-AM, the Top 40 country station in Dayton. As the years passed, I absorbed more and more of the legacy and culture of southwestern Ohio. I was happy that while raising a family and building a career in management and consulting I could also indulge my musical passions in one of the world's great meccas for bluegrass.

Fifteen years into my Ohio residence, it became evident that the glory years were coming to an end. Not only was the industrial base of the region shifting, but bars were dropping live entertainment, prominent bands and record companies were locating elsewhere, the recorded legacy of the area was not making the transition from vinyl LPs and cassette tapes to CDs, and the legendary figures of the 1940s, '50s, and '60s were starting to pass from the scene. There was still a lot of bluegrass on local airwaves, and plenty at nearby concerts and festivals, but Cincinnati/Dayton had ceased to be the creative nexus it once had been.

Two notable events marked the passing of an era. The City of Middletown's Division of Parks and Recreation, with support from the Ohio Arts and Humanities Councils and Miller Brewing Company, put on an event called "Middletown Traditions: Appalachian Ties" on June 11 and 12, 1983. That program included numerous regional performers, among them former legendary WPFB personalities Smokey Ward, "Old Joe" Clark, and Paul "Moon" Mullins. A twelve-page program book described the area's bluegrass music heritage with well-researched text and photographs. On April 22, 1989, Cityfolk, Dayton's traditional arts organization, presented "The Dayton Bluegrass Reunion: An All-Star Salute to Dayton's 40-Year Bluegrass Legacy." Supporters included the Ohio Arts Council, the *Dayton Daily News*, and Our Common Heritage (Dayton's Appalachian community development organization).[1] Many of the important bluegrass artists whose careers started in southwestern Ohio—still at the height of their musical ability—gathered at Memorial Hall, the very location where Bill Monroe's classic band had kicked off the regional boom in 1947. I was a participant in both the Middletown and the Dayton events.

In December 2002 I was invited to join the board of Bgrass Inc., an organization seeking to document the rich history of bluegrass in the Cincinnati/Dayton region. I would ultimately become its chair. Notable accomplishments included a partnership with Miami University; creation of a website encyclopedia profiling significant individuals, organizations, and locations in bluegrass history;[2] and a nationally distributed radio special on the history of the Osborne Brothers. Some of the most active participants were Barbara Brady, Wayne Clyburn, Joe Colvin, Kevin Feazell, Bernie Fisher, Al Jamison, Grady Kirkpatrick, Tom Kopp Katie Laur, Mary Jo Leet, Mac McDivitt,[3] Joe Mullins, Lisa Mullins (no relation to Joe), and Jon Weisberger. After a period of inactivity, Bgrass Inc. evolved into the Southwestern Ohio Bluegrass Music Heritage Project.

One catalyst for the successor project—and ultimately this volume—was the publication of *Bluegrass in Baltimore: The Hard Drivin' Sound and Its Legacy*, by journalist Tim Newby.[4] I knew that Baltimore/Washington on the east and Cincinnati/Dayton on the west were the essential urban forges in which the emergent bluegrass genre developed during its first half century. If Baltimore could have a book documenting events and accomplishments of that region, we should have one too. And I was aware that not only were there fewer surviving participants of the 1947–1989 scene, but its documentation—preceding the digital age—was typically from ephemeral and disappearing sources.

Having organized four other books over the last decade, I knew what a huge task it would be to pull together a credible regional history. Knowing that Curt Ellison, a historian and author with a focus on country music, was preparing to retire from Miami University, I tried convincing him to author the book, offering to donate my services as a researcher. He countered with an alternative proposal: a public lecture series that would commission multiple authors to each prepare a topic about the region's bluegrass legacy and then submit their work in chapters that could be anthologized. Luckily, we knew knowledgeable scholars, artists, journalists, and professional as well as amateur historians who would be willing to research, present, and write about key topics in the story of this region's rich bluegrass music history. Miami University Regionals Appalachian Studies endorsed the project and became its primary sponsor.

The Southwestern Ohio Bluegrass Music Heritage Project turned into a multifaceted, ongoing initiative. A coordinating committee includes Bgrass Inc. stalwarts Mac McDivitt and broadcaster/bandleader Joe Mullins, artist and local historian Sam Ashworth of the Middletown Historical Society, Valerie Elliott of the Smith Library of Regional History in Oxford, Brian Powers of the Public Library of Greater Cincinnati and Hamilton County, and Matthew Smith of Miami Appalachian Studies. Curt Ellison (the previous head of Miami Appalachian Studies) and I cochair the project and serve as editors for this anthology.

Beyond the lecture series and book, project achievements to date include a live concert with Joe Mullins and the Radio Ramblers and guest Bobby Osborne, an updated online encyclopedia, and an eight-panel traveling display supported by Miami University, the Smith Library of Regional History, and the Greene County Public Library. A permanent archival collection is held in Oxford at the Smith History Library. With Miami's support, Joe Mullins is spearheading a Smithsonian Folkways recording project to showcase important bluegrass songs associated with the region.

This anthology documents much, but not all, of the bluegrass legacy of southwestern Ohio. Professionally recorded and performed bluegrass is the tip of an iceberg. As in baseball, there is a vast substrate of amateur, semiprofessional, and avocational music making that the book barely covers. Great performing artists learn their craft and build a following within that environment, but most of the "weekend warriors" of bluegrass perform for their own enjoyment and that of friends, family, and neighbors. There are informal jam sessions in the Cincinnati/Dayton region that have continued on a weekly or monthly basis for decades at word-of-mouth venues: VFW halls, FOP lodges, vehicle repair shops, hardware stores, and the like. While the history, sociology, anthropology, and musicology of such phenomena have yet to be fully studied, we observe that many of the participants, certainly the older ones, are first- and second-generation Appalachian migrants who impart their skills and repertoire to younger enthusiasts.[5]

I am proud to have played a role in documenting the important part that southwestern Ohio bluegrass has played in the evolution of the genre and am grateful for the years of enjoyment and camaraderie I have experienced here as a witness, listener, and participant.

—FRED BARTENSTEIN

Before his iconic voice gained mass-culture fame in the Coen Brothers' movie *O Brother, Where Art Thou?* Dr. Ralph Stanley of Dickenson County, Virginia, had earned a place in the hearts of Appalachian migrants who improved their lives financially in southwestern Ohio but carried lifelong emotional attachments to former family homes in the mountains.[6] My introduction to Dr. Ralph came in the early 1990s, at an old movie house rechristened the Hamilton Music Theatre, in a postindustrial Ohio town where he often packed the house with working people. By that time Stanley had traveled across southwestern Ohio hundreds of times and knew it intimately as the home of a major fan base; a region with congenial recording studios; a source of musicians for his band, the Clinch Mountain Boys; and the place where he met his wife, Jimmi. But Dr. Ralph's deepest connection with fans occurred when he was on stage. In more than two decades of following him to diverse venues, I've seen tears run down the faces of Appalachian migrants as this master circuit rider of the past enchantingly wove an aural vision of enduring mountain life.

I grew up in an Appalachian North Alabama coal-mining town not far from the Birmingham steel mills, and I've listened to country and bluegrass music all my life. Well before the days of television, I tuned in faithfully to radio station WVOK in Birmingham. I remember its hushed reports on the day Hank Williams died. And because I thought it exotic to be able to hear them at such a distance, I often listened late at night to country songs beaming south across the mountains from WCKY in Cincinnati.

The early rock and roll bands I played in during high school often performed (without knowing the term) crossover country tunes. Then after attending the University of Alabama during the heart of the civil rights era, I "went off up North" to the University of Minnesota for a graduate degree in American Studies. Ironically, I used to think, it was there I discovered my deeper appreciation for country music. Today I know that physical distance from one's Appalachian home can sometimes magnify its attraction.

Taking a position at Miami University in 1970 placed me in fertile ground for seeing live performances of country and bluegrass artists in towns and cities across Ohio's Miami River Valley. While teaching for years a course about the history of country music, I discovered that Neil V. Rosenberg's *Bluegrass: A History* could make lifelong converts of students whom it first introduced to the music.

Living here also allowed me the academic pleasure of firsthand ethnographic observation focused on the performance of an engaging popular musical art. My formal efforts along those lines began inadvertently in Dayton at a 1991 Hara Arena concert by Conway Twitty and George Jones, where I absorbed their music but was even more fascinated by behavior patterns of the audience while they were on stage. Four years later, with notes from more than seventy-five such encounters across southwestern Ohio and six other states in a variety of concerts, gospel singings, music festivals, theme parks, historic sites, shrines, music museums, theaters, and tourist destinations to ponder, I wrote up what I had found. *Country Music Culture: From Hard Times to Heaven* was a book about mainstream country music that combined a survey of key figures in the music's history with ethnographic observation of fan and artist interactions at a moment when the music was breaking new ground in pop culture.[7] That project ultimately taught me, however, that this particular music can play distinctly critical roles in the actual lives of working- and middle-class Americans.

Even though venues in southwestern Ohio figured importantly in my first effort to write significantly about the topic, *Country Music Culture* did not do justice to the importance of this region in fostering bluegrass music. Fortunately, in this project I'm privileged to join a group of scholars, artists, musicians, and archivists who are determined to tell the regional and national story of bluegrass music in southwestern Ohio during its formative years. And I'm honored to team up with Fred Bartenstein, whose vast knowledge of bluegrass music and zeal for sharing it has inspired both the Southwestern Ohio Bluegrass Music Heritage Project generally and this volume particularly.

The story of bluegrass music outside the mountains magnifies a larger one of how Appalachian migrants and their descendants helped reshape American life in the twentieth century. It began with migration to the central Midwest and elsewhere and includes the spreading influence of their work ethic, religion, literature, language, folkways, foodways, and family structures. And that influence certainly includes the novel music business created to serve them: the radio stations, recording studios, record labels, nightclubs and other performance venues, churches, gospel music showcases, and music festivals that gave rise to prominent artists and built the national visibility of bluegrass music. This project and this book were born to tell that story, and I'm proud to be part of it.

—CURTIS W. ELLISON

Notes

1. Neil V. Rosenberg's essay in the Dayton Bluegrass Reunion program book was updated as the foreword of this volume.

2. Cincinnati-Dayton Ohio Bluegrass Heritage, swohiobluegrass.com.

3. Mac McDivitt, a retired IRS auditor who first attended local Stanley Brothers concerts in the late 1940s, is an amazing expert on local recordings and performances and the principal author of our online encyclopedia.

4. Tim Newby, *Bluegrass in Baltimore: The Hard Drivin' Sound and Its Legacy* (Jefferson, NC: McFarland, 2015).

5. The online encyclopedia includes this entry for "OKI Bluegrass Association": "The Ohio, Kentucky, Indiana Bluegrass Association was established in October of 1980 with the purpose of promoting, encouraging, and preserving bluegrass music. To those ends the organization has held monthly meetings, jam sessions, and issued a newsletter. It has organized and held bluegrass festivals at Roundeye's Park near Laura, and at the Polish Club park at 3690 Needmore Road in Dayton, to raise funds as well as give local bands a chance to play and earn some money." swohiobluegrass.com.

6. Ralph Stanley was awarded an honorary doctorate in music from Lincoln Memorial University of Harrogate, Tennessee, in 1976 and another from Yale University in 2014.

7. Curtis W. Ellison, *Country Music Culture: From Hard Times to Heaven* (Jackson: University Press of Mississippi, 1995).

Acknowledgments

MANY PEOPLE AND ORGANIZATIONS made this book possible. It was initiated in a conversation between the editors during the May 2016 International Country Music Conference at Belmont University in Nashville. Miami University Regionals Appalachian Studies subsequently agreed to underwrite a lecture series where invited speakers would also submit their presentations for possible publication. We especially thank Moira Casey, Ellen Paxton, Matthew Smith, Jackie Webb, and Sheila Williams, as well as Scott Berry, Howard Epstein, Ladonna Hoskins, and Perry Richardson at Miami Regionals for their support of the lecture series, as well as the larger project that has evolved from it.

After we proposed a set of speakers and Fred Bartenstein initially contacted them, Curt Ellison and Miami Appalachian Studies staff organized well-attended public lectures in Hamilton and Cincinnati that began in spring 2017. Speakers Mac McDivitt, Nathan McGee, Daniel Mullins, Larry Nager, and Phillip J. Obermiller expanded their presentations into chapters for the anthology. Fred Bartenstein, Jon Hartley Fox, Rick Good, and Ben Krakauer authored chapters about other key topics. Lily Isaacs and Neil V. Rosenberg generously allowed use of material from their previous publications, and Joe Mullins and Bobby Osborne agreed to let us include a transcript of their onstage discussion held during a public concert for the series.

Valerie Elliott, Mac McDivitt, Joe Mullins, and Brian Powers graciously lent their knowledge and research skills for this anthology. Shelby Dixon was an early research assistant. Sam Ashworth, who had previously designed the project's traveling exhibit, managed and organized illustrations. We are grateful to the photographers, archives, museums, and private collectors who generously provided visual images.

We thank Director Laurie Matheson and her staff at the University of Illinois Press for their keen interest and fine support, especially Angela Burton, Kevin Cunningham, Ellie Hinton, Dustin Hubbart, Tad Ringo, Michael Roux, Roberta Sparenberg, and copyeditor Jill Hughes. We're grateful to Charley Pennell for preparing the index.

Fred Bartenstein thanks Joy Bartenstein for attracting him to and keeping him in southwestern Ohio, as well as for her partnership in many bluegrass endeavors. Curt Ellison thanks Celia Ellison for unfailing editorial assistance, for willingness to hear endless country and bluegrass tunes, and for learning to like many of them.

A Southwestern Ohio Bluegrass Timeline

All locations in Ohio unless noted.

The Migration (1900–1946)

1926	Jimmie Skinner migrates to Hamilton
1937	*Renfro Valley Barn Dance* first broadcasts over WLW, Cincinnati
1938	Aubrey Holt born, Milan, Indiana
	Pete Steele records for the Library of Congress, Hamilton
	Boone County Jamboree first broadcasts over WLW, Cincinnati
1939	Lillimae Whitaker born, Roundhead
1942	Osborne family migrates to Dayton
1943	Syd Nathan founds King Records, Cincinnati
1946	Nelson King arrives at WCKY, Cincinnati

Establishment of a Bluegrass Epicenter (1947–1965)

1947	WPFB goes on the air, Middletown
	Bill Monroe's classic bluegrass band sells out Memorial Hall, Dayton
	Larry Sparks born, Lebanon
1948	"Hylo" Brown gets his nickname at *WPFB Jamboree*, Middletown
1949	Jimmie Skinner opens a record shop in Cincinnati
	Noah Crase's family migrates to Middletown
	Red Allen migrates to Middletown
	Flatt and Scruggs record "Foggy Mountain Breakdown," Cincinnati
1950	Frank Wakefield migrates to Dayton
	Carl Burkhardt founds Gateway-Rite Studio, Cincinnati

1951 Jimmy Martin and Bobby Osborne record for King, Cincinnati
Jim and Jesse McReynolds first record for Kentucky Records as the Virginia Trio, Cincinnati
Louise, Sonny, and Bobby Osborne record "New Freedom Bell" for Kitty Records, Dayton
1952 Reno and Smiley first record under their own name for King, Cincinnati
Rusty York migrates to Cincinnati
1953 Joe "Cannonball" Lewis cowrites and records "Before I Met You," Cincinnati
1954 Jimmy Martin and J. D. Crowe first play together at *WPFB Jamboree*, Middletown
1956 Wayne Raney joins WCKY, Cincinnati
Harley Allen born, Dayton
1958 Stanley Brothers first record for King, Cincinnati
WYSO goes on the air, Antioch College, Yellow Springs
1959 J. D. Jarvis migrates to Hamilton
1960 Osborne Brothers play the first college bluegrass concert, Yellow Springs
Earl Taylor, Jim McCall, Walter Hensley, "Boatwhistle" McIntyre and his son, "Junior," move from Baltimore to play six nights a week at the Ken-Mill Café, Cincinnati
1961 Rusty York founds Jewel Records, Mt. Healthy
Ralph and Jimmi Stanley meet at the Ken-Mill Café, Cincinnati
1962 Moore and Napier first record for King, Cincinnati
1963 Reno and Smiley last record for King, Cincinnati
Jack Lynch founds Jalyn Records, Dayton

A Bluegrass Scene with National Reach (1964–1972)

1964 Paul "Moon" Mullins arrives at WPFB, Middletown
Last broadcast of *WCKY Jamboree*, Cincinnati
Osborne Brothers leave Dayton for Nashville
Rev. William M. Jones founds Melody Records, Hamilton
1965 Joe Mullins born, Middletown
Stanley Brothers last record for King, Cincinnati
1966 Moore and Napier last record for King, Cincinnati
1967 Larry Sparks joins Ralph Stanley's Clinch Mountain Boys, Dayton
Steve Lake stages Ohio's first bluegrass festival at Chautauqua Park, Franklin
Valley Ramblers first record for Jalyn, Dayton

1968 Syd Nathan, founder of King Records, dies, Cincinnati
Lou Ukelson founds Vetco Records, Cincinnati
1969 Mike Zunis opens Sam's Bar and Grill, Dayton
1970 Joe and Lily Isaacs marry, Lebanon
First Appalachian Festival, Cincinnati
Larry Sparks forms the Lonesome Ramblers, Lebanon
Roy Lee Centers joins Ralph Stanley's Clinch Mountain Boys, Dayton
Hotmud Family organizes as a band, Yellow Springs
Rev. William M. Jones purchases Pine Tree Records and records Larry Sparks, Hamilton
1971 Lou Ukelson opens Aunt Maudie's Country Garden, Cincinnati
Ricky Skaggs and Keith Whitley first record for Jalyn, Dayton
1972 Harry Sparks and Mack Smith open Famous Old-Time Music Company, Cincinnati

New Generations (1973–1989)

1973 Boys from Indiana first record for Jewel, Cincinnati
Allen Brothers first record with their father, Red Allen, for Lemco Records, Dayton
1974 *WYSO Country Jamboree* begins live broadcasts, Dayton
1975 Katie Laur Band first records for Vetco, Cincinnati
1976 Ron Thomason organizes Dry Branch Fire Squad, Springfield
1979 Dave Evans first records for Vetco, Cincinnati
Miami University Regionals Artist Series begins programming bluegrass, Hamilton
1980 Ohio, Kentucky, Indiana (OKI) Bluegrass Association founded, Dayton
1981 Ben, Becky, and Sonya Isaacs first record with their parents for Old Homestead Records, Hamilton
Jan McLaughlin begins *Oak Street Ramble* broadcasts at WMUB, Oxford
Mick Montgomery opens Canal Street Tavern, Dayton
1983 "Middletown Traditions: Appalachian Ties" staged by City of Middletown
1985 Traditional Grass first records for private label, Middletown
1986 WOBO begins broadcasting, Batavia
Our Common Heritage produces first Mountain Days festival, Dayton
1989 Paul "Moon" Mullins leaves WPFB, Middletown
Dayton Bluegrass Reunion staged by Cityfolk, Dayton

1. Appalachian Migration

Setting the Musical Stage in Southwestern Ohio

PHILLIP J. OBERMILLER

INTERNAL MIGRATION REMAINS a hallmark of twentieth-century America. Farm families impoverished by Dust Bowl droughts sought agricultural work in California's Central Valley. The imposition of Jim Crow laws and the boll weevil infestation in the cotton-growing South forced many Black families to seek employment in the nation's cities. High birth rates and changes in the economics of both agriculture and the extractive industries impelled migration from Southern Appalachia to many of those same cities.[1]

These population movements included men, women, and children, swelling the migration streams to hundreds of thousands of people. They included the poor, blue-collar workers, and many middle-class folks as well. Nearly everyone in small-town and rural America was affected by these conditions.[2] In every case the migrants took their music with them: western swing found its way to California, while jazz and bluegrass flourished in the destination cities of Southern Black and Appalachian migrants respectively.[3]

Appalachian Migration

Migration underpins the spread of bluegrass music throughout southwestern Ohio. People have been moving into and out of what became known as the Appalachian region for centuries. Streams of migrants began to flow out of the Southern mountains after World War I, but these were mere trickles compared to what came later. The flood of out-migrants that occurred between 1940 and 1970 would be part of what became known as the Great Migration.

The downturn in the Appalachian regional economy had begun as early as the 1920s, affecting farmers in eastern Tennessee, timber workers in western

North Carolina, and coal miners in eastern Kentucky and West Virginia. Among the first to leave were African Americans and European immigrants who had been attracted to the coalfields by opportunities for work and wages but had few strong ties to the region.

Early on, some Appalachians were seasonal farmworkers who worked the onion crops in Ohio or the tomato crops in Indiana, returning home after the harvest. This back-and-forth movement is known as shuttle migration. Maintaining a homestead in the region, shuttle migrants became temporary laborers akin to the migrant farmworkers of today, although this type of migration involved both agricultural and industrial workers. During the Depression, for instance, Detroit autoworkers worked only a few months each year until the corporate quota for expected new car demand was met. For the most part, Appalachian workers returned to their home places in the mountains until they were called back to field or factory. The Depression era only increased shuttle migration. In 2004 I described typical shuttle routes:

> The first surfaced highways in the mountains brought bus lines into the Appalachian region in the late 1920s. The road-building programs of the Roosevelt administration came into the mountains in the late 1930s; north-south arteries such as Routes 23, 25, and 27 and east-west corridors such as Routes 50 and 52 made the mountains and many outlying cities accessible to each other. Although these roads were ostensibly built for commerce, they began to be used heavily by individual commuters as routes out of the mountains. An oft-repeated mountain maxim prescribes a knowledge of "readin', writin', and Route 23" as key elements for success. This bit of popular wisdom promoted the paradox that the only way to survive in the mountains was to leave them.[4]

World War II drew thousands of women and men out of the mountains into the military and the war industries. The Wright Aeronautical plant in southwestern Ohio, for example, encompassed thirty-seven acres under one roof. At its peak it employed twenty thousand workers, many of them Appalachian migrants, who turned out a total of sixty thousand military aircraft engines. Today it is the site of General Electric Evendale.[5]

Following the war, the economic bottom dropped out in the Appalachian coalfields as diesel fuel replaced coal for marine and railroad engines, oil and natural gas replaced coal for home heating, electricity replaced coal in the steel industry, and mechanization replaced miners across the board. At the same time, factories in and near cities outside the region were booming. The Great Migration involving millions of Appalachians began in earnest.

These migration streams brought hundreds of thousands of Appalachians to the Midwest. The migrants frequently started out in port-of-entry neighborhoods such as Fifth and Wayne in Dayton, Over-the-Rhine in Cincinnati,

Uptown in Chicago, or the Briggs neighborhood in Detroit. Some migrant families became trapped in a cycle of poverty that still affects them several generations later. Most, however, did not stay in the city centers for long, because their jobs were often in suburban or exurban locations. In southwestern Ohio, industrial work was plentiful at Armco, the Delco and Frigidaire Divisions of General Motors, Ford, Formica, Nutone, National Cash Register, U.S. Shoe, and Champion Paper.

The draw of Champion Paper provides a good example of why, at least in some counties of eastern Kentucky, a suitcase was commonly called a "Hamilton":

> Migrants from Kentucky were arriving in Hamilton, Ohio, as early as 1900 to take jobs at Champion Paper and other area industries. Hamilton companies actively recruited the migrants because of their mechanical skills. Local newspaper editor James Blount notes: "Some of the other industries here . . . figured that Champion was drawing enough people that they would get some of the spillover. . . . Mosler [Safe] might pick them up or some other factory." The *Hamilton Evening Journal* reported that 138 families arrived from Kentucky seeking jobs in one two-week period in 1924. "Kentuckians took Ohio without firing a shot," one Appalachian migrant recalled in a 1983 *Journal* feature on Appalachian origins.[6]

Regular industrial wages gave Southern migrants the wherewithal to enjoy their musical heritage through the purchase of instruments, records, phonographs, and radios, along with listening to jukeboxes, attending live concerts, or enjoying both live and recorded music in local churches, clubs, pubs, and restaurants. Referencing the "father of bluegrass," Bill Monroe, historian Chad Berry writes, "Monroe's new music—bluegrass, according to the film *High Lonesome*—a blend of sacred and secular, urban and rural, hill and ragtime, sentimental and blue, may have been born in the South, but it was nurtured in the North."[7]

Migration Flows

Appalachian migration flows in the 1950s and '60s were one of the largest internal migrations in our nation's history (map 1). We should imagine arrowheads at both ends of migration streams, because shuttle migration typified, at least initially, people's movements to and from the mountains. Relocation to the city was often accompanied by frequent, sometimes weekly, visits back home. The energy crisis of the 1970s put a premium on coal production and drew many migrants back to the coalfields. By the 1980s, however, the outward flows began again and have not changed direction since.

Some migrants, however, moved back to the mountains. This could be due to a family breakup where one or both spouses couldn't abide city life, for

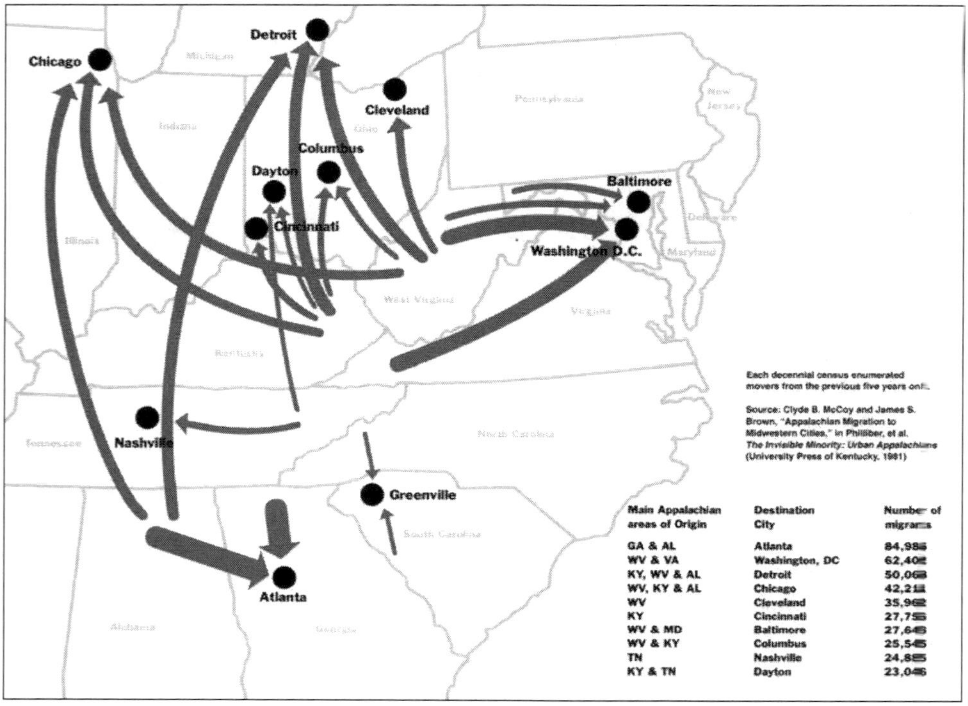

MAP 1. Migration Flows from Appalachia to Selected Cities, 1955–1960 and 1965–1970

economic reasons, or simply a preference for life as they had experienced it "down home."

Now imagine arrows running between some of the cities (map 2). Cincinnati, for example, was a major Midwestern transportation node for Appalachians on the move. The city was often a waypoint for migration to Hamilton, Dayton, Detroit, or Chicago. Folks would check in with relatives or friends to test the local job market before moving on.

This pattern of movement between and among points of origin and destinations is described as the "stem and branch" system. With a family base in the mountains and support groups along the way, people prospecting for work could branch out and seek new opportunities. The stem and branch system provided a means of communication and a safety net that reduced risk. Money also flowed through this system as those who found work sent remittances to kinfolk to enable their migration or to help support those remaining back home.

Map 3 shows the relative size of the destination city rather than the absolute number of Appalachians, but the gravity theory of migration is pretty clearly

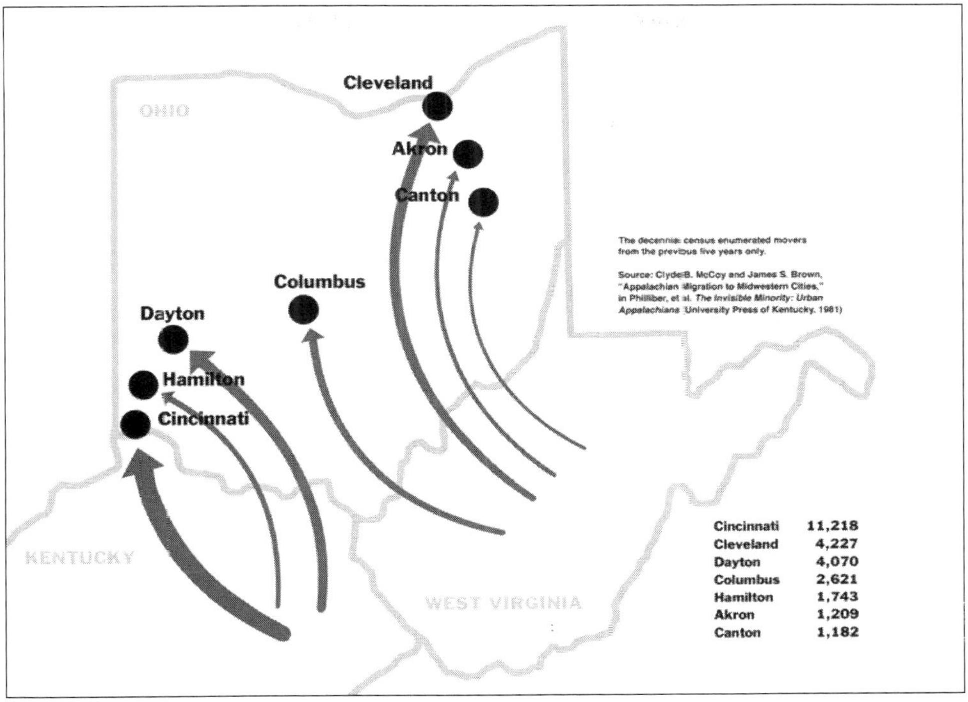

MAP 2. Migration Flows from Appalachia to Selected Cities in Ohio, 1965–1970

demonstrated, where larger populations have more opportunities that attract more migrants.

Once they got their feet on the ground, most migrants moved to the suburbs, exurbs, and small towns near major cities, as commuting to work became an option. They also started a variety of civic and social groups in southwestern Ohio, including Cincinnati's Appalachian Community Development Association and the Urban Appalachian Council (or UAC, now the Urban Appalachian Community Coalition), Dayton's Our Common Heritage, and Hamilton's O'Tucks (Ohioans from Kentucky). These groups celebrated Appalachian arts and crafts, foodways, and musical heritage through the Appalachian Festival in Cincinnati, Mountain Days in Dayton, and annual events in Hamilton.[8]

Housing played almost as important a part as job availability in determining migrant destinations. Affordable housing within reasonable driving distance of worksites allowed migrants to disperse widely across southwestern Ohio. Many migrants had moved from place to place in the coalfields, following available work, and home ownership would have hindered that flexibility. Likewise, in

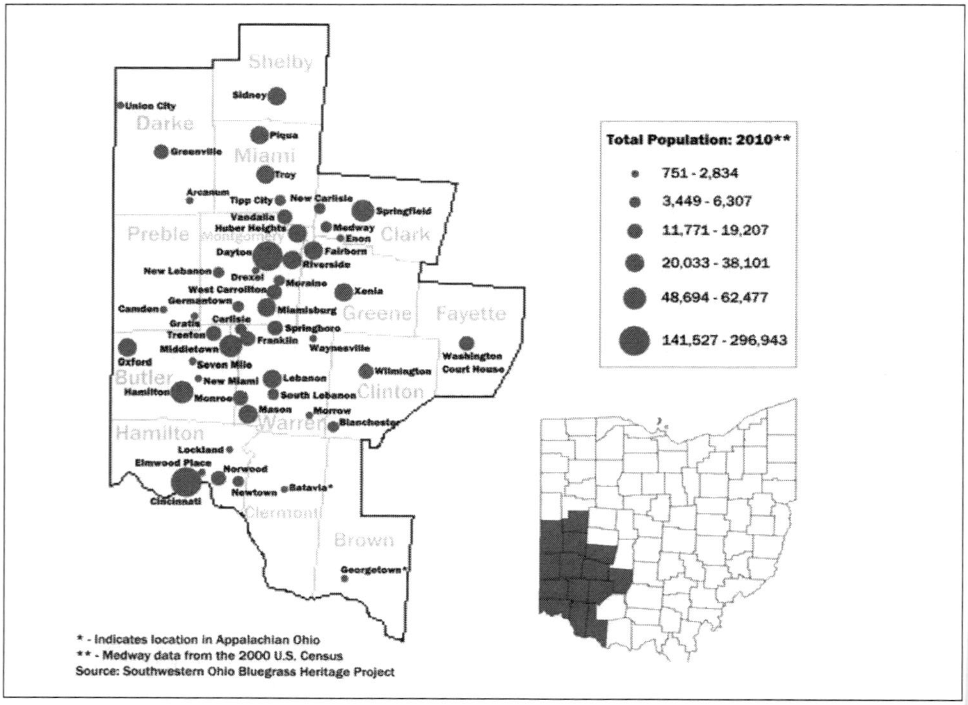

MAP 3. Selected Towns and Cities in Southwestern Ohio with High Numbers of Appalachian Residents

the cities, renting was preferred until a stable occupation and income made buying a house, however modest, feasible. Making such a purchase indicated a commitment to the new location, a difficult decision for many, but one that more often than not turned mountain migrants into urban Appalachians.

Movement along the stem and branch system evolved from an economic survival strategy to take on a personal aspect as well:

> In later years, however, returns home took on social dimensions beyond the purely pragmatic aspect of having a refuge in hard times. Visits home became a form of cultural refreshment and social renewal apart from the rigors of city life. In the words of Louisville *Courier-Journal* reporter Ora Spaid: "They find the big cities cold, impersonal, and unwelcoming. So they come back home. Not necessarily to stay, but to be emotionally restored in the warmer, friendlier surrounding of people who care."[9]

Migrants and Music

The individual experience of migration is hidden within data about large migration flows. Personal accounts provide a sense of who the migrants were and the key role that music played in their lives.

Ron Eller, a first-generation migrant, became a nationally recognized historian at the University of Kentucky. He is emblematic of thousands of migrants who achieved a secure middle-class life. Eller devoted his career to understanding the history of the region and examining the structural causes of its economic difficulties: "My people, of course, were hillbillies, and we had just moved from West Virginia to Ohio. Along with 3.5 million other Appalachians who migrated to the industrial cities of the Midwest after World War II, we were often received with suspicion and frequently cautioned to speak correctly, dress properly, and listen to the right kind of music."[10]

Mike Maloney is a first-generation migrant from Breathitt County, Kentucky. Coming from a large extended family, he was vitally aware that migration was not successful for everyone; some migrants failed to "make it" and became part of the urban underclass. Maloney has devoted a lifetime to advocacy for the rural and urban poor: "Family reunions are held in Warren County, Ohio. The relationship to the mountains is weakening, but when we get together some of the young people get out their guitars and make music with the elders as we sing the songs of the mountains."[11]

Harriet Marsh Page, an African American, grew up in Number 9 Camp, a coal town in Logan County, West Virginia. With master's degrees in music and arts administration, she taught in schools across the Midwest. She also directed the Marsh Series in Cincinnati, a recital program she founded in 1978. Page's story illustrates that Appalachian migrants were men and women, Black and white, of many social classes, and with many different tastes in music. Nor did everyone follow typical migratory patterns. Page, for instance, taught music in Michigan before settling in southwestern Ohio. In her travels, however, she never lost touch with people from her home place:

> Actually, I never broke any ties with home because there were always people from home wherever I was. We still have high school reunions every year. In the odd years they're in Logan, and even years they're in some major city. This summer it's going to be in Detroit. Last time it was in Washington. New York, LA, Denver. Wherever there are ten people from Aracoma [High School] they form a chapter of the alumni association.[12]

Five-string banjo player Noah Crase moved with his parents from eastern Kentucky to Middletown, Ohio, in 1949, when he was fifteen. One of Bill Monroe's Blue Grass Boys between 1954 and 1956, Crase later played across southwestern Ohio with the Valley Ramblers, the Nu-Grass Pickers, the Boys from Indiana, and the Bluegrass Legends. Crase is a good example of an Appalachian migrant who came from a musical family, was inspired by other musicians, and clearly had the requisite talent but actually learned his musical craft through diligent practice and perseverance:

> Smokey Ward had a tent show in Middletown on WPFB. Dad would go out there and play the fiddle, with my sister on guitar. He wanted me to go out and play the banjo. I went up there one night but I wouldn't play. I said, "I'm not doing it right. I'm going to go back home and learn to play a banjo."
>
> The next day I went downtown to Goldflies Music Store, got me some fingerpicks, bought twelve 78-rpm records, all by Lester [Flatt] and Earl [Scruggs] and Don Reno, and one of those little record players. I was working in a grocery store after school and had saved twenty-some dollars. I brought those records back to the house and started to learn to play. By myself. Nobody around.
>
> I thought I'd figured it out. I'd seen somebody use picks, or heard about it. That old banjo laid there on the couch all the time. I don't think I even had a case for it. I'd get up every morning before I went to school and play it. I'd come home from school and play it until I went to work in the grocery store. Then I'd come home about 7:30 and play it until I went to bed.[13]

Most Appalachians in southwestern Ohio today are no longer first-generation migrants but multigenerational urban families with roots in the region—urban Appalachians, firmly embedded among their children, grandchildren, neighbors, coworkers, and friends. Vocalist Jennifer Brierly is a second-generation migrant who discovered her Appalachian heritage through music:

> The first time I connected with it was when an old fellow sang at my church. He sang the old mountain-type tunes, and I was really drawn to it. I thought it was weird because I never liked country music, but I liked the music I was hearing. I started singing with him, and he said my voice was made for this kind of music, and that I had to be from Kentucky. I argued with him, of course.[14]

Taylor Farley Jr. was a third-generation migrant. He played a banjo that his grandfather brought with him to Cincinnati from Breathitt County, Kentucky, in 1922. Aunt Maudie's was a bluegrass venue in Cincinnati's Over-the-Rhine neighborhood where Earl Taylor and some combination of the Stoney Mountain Boys would often play. Farley's grandfather was old-school—nothing but the traditional tunes and arrangements for him. Farley, on the other hand, was inclined to slip in a few Grateful Dead, Pink Floyd, or "Dueling Banjos" riffs during his performances. Both were Appalachian migrants who had their own take on their musical heritage:

> Well, my grandfather, when I was a little-bitty kid, I can remember he lived—it's really funny—he lived right over the top of what turned out to be Aunt

Maudie's. . . . I'd been listening to the Beatles and rock 'n' roll and everything like that, and when I heard Lester [Flatt] and Earl [Scruggs], that was just it right there. Ever since then that's all I've been interested in, was the five-string banjo.[15]

Sherrill Jennings, a vocalist and banjo player who performs with his wife, Judy, is a first-generation migrant from East Tennessee:

My mom and dad met in Kingsport, Tennessee. They both migrated to that area from Southwest Virginia and got married in 1936. My dad was a musician. He was primarily a guitar player but could play some on the banjo, mandolin, and fiddle. He was a carpenter, but earlier he worked at the glass plant and Holston Ordinance in Kingsport. He played music with his two brothers. There were eight siblings in his family, three boys and five girls, and almost all of them played music and sang.

I was born in 1950 in Kingsport. I have two brothers and a sister, all older. They all played except for my oldest brother, but we all loved music. We grew up with music in the house all the time. We moved to Ohio just before I was ten years old. As a matter of fact, we moved on Christmas day in 1959. My dad got a job at Gentile Air Force Station, later known as Defense Electronic Supply Center. It was a government facility in Kettering, Ohio. A friend offered him a job there and so we moved to New Carlisle, Ohio, because we were hungry, I guess [laughs]. That's basically the best way to put it.

He worked there until he retired in the early '80s. He got us kids interested in playing music too. Actually, I don't even remember trying to sit down and learn how to play anything much, because music was always around and it was just a second nature to us.

We would go to church and sing. That's how we got started singing. It was a natural thing. My dad was singing lead and I would sing tenor and my sister, well, she would sing whatever I sang. Singing harmony parts was natural for me, so she just sang what I would sing, and my brother would sing the low part. We did that for a few years till my brother was drafted and, soon after, my sister got married.

In the Franklin-Carlisle Ohio area, there is a small community called Chautauqua. In the mid-'60s, the Lake family of Franklin began to sponsor shows featuring top country and bluegrass performers. Before I was even old enough to drive, my Dad would drive me down to Chautauqua Park, and I got to first see professional musicians and I really got hooked on bluegrass music in particular.

When I graduated from high school, I got a job in a tool shop as a toolmaker apprentice and later became a toolmaker. I did that for a few years, then I started to work for a nuclear weapons facility called Mound Laboratory in Miamisburg, Ohio. While there I worked in different areas of manufacturing and metrology while taking some college at night.

My career evolved over the years and I retired as a design engineer. But music was always my love. Over the years I participated in several bands, primarily as a banjo player but frequently filling in on guitar and mandolin. My longest running band was a gospel bluegrass band, the Beacons. We ministered from the early '90s to the mid-2000s, regularly, at many churches in Ohio, Kentucky, Indiana, and West Virginia. We performed also at various events like bluegrass festivals, fairs, and such.[16]

Judy Jennings, a vocalist and bass player, is a second-generation migrant from Kentucky who grew up in Lockland, just north of Cincinnati. Lockland was the site of the Stearns and Foster bedding factory that employed some twelve hundred workers, mostly Black and white Southerners.[17] After high school, Judy Jennings worked there, as did her father:

> My dad's family were farmers. My dad always loved music. My mom said she could remember my dad going around with a mandolin around his neck when he was young, because they knew each other in their early years.
>
> Then he served in the Navy, and they were engaged while he was in the Navy. Then when they got married in 1948 they came to Ohio. Actually, a little town about twelve miles north of Cincinnati called Lockland. He came up here to get a job, because there was not a lot of work around Mt. Vernon, Kentucky. He got a job at Stearns and Foster making hand-tied box springs. Neither one of them drove, so we lived in Lockland where he could walk to work all the time.
>
> Then I was born in August of '49. I lived in Lockland until I got married. I started school there, graduated from there. For graduation my parents bought me a new car, so we finally had a way to [laughs] get around besides buses or walking or whatever.
>
> My dad [Paris Decker] played music as long as I can remember. He played music with lots of different people and practices were usually at our house. Our home was where they would meet and play and jam. He also would go do some shows, if somebody had somewhere to play.
>
> I grew up with music. My mom said she could remember me dancing on his mandolin case when I was real little. I don't remember that, but she did. I always liked the music. He did country. He did bluegrass. Mostly a mandolin player, but he played guitar and he could play banjo a little.
>
> I grew up with it. Of course, as a teenager, I liked rock and roll. I was into rock and roll until I got about sixteen or seventeen years old. There was a guy in Franklin, Ohio, that had shows at Chautauqua Park. He would bring in country stars, he would bring in bluegrass stars. My mom and dad and I started going to these shows. I saw tons of people I would never have been able to see otherwise except driving up there to those shows. They were great.
>
> I really started getting interested in playing, because there was a couple of people there I would sit and I would watch [them] play. I told my mom and dad, "I think I can do that."
>
> By that time, I was out of high school; I was working. I said, "I'm going to buy me a new bass and amplifier." I did. My dad helped me learn to play. That's

how I got started playing music. I really got interested in bluegrass, but I did some country songs too.

Sometimes we would rent a place and have a show. Our band was Dave Woolum, Paris Decker, and the Laurel County Partners. My parents and I were all in the band. At one show in Trenton, Ohio, I met Sherrill. He was playing the same show in a different group. We needed a banjo player [laughs], and so I invited him to come down to one of our practices.

I said, "We always get together on Saturday nights and practice, if you want to come down." He did, and he ended up being our banjo player and my husband. That's how we got started in the music.[18]

Although they have much in common, as seen throughout these vignettes, there is no rigid template for Appalachian migrants of any generation.

Possible Futures

Much has been written about the history of Appalachian migration, yet it is still possible to ask questions about its future. Is population stability a new motif across Appalachia, making the Great Migration truly a past phenomenon, or can another wave of migrants be expected to begin flowing from the region?

Out-migration was a key demographic feature of the Appalachian region throughout the twentieth century. In the early decades of the twenty-first century, however, migration streams have subsided to the point where out-migration is negligible. Much of last century's population movement was associated with economic highs and lows in the coalfields as well as the availability of job opportunities outside the region.[19] The factors affecting Appalachian migration today may be significantly different, and the scope and direction of new migration are not yet evident. One thing is certain, however. Wherever Appalachians are to be found, they will have their music with them.

Notes

1. James N. Gregory, *American Exodus: The Dust Bowl Migration and Okie Culture in California* (Oxford: Oxford University Press, 1991); Fabian Lange, Alan L. Olmstead and Paul W. Rhode, "The Impact of the Boll Weevil, 1892–1932," *Journal of Economic History* 69, no. 3 (2009): 685–718; Philip J. Obermiller, "Migration," in *High Mountains Rising: Appalachia in Time and Place*, ed. Richard A. Straw and H. Tyler Blethen, 88–100 (Urbana: University of Illinois Press, 2004).

2. Chad Berry, *Southern Migrants, Northern Exiles* (Urbana: University of Illinois Press, 2000).

3. Gerald W. Haslan, *Workin' Man Blues: Country Music in California* (Berkeley: University of California Press, 1999); Ken Burns and Geoffrey C. Ward, *Jazz: A History of America's Music* (New York: Alfred A. Knopf, 2000); Nathan McGee, "Sounds Like

Home: Bluegrass Music and Appalachian Migration in American Cities, 1945–1980," PhD diss., University of Cincinnati, 2016.

4. Obermiller, "Migration," 92.

5. Pamela C. Twiss and Phillip J. Obermiller, "'Civilians Came Second': The Impact of World War II Defense Plants on African American and Appalachian Neighborhoods in Pittsburgh and Cincinnati," *Appalachian Journal* 41, nos. 3–4 (2014): 284–309.

6. Thomas E. Wagner and Phillip J. Obermiller, "Going Home without the Trip: Appalachian Migrant Organizations," in *Appalachian Odyssey: Historical Perspectives on the Great Migration*, ed. Phillip J. Obermiller, Thomas E. Wagner, and E. Bruce Tucker, 215–30 (Westport, CT: Praeger, 2000).

7. Berry, *Southern Migrants, Northern Exiles*, 158; McGee, "Sounds Like Home."

8. Wagner and Obermiller, "Going Home without the Trip," 222.

9. Obermiller, "Migration," 94.

10. Ron Eller, "America and Appalachia," in *Perceptions of Home: The Urban Appalachian Spirit* (Cincinnati: Urban Appalachian Council, 1996). This is an unpaginated booklet that accompanied a photo exhibition.

11. Michael Maloney, "Who Are the Urban Appalachians?" in *Perceptions of Home.*

12. Harriet Marsh Page, interviewed by Dan Corathers in *Perceptions of Home.*

13. Noah Crase, interviewed by Fred Bartenstein in "Noah Crase: It's Not Easy Done, Part I," *Bluegrass Unlimited*, June 1985, 49–50.

14. Jennifer Henderson Brierly, interviewed by Don Corathers in *Perceptions of Home.*

15. Taylor Farley Jr., interviewed by Don Corathers in *Perceptions of Home.*

16. Sherrill Jennings, interviewed by Phillip Obermiller (2017). Transcript in author's possession.

17. To this day there are many Protestant churches in Lockland but no Catholic church, because internal migration from the South meant few job opportunities for European or Hispanic immigrants. Twiss and Obermiller, "'Civilians Came Second.'"

18. Judy Jennings, interviewed by Phillip Obermiller (2017). Transcript in author's possession.

19. Obermiller, "Migration," 88–100; Berry, *Southern Migrants, Northern Exiles.*

2. Bobby Osborne Remembers How It Was

BOBBY OSBORNE AND JOE MULLINS

BOBBY OSBORNE *(1931–) migrated with his family from rural Leslie County, Kentucky, to Dayton in 1942. He played bluegrass professionally with the Lonesome Pine Fiddlers, Jimmy Martin, the Stanley Brothers, and the Osborne Brothers before founding his own Rocky Top X-Press in 2003. This chapter was excerpted from an interview conducted by Joe Mullins on April 25, 2017, at the Wilks Conference Center of Miami University Hamilton, in Hamilton, Ohio.*[1]

MULLINS: Tell me what life was like in Thousandsticks, Kentucky, about 1939 or '40.

OSBORNE: Son, it was R-O-U-G-H, "rough." I was there until I was about seven or eight years old when my dad moved away, and so it was not until I got much older that I realized how tough it was for people in Thousandsticks, and not only that part of Kentucky but Tennessee and West Virginia and the Carolinas. It was rough about every place back in those days. There was no transportation much or roads to drive on if you did have transportation, so a lot of places were just as bad as it was there in Leslie County, or Hyden, or Bull Creek.

I never seen a car or anything until I was close to ten years old. I was out in the yard one day playing. Our house stood way up on the hill from the creek, and so I looked down the creek . . . and of course all the roads were mostly in the creek bed then. I looked down the road and saw the doggest thing coming up the road I'd ever seen. I had a little old truck that my dad had bought me. It looked like that truck but it was huge, a big truck. He went on past, went up the creek, and come back with a load of logs after a while. It was a big red Chevrolet truck. I never will forget that. As it went by the house, I watched them back tires roll over and over, and the water run off the back of them. I followed that truck a mile or two down the road. That was the first vehicle that I ever seen.

It was four miles across the hills to Hyden, and just a wagon road was all there was. You couldn't get a car over it, or a truck or anything like that. My granddad had a store there at Thousandsticks, and if it hadn't been for that store, a lot of people would have probably starved to death, because they depended on dry goods, canned goods, and meal, flour, things like that. No refrigeration . . . unheard of. What you raised in the summertime is how you lived in the wintertime.

MULLINS: So there was your daddy, Robert Osborne, and he had your sister, Louise; and you; and your brother, Sonny, with no electricity, no running water, and he wanted to find a better life for his family, didn't he?

OSBORNE: He did. And I tell you, there was a man lived over there whose name was Keen Sizemore. He had heard about work in Dayton, Cincinnati, and Michigan. He went to Dayton and he found work there, and he come back and told everybody up and down the creek, "If you want to work, there's work in Ohio." My dad borrowed fifty bucks and took off for Dayton. And the first place he came to was National Cash Register. It was one of the biggest companies back in the day. He stopped there and filled out an application, I assume, and they put him to work. In about eight weeks or something like that, we got the money. He come back and got the rest of us, and we moved to Dayton, Ohio. And so that was my life. It changed then.

MULLINS: Changed dramatically. You said that was probably about 1942, when you were around ten years old. A few years later, after you and Louise and Sonny started playing and singing around there a little bit, you told me you had very little exposure to music but you did get to hear the Grand Ole Opry. I know Ernest Tubb was a big influence on you.

OSBORNE: Yeah, I got to listen to the Grand Ole Opry with my dad. There wasn't anything else to do other than meals on Saturday night. When the lights went out, you had to go to bed or set up in the dark, one of the two. You couldn't see much in the dark. The Grand Ole Opry is about the only entertainment that we could hear. And ever who had the biggest living room and had a place to seat all the people, why, everybody'd gather to that guy's house on a Saturday night. I'd listen to the Opry. I'm a member of it and I still listen to it.

MULLINS: There was two influences you told me about. One was the Grand Ole Opry and the other one you called the "ginny barn." What's a ginny barn?

OSBORNE: A "gin barn" is a nice way to say it. A ginny barn is a nightclub, and everybody drinks and carries on in there just like you do at a club nowadays. Somebody would say, "Where is so and so?" "Ah, he went off to a ginny barn somewhere."

My mom's sister lived right up on the hill in Hyden and her brother had a little restaurant-type place. Back in those days Hyden, Kentucky, was wet. In case you don't know, it's where they drink and carry on all the time. Anything they can get their hands on, from moonshine to some kind of alcohol. Anyway, that little restaurant was open through the daytime and half the night, and he had records on there by different people, and Cousin Emmy had a record on there. She was picking, clawing the banjo. She was a member of the Renfro Valley Barn Dance for a while, and she had recorded. Also, the original cut of Bill Monroe's "Footprints in the Snow" was on that jukebox. Those two records went from the time the doors opened until they closed at night: "Ruby" by Cousin Emmy and "Footprints in the Snow" by Bill Monroe.

MULLINS: After the Osborne bunch landed in Dayton and you were a teenager, you told me somebody heard you and Louise and Sonny playing around the house a little bit and they said they'd take you to the big tent down at WPFB. WPFB went on the radio in 1947, so by 1948 or '49 you're sixteen or seventeen years old, and you wound up in that big tent down there. Went down to try out?

OSBORNE: Yeah, the guy had told me he had a wire recorder. He come over there and recorded us. Of course I knew about the thing in Middletown, about the [*WPFB*] *Jamboree* down there, and I knew the tent show. But I never give no thought about it or ever going down there to that.

This guy said, "I know somebody down there. You sing good enough to be on that show. If you want to go, I'll see if that can't happen." I said, "Well, I can't lose on that, so go ahead." Me and two other guys was playing together around there, and we'd meet at each other's houses and play when we had a chance.

To make a long story short, we went down to the tent show at Middletown.[2] And we only knew one song, "Summertime Is Past and Gone," one of the old songs that Bill Monroe put out years ago. I thought we did a pretty good job of singing it. Everybody in the crowd stood up and it scared me to death. Somebody stands up, you don't know whether you're gonna get hit. Anyway, the emcee said, "They want you to sing another one." And I said, "That's the only one we know." He said, "How come you don't know more?" I said, "That's the only one we have learned. We just sing it all the time we're together."

So I got to thinking about that time I'd heard "Ruby" down there at Hyden. I said, "I know one other old song, but I never even tried to sing it." He said, "Well, whatever it is, sing it." And so how I did that God knows, but I don't. I got out there and must have took a brave streak that day or something, but I sang "Ruby" and that crowd just stood up and hollered again. I thought, "Man, I hope I'm doing right. I don't know whether I am or not, but I hope I am." When people got to clapping, I knew I was home free.

The manager of the radio station was named Mr. Ranny Daly; he was a big-built man. We got such a good applause, why he come down there and said, "I want to know who sung that stupid song 'Ruby' a while ago." Well, I kept my mouth shut; I never said a word. I knew I'd messed up anyway; I wasn't gonna make it no worse. He said, "Somebody here sung it. Ain't nobody gonna say nothing?" I stood right there. Finally he said, "Well, ever who sung it, get out there and sing it again, 'cause we're on the air and broadcasting." He said, "I've got five phone calls on my desk up there saying if they don't do that song again, they're going to turn it off." And he said, "We don't allow that around here, turn a radio off." So I got out there and sang "Ruby" again. And they paid me four dollars; best four dollars I ever got paid in my life!

MULLINS: Well, that kind of started a career that's blessed millions of people now. I know the Osborne Brothers story, many folks do. I know you've continued to evolve and develop as a player and a singer. You wound up leaving Dayton just for a little while, working down in the Blue Ridge Mountains with the Lonesome Pine Fiddlers, a little while with the Stanley Brothers down in southern Virginia, and then you wound up making a career decision that involved Uncle Sam, didn't you?

OSBORNE: Yeah. I was called. I was in Bluefield, West Virginia, at the time, working with the Lonesome Pine Fiddlers, and I was in the age where you registered for the draft, so I knew I was going to get called. I didn't know when. I left the Lonesome Pine Fiddlers and got a chance to work with Carter and Ralph Stanley. They had heard of me singing, and Pee Wee Lambert had left them, so they asked if I would play the mandolin and sing his parts. I took that chance because I knew Carter and Ralph well. I only got to work with them three months, but that was just as good a three months as I ever spent. I liked that, really did.

MULLINS: Well, the draft notice came up and you chose the United States Marine Corps?

OSBORNE: My mom had five brothers that had been in the service, and they knew I had been called. They all told me, "Don't get in the Marine Corps, because boy, that's a rough outfit." I was drafted right out of Cincinnati and I had it in my mind I was gonna be in the Army, if I could pass its physical. So we're in this room and this big-built guy come out there and said, "The Army is pretty well filled up. All of you can't go to the Army; we ain't got room for all of you. Somebody's gonna have to go in the Marine Corps." He said, "Now you can go in the Army and you'll be sent to Fort Meade, Maryland, and freeze your can off up there, or you can take the Marine Corps and go to good old sunny California." It was the month of November, and I thought, "I want to go to sunny California." I went back home that night and my daddy said, "Well, did you get in the Army?" I said "No, I took the Marines." He said, "I knew you were gonna do that."

MULLINS: Well, Bobby had a very distinguished career as a United States Marine. You earned the Purple Heart, didn't you, too?

OSBORNE: I did that, the hard way. I was gone two years.

MULLINS: While you were in Korea, that little brother of yours had stuff going on back here, didn't he?

OSBORNE: Yeah, he wanted to be a football player, you know. Larry Richardson, who played the banjo with me for a while, came to the house and

Sonny watched him play the banjo. [Sonny] wanted to talk my daddy into going and buying him a banjo; he'd learn how to play. So his career started. He kinda learned how to play one just before I went into the Marine Corps.

MULLINS: Well, while you were fighting the Communists, Sonny wound up spending a summer with Bill Monroe when he was only fourteen years old. That's a real education for any young man, riding around with Jimmy Martin and Bill Monroe. He got back to Cincinnati to make a bunch of good records with Enos Johnson and Carlos Brock. He even had a kind of hit called "A Brother in Korea" that was distributed on a record label right here in Cincinnati in the early 1950s.[3] When you got back from Korea, all of a sudden it's gonna be you and Sonny. You guys hit the road in '53, right off the bat?

OSBORNE: I had in mind to go back to Carter and Ralph Stanley, to work with them. I didn't know Sonny was serious about it, but by the time I got back he'd done all this recording and everything, and I thought to myself, "There ain't no use; there's your banjo player, right there." So I told Sonny, "Let's just start together now and not have to do it later."

MULLINS: Well, there was plenty of work because of all them hillbillies. Just like the Osborne bunch, there was all kinds of people poured out of them factories in Dayton and they liked to drink beer, didn't they?

OSBORNE: Most of 'em did, yeah.

MULLINS: And you provided the entertainment for all them hillbillies, didn't you?

OSBORNE: We sure did. Played every club in Dayton, I reckon.[4] We got together, and Enos Johnson came to work with us, playing, pickin' together, and everything. I had to learn to play the mandolin again. I took one to Korea with me but it got ruined over there, so that ended my mandolin playing until I got back. We got started again and got a job down there in Dayton. It was called Little Mickey's nightclub.

MULLINS: A real nice place?

OSBORNE: Oh yeah. Ah, there's a million things I could tell you about that place. Anyway, we played it one night, and Enos Johnson says, "Boys, I've got to go home"—Enos is from East Tennessee—"I don't want to play around where they're drinking alcohol." I said, "Enos, let them go ahead and drink; we're gonna do the picking for 'em." He said, "I just don't want to be around where it's at." Well, we lost him right there; he left. And so we was looking for a third guy to sing with us. Red Allen was born and raised around Pigeon Roost, Kentucky. He's just like us; he come right out of a holler where there wasn't nothing going on. It's pretty close to Hazard, so Red and us grew up just practically twenty-five or thirty miles apart. Red came to work with us.

MULLINS: You told me one time there were so many of those beer joints in downtown Dayton that you and Sonny had a job for a while playing on one side of the street and Red and Frank Wakefield had a job on the other side of the street.

OSBORNE: Yeah, Red had Noah Crase playing a banjo with him and Frank Wakefield playing mandolin and Billy Thomas playing a fiddle. We were playing right across the street. During their break, Red's guys would come over and listen to us. Well, when we got a break we'd go over and listen to them.

MULLINS: Well, you're playing the nightclubs in Dayton, and you wound up recording for MGM Records. You and Red and Sonny established a new trio style when you got a song called "Once More," and it became a hit, didn't it?

OSBORNE: Yeah, it did. Back in those days, we found the song in Wheeling, West Virginia. A man up there wrote it.[5] He was an entertainer himself and I asked him if he cared if we sang his song. He said no, so I got the words to it and I knew the melody to it. Red, me, and Sonny was on our way back home to Dayton and we got to singing that song, going along in the car. All of a sudden I just started singing the lead to it in a higher-pitch lead voice. All our instruments was in the trunk, so we didn't know what key we was in. But I started singing the lead to it just way up higher, in higher range. Red knew the tenor part of it, so he did that in a lower range. Well, that put Sonny in the middle part, and Sonny knew that part like the back of his hand. So we got to singing it like that right there, you know.

We got the guitar out and found out what key it was in, and so we just kept on. We sung "Once More" all the way from Cambridge, Ohio, to Dayton; we didn't want to forget that. I'd never heard nobody sing that type of harmony, and we kept that in our minds. We finally approached the man at MGM Records. He said, "Uh, uh, no we can't have that. That ain't no kind of trio there. It's not good singing," or whatever he said. So we kept on. We said, "No, it's different. We don't want to be like Bill Monroe or anybody." He said at MGM they just won't put up with you changing your harmony around like that. "If you want to take a chance on it, you may lose your contract." So we recorded "Once More" and it came out like that. It made it to number thirteen on the Top 40 charts on country stations. We never heard nothing else out of MGM.

MULLINS: So you and Sonny and Red were established enough to have an MGM contract. I think when you first went down there to record, they wanted you to record "Ruby" for the first time. You've recorded it three times in your career.

OSBORNE: Yeah, there used to be a DJ in Dayton; Tommy Sutton was his name.[6] Red knew Tommy some way or another, so we got acquainted with Tommy and went over to his house. He said, "If you'll make me a tape and pay my way to Nashville, I know some people; I might get you a recording contract." So we did that and Tommy took off; we paid his train fare. He came back and told us, he said, "I've got you a contract with MGM Records." Before that we had told Tommy about the two banjos. Sonny and Noah Crase had been playing the banjos together and had "Ruby," playing two banjos on it.

Tommy told Wesley Rose of MGM Records, "They've got two banjos and they're gonna play harmony." He said, "I'd like to have that." So Tommy brought the news back to us. Well, about a month or something like that before we're supposed to go to Nashville, Noah just disappeared. He just completely vanished. We couldn't find him anywhere. Noah and Sonny were about the only two around this area that played the banjo. I'd fool with a banjo a little bit, but never in front of somebody or anything like that. So Sonny said, "Well, we've got to have that contract. Here's you a set of picks. I've got a banjo. Take that banjo; you've got to learn how to play 'Ruby' in about a month." I got to work on it, and I learned. He showed me what to play, how to play it and everything.

In a month we went to Nashville. I don't know . . . fate was with us. We got down there and that guy said he wanted the two banjos; that's the first one he wanted to hear. So Red was with us then, and he and Sonny were both about the same height, but I had to stand on a box so the banjo would be up real close to the mike. So we played "Ruby," and he was sitting in that control room. I was expecting him to come out of there and start pulling his hair any minute, but he didn't. He said, "That's exactly what I want. I like the banjo sound." And I went back to the mandolin again.

MULLINS: That was the first recording of "Ruby," and it went on, as we all know, to be one of the biggest hits in bluegrass music. Let me ask you this. You guys are working for MGM Records, you're playing beer joints in Dayton, and you're members of the Wheeling Jamboree, but were you getting rich?

OSBORNE: Uh, two ways to put that, I guess. "Yes" and "no," but we was on the "no" end of it. I tell you what, we had a lot of fun but we didn't make much money.

MULLINS: Things were not absolutely on the upside for the Osborne Brothers. Red had left the group and you and Sonny persevered with other fellows playing the guitar and singing with you, but MGM wasn't getting it done. They were not getting your music heard where it needed to be heard. By the early 1960s, you guys had to work some day jobs to be able to keep your music career going, didn't you?

OSBORNE: Yeah. I drove a Yellow Cab in Dayton about three years. I liked that as good as any job I ever had, too. You was your own boss; driving a cab, you do what you want to. All the cab companies just wanted that car on the street. But you could get out and work, and you could make a living. That's what I did.

MULLINS: It took a lot of playing in places like Little Mickey's and the Blazing Stump and the Crystal Pistol and Ruby's White Sands. You had to play a lot of those places before you wound up being a star of the Grand Ole Opry, didn't you?

OSBORNE: Yeah, it took us a while to get there. In traveling around a little bit from Wheeling, we run into the Wilburn Brothers. We got to know them real well, and Doyle Wilburn talked to us when we were guesting at the

Opry one night. He said, "How you guys fixed with MGM?" I told him, "We're not making any records right now." He give me a card, and said, "If you ever want to change, call me."

I put that card in my billfold and kept it for, probably, six months, and then—Benny Birchfield was playing with us then—we was playing at a club for a week up in Wilmington, Delaware. We checked into a little motel up there, and we was trying to decide whether to quit or keep going on. We was just in a straight line going across; we weren't going down or up either one. So I looked in my billfold, I found that card, and I said, "Here's a card Doyle Wilburn gave me six months ago, and it was when we was at the Opry." It was nine, ten o'clock at night. Sonny called that number and Doyle answered the phone. We told him our situation.

It was on a Wednesday night. He said, "Give me a week. Call me next Wednesday and I'll see what I can do." So the next Wednesday we was in Columbus, Ohio, playing a club there. And within that week's time, Doyle got us another shot at the Grand Ole Opry, Ralph Emery's early morning TV show, and some records for the Air Force. He got all that done in a week's time, plus the contract with Decca Records. And so that was the start, when he gave me the card. I said, "We want to be members of the Grand Ole Opry." Doyle said, "That will take me some time, but if you'll give me a shot, I'll get that done." And eleven months later we became members of the Opry. Doyle said, "I got you here. It's your job to stay now."

MULLINS: It started right here in Dayton, Ohio, and wound up in Nashville, Tennessee, as Opry members in August of 1964, with that Decca recording contract that put you in the hands of Owen Bradley, one of the most famed record producers in that town, and all the great songwriters then, and the Wilburns and Owen Bradley got you guys the songs you needed to sing, didn't they?

OSBORNE: They sure did, yeah. He looked out for us and Loretta Lynn. We had great songs, and he was a great producer, and of course the Wilburn Brothers had a talent agency and a publishing company. So we signed with them, and that was the best move we ever made.

MULLINS: Before you got to the Opry, you guys made history in 1960, the first time there was a bluegrass band on the stage at a college campus. It was right here in southwestern Ohio. I only live about five miles from the campus of Antioch College in Yellow Springs, Ohio. You told me you didn't know exactly what was going to happen that night, did you?

OSBORNE: Well, you know, back then, I finished the tenth grade, and didn't want to do that. I wanted to do what I'm doing now. I didn't have no time to go to school. I didn't want to go, but I did finish the tenth grade. I'm glad. I wish I'd went further, but that's another story. Back then, when I thought of college, that was uptown people. I mean people that dress nice all the time, you know, surely not people like us. And we went to that college. Neil Rosenberg was a part of that. We thought, going to a college, you want to sing the country songs that Ray Price and people like that did. That would be good. We did about four or five of them country songs, and the kids—it was only young kids; I couldn't figure that out; I mean there was no older people, just college kids—of course, we was at a college.

Well, every time we did one of them songs, you'd hear this [claps hands slowly]. When we took a break, Neil Rosenberg said, "They don't like what you're doing." I said, "Well, what are we supposed to do?" And he says, "When you go back out, try 'Little Maggie,' 'Pretty Polly,' and 'Blue Moon of Kentucky,' something like that." We knew them by my heart, you know. So we started playing them, and that bunch stood up, and we didn't expect nothing like that out of a college, 'cause that's people trying to get an education. We didn't think they'd be interested in "Footprints in the Snow" or nothing like that. But we found out right there that those kids were really into bluegrass music. So that was a first for us. And of course bluegrass then spread just like wildfire through the college circuit. I never seen anything to beat that in my life. And Flatt and Scruggs got to playing colleges, and Monroe. Of course, we played them all the time then.

We played NYU; it was there right on the campus, right in the middle of New York City, and them kids had a big playground, I mean a huge place. And all these college kids, they gathered on that acre of ground, and every one of them is all playing mandolins and guitars and fiddles, and I thought, man, I ain't never seen nothing like that in my life. We learned right there that bluegrass had went to town.

MULLINS: Bobby's got a new song which is one of his favorites in his new CD, which I got in the mail from his record label about ten days ago. I put it in my player in my living room, and when he got through song number three, I was crying. The song tells so much about what this project has been all about. It's about those folks that had to leave those hills and those hollers, and took their music with them, whether they took it to Cincinnati or Middletown or Dayton or Chicago or Detroit or Baltimore. It started in those Appalachian hills where Bobby Osborne started life in 1931. And the conviction, the heart, and the soul that he sings every note with really comes together in this song. And you've never heard a better eighty-five-year-old voice sing a song from the heart than this one. And we're going to share this song with you, a number by Darrell Scott entitled "Kentucky Morning." [This song is the story of a man who follows his brother north to a midnight-shift factory job, but finding that the "bright lights don't shine like a Kentucky morning," he returns home to "a good piece of land and an old cane-back rocker."][7]

Notes

1. The full interview can be viewed in video form at https://www.youtube.com/watch?v=ZnhYXTkf2tg&t=147s.

2. See chapter 3, "All the Way to the Fence."

3. See chapter 4, "Taking the Music Home."

4. See chapter 5, "Sing Me Back Home."

5. Robert "Dusty" Owens (1930–2015), https://www.dignitymemorial.com/obituaries/tampa-fl/robert-owens-6379442.

6. See chapter 3, "All the Way to the Fence."

7. "Kentucky Morning" by Darrell Scott (BMG and Sony Music), as recorded by Bobby Osborne, 2017.

3. All the Way to the Fence

Bluegrass Broadcasting in the Miami Valley

DANIEL MULLINS

EVEN BEFORE BLUEGRASS was recognized as a genre distinct from country music, it found a home on Miami Valley radio dials. Broadcasting played a critical role in building the bluegrass market over decades. Bluegrass music's consistent presence on the radio airwaves of southwestern Ohio is a primary reason for the genre's continuing success in the area.

Everything related to bluegrass in southwestern Ohio can be connected directly or indirectly to Appalachian migration. Transplants from the rural South went looking for jobs in the industrialized North for most of the twentieth century. Tens of thousands of families moved to southwestern Ohio from mountain regions of Kentucky, Tennessee, Virginia, West Virginia, and southeastern Ohio. By 1975 a large proportion of the Miami Valley population was either from or had family ties to Appalachia.[1]

A paycheck was not the only need of these new Miami Valley residents. Transplanted from the familiarity of the "hills of home" to industrialized communities of the North, the migrants sometimes felt like aliens in their own country. Through their music, they were able to maintain both a positive identity and a connection to their former home.

The newcomers were also an underserved consumer demographic. In stark contrast to today, when companies use internet-accessible data to identify a tailor-made audience within a geographic area, the needs and desires of the migrants were often overlooked. Radio, intentionally or not, became a primary means for business to tap into the large Appalachian market throughout southwestern Ohio.

Radio was a cheap form of entertainment and, for those struggling to make ends meet, perhaps their only luxury. Feeling alone in the big city, away from family and friends left behind, listeners felt a special connection to on-air personalities who gave them a little taste of home through familiar music and dialect. They truly felt like "friends and neighbors" of the man behind the microphone.

WLW, John Lair and the *Renfro Valley Barn Dance*, *Boone County Jamboree*, and *Midwestern Hayride*

In the early 1920s, a Cincinnati businessman and radio manufacturer by the name of Powel Crosley Jr. decided to further indulge his passion for radio by starting his own radio station (and, not coincidentally, expanding the market for his receivers). Crosley started WLW at AM frequency 700 on March 22, 1922.[2] WLW began broadcasting at 50 watts but within six years became the country's first radio station to regularly broadcast at 50,000 watts. By 1934 its transmitter was broadcasting at 500,000 watts, making WLW the only US radio station to ever broadcast at that magnitude.[3] The sheer power of WLW's signal was staggering. The Cincinnati station could be heard from New York to Florida, earning it the moniker "The Nation's Station." Although its days as a 500,000-watt juggernaut would last only from 1934 to 1939, those five years became critical in helping to establish the country music business, at both a local and national level.

The first appearance of country music on the airwaves of WLW was the *Top of the Morning* show in 1928. Live country music showed up on the broadcast schedule at various times over the next few years but without the impact and success that radio barn dance programs were achieving elsewhere.[4] WLW station executives decided to add more rural, "down-home" entertainment in order to compete with popular programs such as the *National Barn Dance* on Chicago's WLS and the Grand Ole Opry on Nashville's WSM. Cincinnati's location across the river from Kentucky and the large number of Appalachian migrants already in the Miami Valley would give the new programming a built-in local audience, and WLW's clear channel would take it to the nation at night.

In 1937 WLW engaged with budding radio visionary John Lair, who had been key to the *National Barn Dance*'s initial success during the early 1930s.[5] Lair was a talent contractor; he bought radio time, filled it with the musicians he hired and made money from the advertising he sold within his time slot. It had been Lair's idea to recruit performers from his native Kentucky and bring them to the Windy City to become a part of the cast.[6] The idea paid dividends and added a further level of authenticity to the already established program. When WLW hired John Lair, some of his talented Kentucky friends came with him.[7]

On October 8, 1937, John Lair debuted the *Renfro Valley Barn Dance* on WLW, broadcasting live from the Cincinnati Music Hall's six-thousand-seat auditorium.[8] Featuring such musical acts as the Coon Creek Girls and Red Foley (later to become a national star and eventually a member of the Country Music Hall of Fame) and country comedians such as Whitey Ford, known as "The Duke of Paducah," the *Renfro Valley Barn Dance* delivered high-quality entertainment for both the live audience and those tuned in to WLW airwaves.

"We were an instant hit in Cincinnati," recalled Whitey Ford in a 1972 interview. "This one year in Cincinnati established us as a country music show on the air, and we were drawing tremendous crowds in theaters around the country." Even more crucial to the program's viability was Lair's ability to secure sponsorships for the *Barn Dance*. "We had every minute of our time sponsored," remembered Ford.[9] The opportunity for businesses in southwestern Ohio to experience the untapped economic potential of the hillbilly music market would pay future dividends for Appalachian migrants and their search for respect and relevance in the Miami Valley.

Lair's success with the *Renfro Valley Barn Dance* raised more than a few eyebrows among WLW executives, particularly since they were not sharing in the program's profits outside of the fee Lair paid for air time. After seeing how profitable a high-quality barn dance–style program could be, they were determined to get a piece of the pie. In 1938 the station hired George Biggar, who, like Lair, had previously worked for Chicago's WLS, to develop a new barn dance show specifically for WLW.

On September 16, 1938, a little less than a year after the *Renfro Valley Barn Dance* became the hottest thing on WLW, the station debuted the *Boone County Jamboree* at Cincinnati's twenty-two-hundred-seat Emery Auditorium.[10] Attendance at the *Renfro Valley Barn Dance* began to decrease, so Lair moved his show fifty miles north to Dayton's Memorial Hall on October 22. The *Boone County Jamboree* then moved to the much larger Cincinnati Music Hall.

Nearly a year later, on November 4, 1939, with a reliable broadcast infrastructure in place, Lair relocated the *Renfro Valley Barn Dance*—as had always been his intention—to a location remembered from his childhood on Renfro Creek in Rockcastle County, Kentucky.[11] Success of the program in Ohio allowed him to achieve his dream and raise adequate funds to construct an actual barn that would host the barn dance. WLW broadcast the live show remotely from Renfro Valley for a few more years, and then CBS began carrying the program on its network of stations through WHAS in Louisville.

Although by 1939 WLW was required to scale its 500,000-watt signal down to 50,000 watts, *Boone County Jamboree* continued to be the region's premier vehicle of rural entertainment and achieved nationwide popularity.[12] In 1951 the program was sold to the NBC television network as a summer replacement for Sid Caesar's *Show of Shows*. The name was changed to *Midwestern Hayride* in order to de-localize the moniker and give the show broader appeal. Production moved to a studio rather than an auditorium, but the program occasionally broadcast on location from state and county fairs around the region. *Midwestern Hayride* remained a staple of WLW's Saturday night schedule for several decades.[13] The program helped to catapult careers of Chet Atkins, Cowboy Copas, the Delmore Brothers, Grandpa Jones, Merle Travis, and many other early country stars.[14] It remained on the air until 1972, when WLW ceased live programming.

It was no coincidence that Cincinnati's King Records began operation just as the *Boone County Jamboree/Midwestern Hayride* soared in popularity. King Records would quickly establish itself as one of the top independent country labels of the era, largely because of its proximity to WLW's "Cradle of Stars" (a nickname given to the station). Over the coming decades, King would become a legendary bluegrass label as well.[15]

The *WCKY Jamboree*, Nelson King, Wayne Raney, and the Jimmie Skinner Music Center

Across the river from Cincinnati were the tower and transmitter of Covington, Kentucky's WCKY. Beginning in 1939, WCKY was able to blast a 50,000-watt signal into Ohio, where its studios were located in downtown Cincinnati, and compete directly with WLW. WCKY could be heard in Columbus, Indianapolis, Lexington, and Louisville, along with the burgs, suburbs, hills, and hollers of three states during the daytime and many more at night.[16] While WLW remained the king of live hillbilly radio entertainment in the region, WCKY in the 1940s became the earliest significant presence of recorded country music on southern Ohio radio airwaves.[17]

This reputation was largely due to the contributions of legendary disc jockey Nelson King. Born Charles Schroeder in Portsmouth, Ohio, he got his start on radio in the 1930s at WPAY in Portsmouth before moving to WCPO in Cincinnati and eventually landing at WCKY in 1946. It was at WCKY that Schroeder adopted the pseudonym "Nelson King" after skimming through a local phone book.[18]

At the time, the role of a disc jockey was relatively new and often looked down upon within the broadcasting community. Most radio stations were still focusing on live entertainment, but after World War II, DJs who played recorded hits of the day started to become more popular.[19] This new program structure was both practical and economical: more artists could be featured, and one DJ was much cheaper than a regular cast of performers. King played popular hits during the day, but his evening record program, the *WCKY Jamboree*, focused on country music and the new acoustic style that later became known as bluegrass.

In the mid-1940s, Bill Monroe introduced to Grand Ole Opry airwaves an edition of his band that included Lester Flatt, Earl Scruggs, Chubby Wise, and

Howard Watts. After that, performers everywhere began adopting the high-energy sound that was equal parts new and old, classic and contemporary, traditional and groundbreaking. Throughout the 1940s and '50s, WCKY was one of the most ardent broadcasters of early bluegrass music.[20]

The *WCKY Jamboree* began shortly after King arrived at WCKY in 1946 and ran through 1964. To say the program was a success would be an understatement. The style of country music King featured resonated with Appalachians who lived throughout the listening area—both the migrants who had moved to metropolitan areas of southwestern Ohio and those who had never left the hills and hollers of Kentucky.

Rather than having typical paid sponsors, King sold "per inquiry." He would pitch a product to his listeners and tell them to mail payment to the radio station, which would keep a commission and send orders on to the retailer. King peddled everything from Bibles to baby chickens. His program was so popular, and the response to these per-inquiry ads so immense, that proceeds from the *WCKY Jamboree* were enough to fund the entire operating expenses of the radio station, turning revenues from the other programs into pure profit.[21] King and WCKY proved that hillbilly music could be profitable. This earned legitimacy for the format and also for its Appalachian listeners, both formerly viewed as somewhat disreputable within the broadcast industry and local power structure.[22]

The *WCKY Jamboree* helped pave the way for regional growth of the burgeoning style of country music now known as bluegrass. Proximity to Cincinnati's King Records, which now boasted such bluegrass legends as the Stanley Brothers and Reno and Smiley, made it easy for Nelson King to feature bluegrass records. It is no coincidence that the second song that Reno and Smiley recorded for King Records, "I'm Using My Bible for a Roadmap," lists Nelson King as a cowriter (under his real name, Charles Schroeder). According to Carlton Haney—Reno and Smiley's manager at the time—when the duo came to Cincinnati to record, they paid a visit to WCKY. "Nelson King wanted to know what they was gonna record, and Don sung 'I'm Using My Bible for a Roadmap' for him," said Haney. "I am told that Don decided to put his [King's] name on it, [so] that Nelson would play the hell out of it."[23] The strategy must have worked, as the song became a signature Reno and Smiley hit.

The *WCKY Jamboree* was a game changer for broadcasting in the Miami Valley. The profitability of the program, along with the popularity of WCKY's recorded country music format, forced Cincinnati's WLW to follow suit, hire disc jockeys, and deemphasize live entertainment by the early 1950s.[24]

The program's success also propelled Nelson King into the national spotlight. For eight years straight he was named Most Popular Country Disc Jockey by *Billboard* magazine. He was also a founder and officer of the Country Music Disc Jockey Association, a forerunner of the Country Music Association. King's attention to the *WCKY Jamboree* began to wane, and substitute host Marty Roberts was soon appearing more often than King. Nelson King left WCKY in 1957, passed away from lung cancer in 1974, and the following year was posthumously inducted into the inaugural class of the Country Music Disc Jockey Hall of Fame.[25]

Upon King's departure, the regular host of the *WCKY Jamboree* became Wayne Raney, an ace harmonica player who recorded for King Records and also toured and recorded with the Delmore Brothers. His most notable recordings with them were the classics "Freight Train Boogie" and "Blues Stay Away from Me."[26] He hosted the radio program until health issues forced him to leave and return in 1961 to his native Arkansas. The *Jamboree*, subsequently hosted by Jimmie Williams and Jimmie Logsdon, ended in 1964.

Both King and Raney exhorted listeners to order the records they heard over WCKY by mail from the Jimmie Skinner Music Center in Cincinnati. Founded in 1950, the center initially struggled but soon became a prominent outlet for country, bluegrass, and hillbilly records.[27] Jimmie Skinner's successful performing career straddled the line between bluegrass and country. He wrote many often-recorded songs in both genres, including "Doin' My Time," "Don't Give Your Heart to a Rambler," "He Died a Rounder at 21," and "Will You Be Satisfied That Way?"

"Jimmie Skinner had a record shop where we bought all our records," remembered Bluegrass Hall of Famer J. D. Crowe, who lived in nearby Newport, Kentucky, for a time during high school before relocating to the Miami Valley during his earliest years as a professional musician. "[Skinner] was not going full force with his recording career, and he broadcast live every Saturday from his record shop."[28]

Through his live broadcasts on Newport's WNOP, advertising on WCKY, widespread distribution, and effective advertising in country music publications, Skinner's store established a national presence. Mail orders to the Jimmie Skinner Music Center became a popular method for purchasing bluegrass music in the genre's early years.[29] The center's October 1957 advertisement in *Country Song Roundup* was, in fact, one of the first printed appearances of the term "bluegrass."[30]

Paul Braden and WPFB

By the late 1940s, a gentleman named Paul Braden began to notice the immense success that hillbilly music programming was having in the Miami Valley. If weekly programs like WLW's *Midwestern Hayride* and the *WCKY Jamboree* were generating so large a response, he wondered what a radio station dedicated exclusively to this market could do. During the 1940s alone, nearly three million people had migrated from Appalachia to find work in the cities, but the business ventures directed toward this demographic were still minimal.[31]

With the goal of focusing business efforts directly toward migrant communities, Paul Braden founded Middletown radio station WPFB in 1947.[32] While the station's call letters actually stood for Paul F. Braden's initials, they became affectionately reworked as "We Play For Briars." "Briars," short for "briarhoppers," a slang term used to reference Kentuckians, became a badge of honor for those who would rather die than be thought of as "Yankees" or "Buckeyes" (a nickname for Ohioans).[33] WPFB's success surpassed all expectations.

Middletown may have been so named because it is roughly halfway between the larger cities of Dayton and Cincinnati. Not only was Middletown itself a hotbed of migrants looking to put down new roots, but WPFB's signal reached both of the city's big brothers, allowing it to cover two of the region's major industrial centers while still maintaining a local flavor in its delivery.[34] Under the leadership of Braden's program director Ranny Daly, WPFB quickly became one of the primary radio stations in the region.[35]

Smokey Ward, Little Eller, Shorty Hobbs, Fairley Holden, and "Old Joe" Clark

During the early days, WPFB's most prominent radio announcer was Smokey Ward, a fiddle-playing disc jockey with a brash personality that endeared him to audiences. Ward came to Middletown from John Lair's *Renfro Valley Barn Dance*. He was so well liked by the Renfro Valley cast that several entertainers accompanied him to Middletown, including Fairley Holden and Manuel "Old Joe" Clark.[36]

Smokey Ward was short in stature, while his wife, Little Eller, stood about six feet six.[37] Bluegrass Hall of Famer Jesse McReynolds, who worked at WPFB in 1950 alongside his brother, Jim, recalled, "He [Smokey] would be talking, and she [Little Eller] would walk up and throw up her legs over his head! That's how tall she was!"[38] Mandolin player Shorty Hobbs often performed with Smokey and Little Eller. Shorty's hat was rigged with a spring that moved the hat up and down while he played.[39] Fairley Holden was a beloved entertainer with Smokey's troupe as well. "He was kind of a comedian," said Jesse McReynolds. "He was a character. . . . Everything he did, he could make a show out of it." Their lively showmanship made Ward and his company stars on stage and on area airwaves.[40]

In the early 1950s, live endorsement ads were a natural part of radio, and Smokey Ward delivered them differently from everyone else. "Smokey Ward could sell an igloo or a refrigerator to the Eskimos," remembered J. D. Crowe. "He had the craziest sayings. . . . You never heard stuff like it—he'd talk about sponsors, and when you'd go by there, you couldn't get in the parking lot. Every sponsor he had did great business. There were tire stores, restaurants, service stations, furniture stores, everything."[41] Smokey's humor, big personality, and ability to connect listeners to sponsors were great assets to WPFB during the early years.

The loud personality that made Ward popular among WPFB's listening audiences would also prove to be his downfall. After having a lot of trouble with a vehicle bought from a dealer that advertised with the station, Smokey painted lemons all over the car, wrote "LEMON" on the side, and parked it in front of the dealership. He also told radio listeners that the dealership was terrible and that they would sell you a lemon! This proved to not be the best career move, and Smokey Ward's time at WPFB came to an end.[42]

Although Ward's tenure at WPFB ended prematurely, he left a huge mark on bluegrass broadcasting in the Miami Valley. It would be nearly a decade before another radio personality captured the public's imagination, created business for his clients, and featured heavy doses of bluegrass as successfully as Smokey Ward.

The *WPFB Jamboree*, Bobby Osborne, Jim and Jesse, Jimmy Martin, and J. D. Crowe

Not long after WPFB began operating in the late 1940s, Paul Braden erected a large tent near the station's studios (housed in a farmhouse) and began hosting the *WPFB Jamboree* on Saturday nights, broadcasting the ensuing shindigs live.[43] This proved to be a catalyst in the growth of the station and the cultivation of bluegrass in the Miami Valley. A talented core group of veteran performers was a rare commodity for a new radio station. The *Jamboree* drew hundreds of fans from across the region to the WPFB property every weekend, with countless more tuned in on the radio. To better accommodate the crowds, particularly during wintertime, toward the end of 1949 Braden moved the *WPFB Jamboree* into a large barn on the property. After the barn burned down, in January of 1950, it was back to the tent.[44]

The music made under the shelter of a tattered old tent in front of a few hundred eager fans proved to be some of the best country and bluegrass the nation had to offer. A great mixture of entertainment was featured, with high-profile country stars popping in from time to time if they happened to be in the area. Little Jimmy Dickens and the mythic Hank Williams made special appearances on the *WPFB Jamboree*.[45] Bluegrass stars such as Mac Wiseman and Reno and Smiley would stop by as well.[46] Yet, despite the impressive list of guest appearances at the *WPFB Jamboree*, it was the station's cast of regional talent that became the stuff of bluegrass legend.

Red Allen, Hylo Brown, Noah Crase, J. D. Crowe, Jim and Jesse, Jimmy Martin, the Osborne Brothers, and Frank Wakefield all spent significant time at WPFB as part of the weekly on-air entertainment.[47] At a time when bluegrass was still in its infancy, and regarded as a style of country music rather than its own genre, it is staggering that no less than seven future Bluegrass Hall of Fame members spent some of their formative years at the same radio station in Middletown, Ohio, a city whose population had yet to exceed fifty thousand.

The *WPFB Jamboree* was the first place that Bobby Osborne ever sang on stage. He was just a teenager, and it was the song "Ruby, Are You Mad?" that he would eventually sing all over the globe alongside his brother, Sonny, as the Osborne Brothers.[48] In 1954 the powerful pairing of Jimmy Martin with J. D. Crowe on the five-string banjo was first heard over the airwaves of WPFB.

Jim and Jesse McReynolds were brought to Middletown by the popular entertainer "Old Joe" Clark and were a part of the on-air cast for about a year. Still going by "the McReynolds Brothers" or "Jesse and James," Jim and Jesse recorded a few demo discs in the WPFB studios.[49] "Our first record was 'Are You Missing Me?,'" recalled Jesse. "[Fairley] Holden had given us that song. Charlie Louvin wrote it and pitched it to Fairley. He never did anything with it and gave it to us, so we recorded it first."

While Jim and Jesse were working at WPFB, they were tuned in to Jimmie Skinner's radio show (most likely on WNOP) and heard that Ken Nelson from Capitol Records was at Jimmie's music shop. The brothers headed to Cincinnati and played their demos made at the WPFB studio for Nelson. He said he would set up a recording session with Capitol. "I thought he was just putting us on," said Jesse. "He called us the next day. It was on a Sunday, and he said he had the session set. This was 1952. From there, that's where Jim and Jesse started." It was Ken Nelson's idea to shorten the future Bluegrass Hall of Fame group's name from "the McReynolds Brothers" to "Jim and Jesse."[50]

Tommy Sutton at WONE, WING, and WPFB

Tommy Sutton was a popular disc jockey in the Miami Valley during the 1950s. His broadcasting pedigree included stints as both a performer and disc jockey. He began his career singing and playing the bass fiddle on WKBF in Indianapolis; WLW's *Renfro Valley Barn Dance*; WWVA in Wheeling, West Virginia; WKBN in Youngstown, Ohio; and KWK in St. Louis during the 1940s, before he landed in Dayton at WING in 1950.[51] While at WING he began his career as a disc jockey.

Tommy Sutton's programming consisted predominantly of country music, but he was also a friend and supporter of the bluegrass community. Sutton used Flatt and Scruggs's "Dear Old Dixie" as his theme song and, through frequent airplay, helped to make Mac Wiseman a star in the Miami Valley.[52] In addition to including bluegrass music during his broadcasts, he was instrumental in several noteworthy bluegrass events in the area during the 1950s.

Tommy Sutton's on-air schedule included hosting a jamboree for WING, similar to the one at Middletown's WPFB.[53] It was on Sutton's live program that Red Allen and Frank Wakefield first performed on stage together. "I saw Frank Wakefield sitting on a porch on the corner of Montgomery and Fifth, playing a cheap mandolin," remembered Red of his and Frank's first encounter. Red was in need of a mandolin player for his radio performance, so he offered young Frank the job. "I told him I'd pay him ten dollars, and he'd never been paid for playing. We played 'Blue Moon of Kentucky' [on the *Jamboree*] in C, and he took a whole mandolin break in B. You couldn't hear for the clapping. He was fifteen years old."[54]

Tommy Sutton was a leader among country music broadcasters of the era. In November of 1953, while still on the air at WING, Sutton helped found the Country Music Disc Jockey Association in Nashville. He served as the association's first secretary.[55] He was rated as one of the nation's top twenty country music DJs, according to a *Billboard* magazine poll. Sutton also worked at Dayton stations WHIO and WONE. A disc jockey of this caliber and experience was a real asset to the radio airwaves of the Miami Valley during a time when the country music business was tenuous at best, due to the popularity of rock and roll.

Part of Sutton's success can be attributed to his passion for people, particularly the "hillbillies" who were often belittled or forgotten by mainstream media of the time. "They [critics] don't seem to realize that hillbilly music is an 'art' and the artists who make this music are sincere, warm and friendly people who believe in what they're singing and playing," said Sutton. "Maybe that's the secret of hillbilly music's popularity. . . . People appreciate the sincerity of hillbilly music and find comfort in its down to earth, homey appeal."[56]

Sutton was embraced by the Appalachian migrant audience and referred to himself as the "Old Corn Bread Eater and Buttermilk Drinker Upper." He would often promote and emcee country package shows at Memorial Hall in Dayton, always including shout-outs to the "hens and roosters up there in the roosts" (the audience in the balcony). Longtime sponsors of Sutton's broadcasts included Zell's East End Radio and Price Stores (downtown clothiers). He encouraged listeners to go see Price's manager, Larry Zusman, who "looked just like Roy Acuff," according to Sutton. He built a studio in the basement of his home and did his shows from there, enabling him to finish one program and begin another within minutes over a different station.[57]

Sutton would eventually land at WPFB for a few years, following the departure of Smokey Ward.[58] It was at WPFB that Tommy Sutton made his greatest contribution to bluegrass music history.

In 1955 Bobby and Sonny Osborne were looking to front their own bluegrass group. They had recently worked with Jimmy Martin. Bobby had previously been with the Lonesome Pine Fiddlers and the Stanley Brothers, and Sonny with Bill Monroe. Ready to make their own mark on bluegrass music, the Osbornes recruited fellow Daytonian Red Allen to round out their trio. Tommy Sutton believed in the act and took some of their demo recordings to Nashville. Sutton's status as a nationally known disc jockey had its perks, and he was able to secure a contract for the Osborne Brothers and Red Allen with MGM Records.[59] Their first release, "Ruby, Are You Mad?," Bobby had sung during his onstage debut at WPFB. Sutton's relationship with the Osbornes and Allen included cowriting credits on several of their recordings, including "Della Mae," "It Hurts to Know," "Teardrops in My Eyes," and "Two Lonely Hearts."[60]

Les Bodine and WBZI, WCNW, and WAVI

Les Bodine was a longtime Dayton-area DJ who in 1964 started and managed full-time country station WBZI-FM in Xenia, Ohio. He operated a music store at 609 East Fifth Street in Dayton, as well as a recording studio in the store's back room. It was there that Red Allen, Frank Wakefield, and Red Spurlock recorded as the Red Heads in 1960.[61] Bodine was also a bandleader and managed a live barn dance show.

WCNW in Fairfield was an all-country station from 1964 to 1975. Its DJs included Charlie Gore, Ray Pennington, Bonnie Lou, and Hamilton/Fairfield legend Pappy Tipton. In a radio response rating by *Billboard* in 1964, WCNW was the top country station in the Cincinnati area.

WAVI, in Dayton, was an all-country station for several years. It began as WWSO in Springfield, where it had been owned by the famous old-time singer Bradley Kincaid. Kincaid sold it to a group that included Tommy Sutton. They moved it to Dayton and changed the call letters. Other DJs at WAVI included Al Morris, who was a fan of the recording "Twenty-One Years" by the Lonesome Pine Fiddlers, and "Cuzzin Bill" Hamby, who was on other Dayton stations as well as doing a second stint at WAVI as program director. In addition to being a much-loved DJ, Hamby had a band and made records that later became favorites of rockabilly collectors around the world.[62]

Paul "Moon" Mullins

After Smokey Ward left WPFB in the mid-1950s, bluegrass music's presence on Miami Valley airwaves fell into decline.[63] Ward's departure coincided with the rise of Elvis Presley, the Beatles, and the rock and roll fever that consumed the nation. WPFB and other radio stations started to feature records they hoped would have more mainstream appeal. Bluegrass and twang were displaced by the lush strings and syrupy background choirs of the "Nashville Sound." Country music went uptown and—at least until 1964—left bluegrass and Appalachian music lovers hungry for their favorite sounds.

In 1964 a radio personality from eastern Kentucky named Paul Mullins came to work at Middletown's WPFB.[64] His beginning in the radio business involved moonshine and a bet. One night during the winter of 1960, Mullins and a buddy were sharing a quart and listening to a local radio station. Elbowing his friend, Mullins said, "I bet you ten dollars I can go get that fellow's job." They shook on it, and within a matter of weeks Paul was live on the radio at WGOH in Grayson, Kentucky.[65] He adopted "Moon" as his radio nickname, after the popular Moon Mullins comic strip character of that era.

Although his assertiveness was to be commended, it had been aided by liquid courage. Moon actually struggled with crippling stage fright. He was known as a fiddle player and had even worked for a time with the Stanley Brothers. Stage fright had cost Mullins his gig with those bluegrass legends, although they would remain close friends. Mullins viewed radio as a less threatening way to overcome his fears of being on stage. After a few weeks on the air, his confidence grew and his fears subsided.[66]

After the initial stint at WGOH, he worked for a short while at WMST in Mt. Sterling, Kentucky, followed by WTCR in Ashland, Kentucky, and a return engagement at WGOH before crossing the river to Ohio in 1964.[67] Moon hit WPFB like lightning. His Kentucky heritage, ad-libbed commercials, and bluegrass pedigree were to make him the local Appalachian migrant community's leading radio voice for the next four decades.

Moon Mullins was originally from Menifee County, Kentucky, one of the poorest counties in the state. Now in southwestern Ohio for work, he was an Appalachian migrant just like his audience. As a transplant himself, he developed a level of trust with the migrant community that was unmatched by any other area businessperson, radio personality, or entertainer. Mullins regularly referenced Southern geography and lore that endeared him to fellow migrants and sounded fascinatingly exotic to non-Southerners. Miami Valley bluegrass bandleader Katie Laur said, "Knowing what he was talking about made you part of the 'in-group.' And as a transplanted hillbilly myself, I know we needed all the self-acceptance we could garner."[68]

Mullins unashamedly spoke with the Appalachian language and humor of a bygone era. Frequent topics included working in his garden (one of Mullins's favorite pastimes), growing tomatoes, hunting ginseng, and reading the mountain signs to predict the weather.

"The sun's as warm as a biscuit."

"The weatherman would do well to quit lookin' at them little scopes and take a look out the winder every now and then."

"It's been dry as a shuck bean lately, ain't it? . . . Have y'all noticed how the trees have been followin' the dogs around?"

"It's hotter than an old lady at a kissing party."[69]

"It's cold. It's like the backside of a witch's lap."

"If y'all have got pop a'sittin' on the back porch, it'll be alright this morning but by tomorrow those bottles'll be froze and busted, don't ya know."[70]

Mullins's country dialect permeated everything he did on the air. Moon often began his radio programs with "We're gonna plow all the way to the fence." It was a recognizable reference for those who grew up looking at the backside of a mule while preparing ground for tobacco, corn, or other crops. It was an Appalachian way of saying "Don't cut any corners." Mullins's colorful expression told audiences that he and they were going to have a good time together, from the time he went on the air until he signed off, and that he was going to give it his all.

It was almost as though Moon had an inside joke with his audience, one that they were in on and from which everybody else was excluded. But regular listeners, whether Appalachian or not, soon came to enjoy and appreciate the special world Moon created on the airwaves. This unique connection and the fierce loyalty it engendered came to serve him well, both in business and in music.

Speaking the same language as the migrants, Moon tailored his ad-lib commercials to his audience in an age before Facebook and Google demonstrated the value of pinpointing specific demographics. His commercials became as entertaining a part of his program as his selection of music—a rare accomplishment in the radio business. People would tune in just to hear Moon do a commercial or give a weather forecast. "In order to be successful, I find you have got to have more than just a record to play," said Moon. "You got to make folks want to listen at you. That's the reason I try to keep humor in my radio program—keep it in my commercials to where it don't get boring."[71]

Moon's listeners were certainly never bored. His audience never knew what he was going to say. One time a local department store had Moon advertising custom-made bras. Moon reported taking his wife, Prudence, to the store to be fitted and advised male listeners to do likewise. As he put it, "Whether they look like Dolly Parton's or two poached eggs, they'll get 'em to look right."[72]

Through his unique insight into migrants' memories and way of life, Mullins developed relationships with business owners who had Appalachian roots and others seeking to penetrate that market. Due to the level of trust he engendered among his audience by being "one of them," he was able to generate business for his sponsors—a lot of business.

Moon's audience trusted him and his judgment, so if Moon endorsed a firm, his listeners flocked to its doors. This old style of personal, ad-lib advertising was truly an art, and Moon was the master. His unique style of phrasing and his no-nonsense approach appealed to the sponsors almost as much as they did to listeners. WPFB management was willing to tolerate a lot of Moon's quirks, as long as he continued to bring in business.

Mom's Restaurant was an old-fashioned country kitchen in the community of Red Lion, a wide spot in the road between Franklin and Lebanon. "Mom" (Hilda Ratliff) bought some ads on Moon's program. Once Moon started telling everybody to head over to Mom's Restaurant to get her biscuits and gravy, the impact was immediate. "Mom" Ratliff recalled standing in the kitchen and crying because she had only one skillet and couldn't keep up with the orders.[73]

Bluegrass singer Dudley Connell (of the Johnson Mountain Boys, Longview, and the Seldom Scene) recalled driving around the Miami Valley in the 1990s. Like other fans of bluegrass and classic country, he tuned in to Moon. Mullins was doing an advertisement for a local gas station that also had a deli serving everything from biscuits to beer. On this particular day Moon was talking about the bologna sandwiches. After listening for just a few minutes, Connell found himself craving a gas station bologna sandwich, leading him to credit Moon as "the greatest salesman who ever lived."[74]

Moon wasn't afraid to push the envelope and was never one to shy away from the "wow" factor. But though he was just a self-proclaimed country boy (and a proud one at that), the level of dignity and professionalism he maintained earned him the respect of people who weren't Appalachian migrants. He said, "I don't know why people have the impression that there's no dignity in being a briar or being from the country."[75]

Moon adamantly fought preconceived notions that many folks had regarding people from Appalachia (stereotypes that, unfortunately, persist in the twenty-first century). "I know that I am country," he said, "and a fellow that don't know what he is don't know very damn much."[76]

Longtime Miami Valley disc jockey Chubby Howard worked with Mullins at WPFB and later at WBZI in Xenia. He remembers one of the salesmen at WPFB taking Moon, wearing a suit and tie, to meet a potential sponsor. "The big guy that owned the entire establishment stepped back a couple of steps and looked [Moon] up and down," said Chubby. "He said, 'You don't look like a hillbilly.'" To which Moon retorted, "What do you think a hillbilly looks like, you no good . . ." followed by a string of choice words. The salesman thought for sure that any particular chance of closing the deal was over, until the business owner said, "Sign me up!"[77]

Moon Mullins was a bona fide country boy and a bluegrass expert. His pedigree as a professional musician added an important level of authority to his commentary about the records he played. His bluegrass performing career did not end after the short stint with the Stanley Brothers. In 1962, while on the air in Ashland, Kentucky, he founded the Bluegrass Playboys, a popular Kentucky band that for a short time included, on bass, future Country Music and Bluegrass Hall of Fame member Tom T. Hall. The band played frequently in eastern Kentucky, West Virginia, and southern Ohio.

With the Bluegrass Playboys, Mullins recorded "Katie Daley," now a bluegrass standard. "Somebody gave me a poem one time," said Moon. "I think there were thirty-seven verses. The gist of the poem was a gal that made whiskey by the name of Katie Daley."[78] Mullins was the first American to record the old Irish poem, bringing it into the bluegrass canon. It became a jukebox hit in the early 1960s for the Bluegrass Playboys and would later be popularized by Ralph Stanley.

During his career as a WPFB disc jockey, Moon would moonlight as a fiddler at bars and nightclubs in the Miami Valley that regularly featured bluegrass music. He worked in bands with other bluegrassers in the area, including Charlie Moore, Bill Napier, Harley Gabbard, Earl Taylor, and Jim McCall. He would even slip down to Lexington, Kentucky, to sit in on fiddle with J. D. Crowe and the Kentucky Mountain Boys. When his former bosses the Stanley Brothers were in the area for one of their frequent local performances, he introduced them to a Miami Valley native named Larry Sparks, who joined the band before becoming a star in his own right.

During the 1970s, while still working at WPFB, Moon Mullins was an integral member of the Boys from Indiana, a popular festival act of the day. Their signature song, "Atlanta Is Burning," became a bluegrass classic. Moon continued his track record of successful bands by founding the Traditional Grass in 1983 with his son, Joe Mullins, and local guitarist Mark Rader. Throughout the 1980s and early '90s, the Traditional Grass was among the hottest bluegrass bands going, with four albums on Rebel Records.

Moon did not make bluegrass successful on Miami Valley airwaves by his expertise alone; he was passionate about the music. When he liked a recording, he would say something like "Grab a hold of something, folks. This un's gonna blow your hat in the creek and make you wanna pat your feet."[79] If it was a record he didn't like, he sometimes simply broke it over the airwaves rather than suffer through listening to it again.[80] If he was feeling generous, he would offer constructive criticism such as "I'd like to know who told that bass player that he could keep time, because whoever that was lied to him." Moon summed up his programming philosophy this way: "I ain't gonna play something I don't like. Especially at 5:30 in the morning."[81]

Mullins believed in integrating bluegrass alongside hit country songs rather than keeping the genres segregated. These were lean times for bluegrass music.

The rock and roll boom had nearly starved out the artists, particularly in the 1960s. Moon's programming style was a major contributor to the success and growth of bluegrass music in the Miami Valley. In most other places, if bluegrass was heard on radio at all, it was relegated to Saturday mornings, Sunday nights, or one particular hour out of the entire week. By playing bluegrass alongside Johnny Cash, Merle Haggard, Loretta Lynn, Dolly Parton, and Ernest Tubb, Moon legitimized the music of bands like the Stanley Brothers and the Country Gentlemen. Mixing in bluegrass every third or fourth song was especially effective in introducing bluegrass music to new listeners who may have tuned in for the country hits or the weather forecast.

Moon Mullins's legacy and impact on the bluegrass musical footprint of the Miami Valley cannot be overstated. His ability to maintain a strong bluegrass presence on radio during the rock and roll era was vitally important to the music's growth in the region. Had Moon not been on radio maintaining a steady pipeline of bluegrass and promoting bluegrass concerts and those of other local promoters, there may not have been a bluegrass market in the Miami Valley by the time the bluegrass festivals rose to prominence in the 1970s. In 1979 Ohio hosted more bluegrass festivals than any state in the country,[82] and by then Mullins had been at WPFB for fifteen years.

After the Traditional Grass became successful in the late 1980s, Moon Mullins and WPFB parted ways. He reappeared on Miami Valley airwaves in 1995 on WBZI and retired in 2005. In 2000 he was named the International Bluegrass Music Association's (IBMA's) Bluegrass Broadcaster of the Year and received their Distinguished Achievement Award. Before his death in 2008 from progressive supranuclear palsy, he received a 2007 Ohio Heritage Fellowship Award for Performing Arts.

Mullins Family Broadcasting Legacy

The Mullins legacy on southwestern Ohio airwaves lives on, for three generations and counting. Moon's son, Joe, began broadcasting at WPFB while a teenager and remained with the station until the late 1980s. In 1995 he purchased WBZI in Xenia, bringing classic country and bluegrass music back to prominence in the Miami Valley. He would eventually add WKFI in Wilmington and WEDI in Eaton. In addition, Joe hosts the nationally syndicated and award-winning bluegrass gospel radio program *Front Porch Fellowship*, heard on over two hundred stations nationwide as part of the Singing News Radio network. He was named Bluegrass Broadcaster of the Year in 2016. Joe also fronts his own award-winning, nationally touring bluegrass band, Joe Mullins and the Radio Ramblers, and is an active leader in the International Bluegrass Music Association.

In 2018 Mullins's Classic Country Radio network underwent a rebranding in order to better connect the roots music of classic country and bluegrass with a new generation. Today, as Real Roots Radio, the network features more bluegrass music than any other radio outlet in the Buckeye State, in addition to playing current and classic country, mountain gospel, and Americana music. This author, Daniel Mullins—Joe's son and Moon's grandson—appears on Real Roots Radio as well, in addition to hosting a bluegrass-themed podcast, continuing the family legacy of broadcasting bluegrass music to the Miami Valley.[83]

The Significance of Southwestern Ohio Radio Bluegrass

The nationwide popularity of the bluegrass sound increased as it established footholds on the radio airwaves of Appalachia, Nashville, the Deep South, the Washington/Baltimore area, and southwestern Ohio. Among these regions, none has experienced the consistently high level of bluegrass radio programming that southwestern Ohio has enjoyed since the 1940s.

The continuous presence of bluegrass on radio airwaves in the Miami Valley played a vital role in the genre's growth. Live southwestern Ohio radio broadcasts provided important early opportunities for musicians who later became pillars of the genre. As industrial southwestern Ohio was increasingly populated by an influx of Appalachian migrants, radio personalities such as John Lair, Smokey Ward, Nelson King, Wayne Raney, Tommy Sutton, Moon Mullins, and Joe Mullins were able to parlay the bluegrass audience into loyal consumers for advertisers. This allowed both the music and its sponsors to flourish.

Radio allowed bluegrass music to be discovered by folks who weren't searching for it, whether they found it by scanning the dial or by initially tuning in to hear the weather forecast, traffic report, or local school closings. Radio also enabled those fans who were actively seeking out the music a way to engage as a community, to learn of area bluegrass events and recordings, and to grow in their knowledge of the music and its artists.

The genre's prominence on radio since the 1940s played a major role in making the southwestern Ohio region one of the world's leading markets for bluegrass musicians, bluegrass festivals, and bluegrass recordings—and a continuing wellspring of musical creativity. While the local recording industry, live performance venues, gospel music scene, and Appalachian community development all played roles in the growth of bluegrass in the Miami Valley, nothing exposed the music to a greater number of people or presented performers with greater opportunities than did radio.

Notes

1. Frank and Marty Godbey, "Paul Mullins: Musician, Disc Jockey and Bluegrass Influence," *Bluegrass Unlimited*, December 1975, 20.

2. John Kiesewetter, "WLW 700 Turns 80," *Cincinnati Enquirer*, March 17, 2002.

3. Ibid.

4. Radio barn dance programs incorporated a mixture of comedy and hillbilly music (as it was known at the time). Their popularity helped form a foundation for the now multimillion-dollar country music business.

5. Pete Stamper, "The History of Renfro Valley," Renfro Valley Entertainment Center, http://www.renfrovalley.com/info/renfrovalley-history.php.

6. Pete Stamper, *It All Happened in Renfro Valley* (Lexington: University Press of Kentucky, 1999), 7–8.

7. Ibid., 13.

8. Stamper, "History of Renfro Valley." In subsequent remodeling, the seating capacity of Cincinnati Music Hall was reduced.

9. Stamper, *It All Happened in Renfro Valley*, 14.

10. In subsequent remodeling, the seating capacity of Emery Theatre was reduced.

11. Stamper, *It All Happened in Renfro Valley*, 14–15.

12. Kiesewetter, "WLW 700 Turns 80."

13. Greg Gaston, "Before 'Hee Haw' was Cincy's 'Midwestern Hayride,'" *USA Today*, https://www.cincinnati.com/story/entertainment/music/2017/09/14/before-hee-haw-cincys-midwestern-hayride/666651001.

14. Alton Delmore, *Truth Is Stranger Than Publicity* (Nashville: Country Music Foundation Press, 1995), 270, 279.

15. See chapter 4, "Taking the Music Home."

16. Theodric Technologies LLC, "Predicted Daytime Coverage Area for WCKY 1530 AM, Cincinnati, OH," map, https://radio-locator.com/cgi-bin/patg?id=WCKY-AM&h=D.

17. "Nelson King: 'King' of Cincinnati Disc Jockeys," *Media Heritage.com*, August 12 2014. http://www.mediaheritage.com/nelson-king-king-of-cincinnati-disc-jockeys.

18. Ibid.

19. Ibid.

20. Neil V. Rosenberg, *Bluegrass: A History, Twentieth Anniversary Edition* (Urbana: University of Illinois Press, 2005), 153, 362.

21. "Nelson King."

22. See chapter 10, "Bluegrass Music and Urban Appalachian Identity in Cincinnati."

23. Gary B. Reid, liner notes to *Reno and Smiley, 1951–1959* (King Records, 1993), 7.

24. "Nelson King."

25. Ibid.

26. Charles K. Wolfe, *Classic Country* (New York: Routledge, 2001), 115–16, 201–202.

27. See chapter 4, "Taking the Music Home."

28. Marty Godbey, *Crowe on the Banjo: The Music Life of J. D. Crowe* (Urbana: University of Illinois Press, 2011), 28.

29. Rosenberg, *Bluegrass: A History*, 102–103.

30. "Best Selling Blue Grass Type Records (featuring 5-string banjo, mandolin, etc.)," in Rosenberg, *Bluegrass: A History*, 114.

31. Glenna Fisher, "Middletown—The Valley Where the Grass Grew," *Middletown Traditions: Appalachian Ties*, program booklet (1983), 1.

32. Ibid.

33. Fred Bartenstein, ed., "Where the Holler Hits the Hardtop: Paul 'Moon' Mullins on WPFB," (2005), https://realrootsradio.com/wp-content/uploads/2013/08/Where-the-Holler-Hits-the-Hardtop.pdf, 3.

34. Theodric Technologies, "Predicted Daytime Coverage Area."

35. Fisher, "Middletown," 1.

36. Ibid., 2.

37. Ibid.

38. Jesse McReynolds, interview by author, Nashville, TN, February 4, 2017.

39. Chubby Howard, interview by author, Xenia, OH, February 25, 2017.

40. McReynolds interview.

41. Godbey, *Crowe on the Banjo*, 33.

42. Howard interview.

43. Fisher, "Middletown," 2.

44. Ibid.

45. Howard interview.

46. Fisher, "Middletown," 2.

47. Ibid.

48. See chapter 2, "Bobby Osborne Remembers How It Was."

49. McReynolds interview.

50. Ibid.

51. "Tommy Sutton," *Hillbilly-Music dawtcom*, http://www.hillbilly-music.com/dj/story/index.php?id=12598.

52. Mac McDivitt, personal communication, July 17, 2018.

53. Godbey, *Crowe on the Banjo*, 34.

54. Ibid.

55. "Tommy Sutton," *Hillbilly-Music dawt com*.

56. Ibid.

57. McDivitt, personal communication, July 17, 2018.

58. Fisher, "Middletown," 4.

59. Bobby Osborne, interview by author, Nashville, TN, September 3, 2016.

60. "Tommy Sutton," *Hillbilly-Music dawt com*.

61. Dennis Satterlee, *Teardrops in My Eyes: The Music of Harley "Red" Allen* (Kensington, MD, Plucked String Foundation: 2007), 43–44.

62. McDivitt, personal communication, July 17, 2018.

63. Fisher, "Middletown," 4.

64. Ibid.

65. Frank and Marty Godbey, "Paul Mullins," 23.

66. Ibid., 22.

67. Ibid., 23–24.

68. Bartenstein, "Where the Holler Hits the Hardtop," 1.
69. Ibid., 6–7.
70. Mullins family records.
71. Frank and Marty Godbey, "Paul Mullins," 20.
72. Mullins family records.
73. Ibid.
74. Ibid.
75. Frank and Marty Godbey, "Paul Mullins," 20.
76. Ibid., 20.
77. Howard interview.
78. Mullins family records.
79. Bartenstein, "Where the Holler Hits the Hardtop," 4.
80. Howard interview.
81. Frank and Marty Godbey, "Paul Mullins," 21.
82. Rosenberg, *Bluegrass: A History*, 362.
83. Additional Miami Valley broadcasters are covered in chapter 8, "Buckeyes in the Briar Patch."

4. Taking the Music Home

Bluegrass Recording Studios, Record Labels, and Record Stores

MAC McDIVITT

IN THE NINETEENTH CENTURY, the only way to hear music was to be there in person when songs were sung or instruments played. Phonograph cylinders (1877) and records (1889) were invented so that people could take the music home with them. This chapter deals with the recording, manufacturing, marketing, and distribution of bluegrass records in southwestern Ohio.

When people think of making records, they usually think of the major companies such as Capitol, Columbia, Decca, and RCA, where the artist is signed to a contract and paid a royalty for each record sold. In southwestern Ohio only King and (probably) Radio Artist operated in this manner. Most other companies in the area were what is known as custom studios or custom labels. Some of the studios both recorded and pressed records, while others did only the recording and subcontracted the manufacture of the discs to a pressing plant or another studio that did pressing as well as recording.

Artists who dreamed of making it in the music business wanted to be able to say they had a record out. If you had a record, you must be on your way to being famous. If you couldn't get signed by a major record company but still wanted to make a record, you could go to a custom studio, and—for a fee—they would record you and provide you with an agreed-upon number of records that you could sell or use for promotional purposes. If the record was unsuccessful, you could use the unsold copies to play Frisbee.

Many artists didn't realize that having a record out was not a guarantee of becoming a star. They didn't think about the necessity of getting their record on the radio so the public could hear it, or that they needed a distribution system so people could buy the record if they did hear and like it. The custom companies were not going to mail DJ copies of the record to radio stations, and they weren't going to market the records. Some offered DJ mailings if you bought additional records to be sent out, but this didn't solve the distribution problem. Radio stations hesitated to play a record if it wasn't in the stores.

For artists who were thinking locally rather than nationally, custom recordings worked out well. In advertising their shows, it helped to be able to say they were recording artists. At their personal appearances, they could sing the songs and sell the records after the show. They could visit local DJs and ask them to play the record. They could go to their local record store and try to talk them into carrying a few copies, but this depended on the artists' ability to sell themselves to the DJs and record store operators and on their having the time to do so. Later on, the proliferation of chain record stores and discount department stores, coupled with national radio chains taking over local radio stations, put an end to local promotion.

Small independent record companies began to spring up shortly after the end of World War II. There were several reasons for this:

- Raw materials for making records were no longer rationed.[1]
- Invention of the tape recorder made it easier and cheaper to record.[2]
- Emergence of the BMI (Broadcast Music Inc.) performing rights organization made it possible for hillbilly and Black artists to record, because BMI didn't exclude them as did ASCAP (American Society of Composers and Publishers).[3]
- The advent of the 45 rpm record, which eventually spelled the demise of the large and fragile 78 rpm record.[4]
- The economy was good and people had money to spend.

Southwestern Ohio was involved early on in the proliferation of small labels and studios. Earl Herzog opened the first commercial recording studio in Cincinnati in 1946,[5] followed by his Radio Artist record label in 1947.[6] Syd Nathan at King made an attempt at issuing records in December of 1943,[7] with a full-fledged release in late 1944.[8]

In discussing independent record labels and their owners, Shelby Singleton, longtime producer and promoter on the national stage, said, "*All* the record men are real characters, real strong, real different people. Some of them go broke, some of them come back, some of them go broke again, come back again. But you know, we're all gamblers."[9] The southwestern Ohio label owners were no different. Syd Nathan's eccentricity has been well documented.[10] He also went broke and came back several times.[11] Carl Burkhardt was in and out of trouble with the law but kept on chugging along.[12] Lou Epstein went into bankruptcy with the Jimmie Skinner Record Shop but came back bigger and better with the Jimmie Skinner Music Center.[13] "Hobo" Jack Adkins acquired his nickname honestly.[14] Estel Lee was in and out of various enterprises.[15] Jack Lynch stories abound.[16] What follows is the story of these men and others, and the enterprises they operated.

Cincinnati Studios and Labels

"Bucky" Herzog, Herzog Studio, and Radio Artist Records

In the late 1940s WLW was the dominant radio station in the Cincinnati market and heavily influential nationally.[17] Numerous network shows were produced at WLW, including soap operas and musical presentations. The station employed many actors and musicians, and most of the shows were broadcast live.[18]

Earl T. "Bucky" Herzog had been an engineer at WLW since 1936.[19] In 1945, deciding to do a little moonlighting, he started a recording business in his home. By June of 1946 his business had grown to the point that he opened the first commercial recording studio in downtown Cincinnati, on the second floor of 811 Race Street. The E. T. Herzog Recording Company was owned by Earl; his brother, Charlie; and Henry Weiss.[20] Because of his connection to WLW artists, "Bucky" was able to record some of them on a label he called Radio Artist Records.[21] The label's motto was "Your Radio Friends on Record."

The studio was just around the corner from WLW. Old-timers joked that Herzog hung a cable out the window at WLW and ran it to Herzog Studio.[22] That was a bit of an exaggeration, since the studio was more than a block away from the radio station. The first four records issued were by the Turner Brothers and the next two were by Dolly Good, all hillbilly artists at WLW.

The bluegrass connection for Radio Artist came late in its existence, when Lou Epstein acquired the label (but not the studio) and used it as a vehicle to promote Jimmie Skinner, an artist he managed.[23] While not strictly a bluegrass artist, Jimmie was close to being one, and years later he did move into straight bluegrass. Eleven of the last twelve records on Radio Artist were by Jimmie Skinner. After Jimmie got a major-label recording contract with Capitol, Epstein allowed Radio Artist to go dormant. In its short life, Radio Artist issued approximately fifty records.[24]

In addition to recording all the Radio Artist releases, Herzog ran an active custom recording business. Major labels came to Herzog because the studio had access to the first house recording band in country music history, predating Nashville's famous "A Team." Jerry Byrd on steel guitar, Louis Innis on rhythm guitar, Tommy Jackson on fiddle, and Zeke Turner on lead guitar had previously worked with the Cumberland Valley Boys, Red Foley's Nashville-based road band. They left for Cincinnati after pay problems with Foley and upon hearing that WLW was looking for a country house band for its radio and TV shows. After arriving in 1948, they became the Pleasant Valley Boys and immediately began picking up recording dates at Herzog.

Producers Fred Rose from MGM Records and Murray Nash from Mercury Records respected the talents of the Pleasant Valley Boys, as well as the friendly and helpful attitude of the engineers at Herzog Studio, so they took artists to Cincinnati to record.[25] On December 22, 1948, Fred Rose brought twenty-five-year-old Hank Williams to Herzog. Hank was looking for his first big hit record and found it that day with "Lovesick Blues," which became his signature song and carried him to the Grand Ole Opry. Williams and Rose returned to Herzog on August 30, 1949, and recorded the poetic "I'm So Lonesome I Could Cry."

The most famous bluegrass session recorded at Herzog was on December 11, 1949, when Murray Nash brought Lester Flatt, Earl Scruggs, and the Foggy Mountain Boys to record. This was the second visit that Lester and Earl had made to the Cincinnati studio.[26] Eight tracks were recorded that day, but the one that stands out is "Foggy Mountain Breakdown," an instrumental featuring Earl's three-finger-style banjo. The tune was popular upon its release, but it gained a new life when actor/producer Warren Beatty used it as the chase theme music for his 1967 movie *Bonnie and Clyde*.

When Syd Nathan formed King Records in the mid-1940s, he didn't have a recording studio; early King records were recorded at Herzog. Eventually, Nathan's abrasive personality alienated the musicians and wore on Earl Herzog, until he finally told Syd that he was no longer welcome at Herzog.[27] This forced Nathan to build his own studio in the King complex on Brewster Avenue.[28]

It was great while it lasted, but in 1951 a couple of things happened that spelled the end of Herzog Studio. Earl's brother, Charlie, who was a partner and did a lot of the engineering, passed away that year. The Pleasant Valley Boys, who had come to Cincinnati for excellent wages as the house band at WLW, were advised by the new owners of WLW that their pay, as well as that of the other station musicians, was being cut in half. Jerry Byrd, Tommy Jackson, and Louis Innis promptly left Cincinnati and returned to Nashville. There they began work at the new Castle Studio in the Tulane Hotel and at WSM Radio. With the Pleasant Valley Boys back in Nashville, producers no longer had to go to Cincinnati for good studio musicians. With Jimmie Skinner's departure from Radio Artist Records, the label went dormant and Herzog lost that source of income. Some sessions were done at Herzog in 1952 but apparently none after that.[29] Herzog Studio had completed a short but historic life, recording a lot of good music.

Syd Nathan, King Studio, and King Records

Syd Nathan had a vision: to start a company that would record local hillbilly artists who worked on Cincinnati's WLW Radio.[30] Syd found that having a vision and fulfilling that vision were two very different things. He had many obstacles to overcome, but his stubbornness and persistence were two of the qualities that carried him through to establishing King Records as the premier independent record company in America.

In 1943 there weren't any commercial recording studios in Cincinnati, so Nathan didn't have much trouble finding locally based artists to record. Grandpa Jones and Merle Travis were regular customers of Syd's Record Shop.[31] They both sang and played on WLW and were willing to try recording. However, WLW had rules about their artists doing any outside work, so they were apprehensive. Finally, Syd and the two artists decided they would go fifty miles north to Dayton and record in what was described as a "makeshift studio" over the Wurlitzer Piano Store on S. Ludlow Street. They accomplished this, apparently in September of 1943,[32] when they cut a total of four songs, two of them duets and the other two Travis solos. The duets were issued under the name of "the Sheppard Brothers" and Merle's solo sides as "Bob McCarthy," apparently to fool WLW.

The next problem was finding a pressing plant, since Cincinnati had none. Syd tried several plants, but the pressing was so bad that a lot of the records wouldn't play. Syd solved this problem by hiring George W. Weitlauf, an engineer from the American Printing House for the Blind in Louisville, Kentucky. Weitlauf was brought to Cincinnati in 1944 to set up a pressing plant in a building that Nathan leased at 1540 Brewster Avenue in Cincinnati's Evanston neighborhood. This became the permanent home of King Records.

Many of the early King recordings had been cut at Cincinnati's Herzog Studio, but not having a studio of his own became a problem for Syd when he was banned from Herzog. After Syd acquired the property on Brewster Avenue, he recorded there at night by turning his accounting department into a temporary recording studio. He eventually built at the complex a permanent studio that was praised over the years by musicians and producers for its acoustics and "presence."[33]

Early recordings on King came almost exclusively from current or former WLW performers. The Carlisle Brothers, Cowboy Copas, the Delmore Brothers, Grandpa Jones, Hank Penny, Bill and Evalina (Stallard), Roy Starkey, and Merle Travis all were or had been members of WLW's *Boone County Jamboree* or the *Top of the Morning* show. A race records division, Queen, was added in 1943 but eventually merged into the King label. Syd Nathan's company was unique in simultaneously and successfully producing both country and rhythm and blues releases.

In the late 1940s King recorded J. E. and Wade Mainer, who were a bridge between old-time country and bluegrass. More near-bluegrass recordings followed, including a 1950 four-song session by Shannon Grayson and the Golden Valley Boys, a gospel group from the Carolinas, and a March 1951 session by Tommy Magness and His Tennessee Buddies. Two of the Buddies were Don Reno and Red Smiley, who in 1952 began recording on their own for King. Reno and Smiley and the Stanley Brothers (signed in 1958) were the most popular bluegrass acts on King Records. In August of 1951 Jimmy Martin and Bob Osborne cut four sides for King, the label's first that completely reflected the new bluegrass style. Other bluegrass artists on King included Bill Duncan, the Easter Brothers, Leon Jackson, Charlie Moore and Bill Napier, Mac O'Dell, Don Reno and Bill Harrell, and Ralph Stanley (following Carter Stanley's death).[33]

After Syd Nathan got his studio up and running, King did a lot of custom recording and pressing for other labels and individual bands. A large pool of excellent musicians in the Cincinnati area could be called upon for professional studio accompaniment.

In later years the number of country and bluegrass acts declined as King's energy was increasingly devoted to promoting rhythm and blues superstar James Brown.[34] However, Reno and Smiley and the Stanley Brothers kept sailing along with frequent King releases. In 1968 Syd Nathan passed away and James Brown's contract, King's publishing rights, and the label were sold.[35]

George Weitlauf, Stephen Shaw, and Shaw Record Processing

When King's Syd Nathan decided to manufacture records as well as produce and record them, he hired George Weitlauf, a mechanical engineer who had experience in establishing manufacturing operations for major labels. Weitlauf set up and for five years operated King's manufacturing operation before leaving in 1949 to develop his own custom pressing facility at 1914 Dana Avenue in Cincinnati. It was named Shaw Record Processing for another King employee, Stephen Shaw, who left with Weitlauf to operate the new company.[36] Because there were no other custom pressing plants in Cincinnati, Shaw was able to corner the pressing business for most of the local labels such as Carl Burkhardt's Big 4 Hits, Gateway, and Kentucky, as well as Echo, Esta, Excellent, Pearl, and Radio Artist. By 1955 Carl Burkhardt was setting up his own pressing operation, which took away a lot of business, and Shaw ceased operations in 1956.[37]

Carl Burkhardt, Gateway-Rite Studios, and Affiliated Record Labels

Sonny Osborne was not quite fifteen years old on an October day in 1952 when he and eighteen-year-old Carlos Brock, along with twenty-four-year-old Enos Johnson, journeyed from Dayton to Carl Burkhardt's Gateway Studio in the Cincinnati neighborhood now known as Northside. Joined by veteran musician and radio personality Smokey Ward and Cincinnati fiddle player Billy Thomas, they were about to embark on a recording adventure that would not conclude until early 1956; it comprised at least six sessions and produced approximately fifty sides.

The musicians were reportedly paid the princely sum of fifty dollars a day, with no residual royalties. They had been playing the Dayton bars and were happy to pick up a little extra money playing the music they loved. That music was bluegrass, but it hadn't yet received that name; advertisements called it "country music with five-string banjo." Sonny Osborne was already a bluegrass music veteran, having played in Bill Monroe's band and recorded with Bill when he was fourteen years old. Sonny and his band recorded fourteen songs on their first session, mostly Flatt and Scruggs and Bill Monroe covers. Ten were issued on Burkhardt's Kentucky label and the other four on Gateway, another Burkhardt label.[38]

Sonny was back again in late 1952 to record another twelve songs. Four were originals, including "A Brother in Korea" by Louise Osborne, about her and Sonny's brother, Bobby, at the time a marine in active service. The other side was an instrumental titled "Sunny Mountain Chimes."[39] This was probably the only actual hit that came out on any of Burkhardt's labels. The record got exposure on WCKY radio in Cincinnati and caught on because it was different, it was exciting, and it capitalized on growing interest in the five-string banjo. Burkhardt ran an ad in *Billboard* that claimed the record had already sold sixty-seven thousand copies. Sonny later said that it eventually sold a total of around eighty thousand copies, unheard of for a local label.[40]

Six of the tracks from that session, the instrumentals and sacred songs, came out on another of Burkhardt's many labels, Big 4 Hits. Big 4 records were actually EPs (extended play records) that had four songs instead of two. The selling point proclaimed on the sleeves was "twice the music for half the price." (At that time, single records with two songs sold for ninety-eight cents, whereas the Big 4s with four songs sold for forty-nine cents.)

During a two-week leave before mustering out, Bobby Osborne returned from Korea in August of 1953,[41] played mandolin, and did some of the lead singing on another of Sonny's sessions.[42] Sonny's stint with Burkhardt ran for two more sessions after that. Most of the releases from those sessions were instrumentals that appeared on the Gateway label.[43] Later some of Sonny's recordings were reissued on another of Burkhardt's labels, Big 6, which had six songs on each record.

The recording studio was located behind Burkhardt's appliance store at 3930 Spring Grove Avenue. In Burkhardt's own words, the studio "was a home-made affair, 20 x 40 x 10, ceiling and side walls covered with acoustic tile and [a] painted cement floor."[44] Jim and Jesse McReynolds and Larry Roll had already recorded bluegrass gospel there as the Virginia Trio, probably in 1951 when they were working at WPFB radio in Middletown, Ohio.[45] Those recordings, ten in all, were issued on Burkhardt's first label, Kentucky Records. The label motto was "Folk Music from the Hills of Old Kentucky." Use of the word "Kentucky" was obviously to let Appalachian migrants in the area know that this was music they would probably like.

Another southwestern Ohio bluegrass artist who recorded for Carl Burkhardt was Red Allen. Red had seven songs released, six on Kentucky and one on Big 4 Hits. Most of the lead singing on these was by fiddle player Johnny McKee, with Red singing lead on "Bouquet in Heaven." All were sacred songs.[46]

Carl Burkhardt was a guy looking for a way to make a buck. He had started an appliance business in 1946 at 3930 Spring Grove Avenue in Cincinnati. By 1950 it was known as Northside Music and Appliance. As was a custom in those days, appliance stores also sold records. Carl Burkhardt didn't limit himself to selling legitimate records; he also sold what were referred to as blue, risqué, or party records.[47]

On June 24, 1950, *Billboard* reported that Burkhardt had been convicted of transportation of obscene records in interstate commerce. He was sentenced to a year and a day in the federal penitentiary at Ashland, Kentucky, but served only four months.[48] He had been caught when Detroit police seized 1,500 obscene records that were linked back to Burkhardt. The FBI estimated that he had distributed 100,000 of the records in sixteen states, describing them as "filthy songs and recitations."[49] These records surfaced again in 1953 when Burkhardt employee Charles "Chuck" Seitz was arrested and fined for having 7,625 pornographic phonograph records at North Side Record Company. Burkhardt later absolved Seitz of having any connection with these records, saying that the records had been in storage under lock and key since 1950.[50]

Carl had another scrape with the authorities in 1955. The US secretary of labor charged him with permitting his employees to work more than forty hours a week at less than the legal overtime rate, employing two minors between the ages of sixteen and eighteen, and failing to make and preserve adequate records concerning his employees and their work.[51]

In 1959 Burkhardt had more trouble. In February he testified before the Senate Rackets Committee, which was investigating a reported gangster plot to counterfeit hit records. Chief counsel for the Senate committee was Robert F. Kennedy, the future US attorney general. It was alleged that Chicago underworld figures contacted Burkhardt with the purpose of having him press bootleg copies of current hits. They would ship him printed labels of the hits, and Burkhardt would apparently affix the labels after the records were pressed. Burkhardt took the Fifth Amendment but did admit to producing up to six thousand records a day in 1957 under labels of various record companies.[52] A former Burkhardt employee said that some of those records were still around in a storeroom at Rite Records in the late 1970s.[53]

Carl Burkhardt built a thriving business in "cover" records. It was common practice for record companies in the 1940s and 1950s to bring out their own versions of another label's hit by one of their major artists. But Burkhardt went them one better: he had local artists make virtually exact copies of hit records. These were then sold in packages of several records at bargain prices, on radio and through *Country Song Roundup* magazine. The advertising pitch didn't actually say that these were the original hits, but it tried to make buyers think they were. Most of the records issued by Big 4 Hits, Big 6, Gateway, and Kentucky were covers.

Carl Burkhardt spawned enough different labels to make a person's head spin. Kentucky recordings were reissued on Alcar with the same numbers as Kentucky, but Alcar also issued records of its own. Gateway had an original series, but it also issued covers on Top Tunes, Gateway Top Tunes, and Gateway Parade of Hits, all using the same numbers. There was also a series called Tunes for Tots, which issued five-inch unbreakable 78 rpm records for children. Burkhardt had a short-lived label called ARC (not to be confused with Artist's Recording Company, which also used those initials, or with Ark Records). ARC started out with originals by artists such as WCKY DJ Marty Roberts, Indianapolis country star Lattie Moore, and Gateway engineer Chuck Seitz's wife, Lucy Traylor. It soon turned into a cover label, with the occasional original thrown in.[54]

The covers were sold in different markets with label names such as Deresco, Four, Hep, Micro, Super-Value, Ultra-sonic, and Worthmore. They were also licensed to budget labels such as Design, Family Library, Hollywood, and many others. In addition, they were issued on Gateway LPs as well as being licensed to numerous other labels for use on their LPs.

After the cover business died down, Carl decided to go into custom recording and pressing. Until this time, most of his pressing was done at Shaw Record Processing in Cincinnati. The owner of Shaw had passed away, and his wife was having difficulty maintaining the business. Burkhardt bought the Shaw equipment and began acquiring the Shaw customers.[55] In 1955 he built a new studio and pressing plant in Lockland, across I-75 from the Cincinnati General Electric plant.

At this time Carl Burkhardt incorporated his custom pressing business as Rite Record Productions Inc. He ran ads in *Billboard* and other publications, offering package prices on various quantities of records.[56] Customers could record in the Rite Studio or supply their own prerecorded tapes, and Rite could handle all aspects of the pressing. Rite pressed records for individuals and bands and for small labels in Indiana, Kentucky, Michigan, Ohio, and West Virginia, as well as for Starday custom labels and for the Texas label Cowtown.[57] By 1984, when they closed down the pressing operation, Rite had pressed twenty-one thousand singles and LPs.[58]

In spite of all his legal problems, Carl Burkhardt was a successful entrepreneur. He was one of the first, if not the first, to press soundalike records to be sold at bargain prices. He also built his custom pressing business into a nationwide operation. Record collectors today are fascinated with trying to catalog and acquire the recordings he pressed for so many different labels.

Estel Lee and Excellent Records

One of the earliest labels in Cincinnati was Excellent Records, owned by Estel Scarborough, who used the stage name Estel Lee. Lee was born at Lock 13 on the Kentucky River, near Beattyville, Kentucky, on November 19, 1915; his father was the lockmaster. Estel's family moved to Hamilton, Ohio, when he was ten years old. As he grew up, Lee showed an interest in dramatics and performing. After seeing magician John Calvert, he became fascinated with magic. When he left Hamilton High School, he went on the road with Calvert's magic show for eight years.[59] After that, he went out on his own and traveled the vaudeville circuit with his wife, Rosa Lee, who sang and performed dances. Estel's magician persona was "The Great Kalahad."[60]

In 1944 he and Rosa were singing and playing on WAGM in Presque Isle, Maine.[61] They left there to play nightclubs in Indiana, Ohio, and Kentucky.[62] By 1945 Estel had two bands, the Arizona Wildcats and the Hollywood Cowboys, and was forming a third one called the Barn Dance Jamboree.[63] The Hollywood Cowboys included Max Terhune and his dummy, Elmer.[64] (Terhune had appeared in movies, as "Lullaby" in the Three Mesquiteers series and as "Alibi" in the Range Busters series.) By 1946 Estel was down to one band, the Arizona Wildcats, and was performing at carnivals and fairs in eastern states: New Jersey, Pennsylvania, and Virginia.

In the early 1950s Lee came to Cincinnati and started working for Jimmie Skinner as a clown on personal appearances and at the Jimmie Skinner Music Center. In 1953 he started the Felicity Barn Dance at the Rex Theater in Felicity, Ohio, a small town about thirty-five miles east of Cincinnati.

In 1952 Estel founded Excellent Records. The new label was announced in the August 9, 1952, issue of *Billboard*: "Estel Lee, who is working personals with Jimmie Skinner around Cincinnati, has started a new diskery, Excellent Records."[65] Three of the first four records issued by Excellent were by Lee himself. *Billboard* wasn't exactly complimentary in their reviews of his records. "Beautiful Rose" / "This or That" (Excellent 202) was described as "a doleful reading by Lee."[66] "Too Much I've Loved You" / "Will You Remember?" (206) received the comment "Lee sings this innocuous item in so-so fashion."[67] After this, Estel Lee seemed to concentrate on recording other people, both bluegrass and country artists.

Excellent started out with a post office box address in Hooven, Ohio, an industrial area just west of Cincinnati near the Indiana state line. Around 1954 the address changed to 224 E. Fifth Street in Cincinnati, next door to the Jimmie Skinner Music Center at 222 E. Fifth.

Music publishing for the early Excellent Records was done through Kentucky Folk Music, a BMI affiliate owned by WCKY DJ Nelson King and songwriter/promoter Joe Grieshop.[68] Around 1956 the publishing shifted to Mooney and Lee Music, also a BMI affiliate, owned by Estel Lee and Bob Mooney.

From the beginning, Excellent had given its pressing business to Shaw Record Processing, the pioneer pressing plant in the Cincinnati area. About the same time that the publishing changed, Excellent took its pressing to Rite Records. This raises the question as to whether Bob Mooney became a partner about this time. Around 1958 Bob Mooney did become a partner with Estel Lee in Arvis Records, which began operations the next year, shortly after the end of Excellent. Arvis had a short life, issuing fewer than twenty records through 1961, with one last release in 1967. Estel Lee died on November 5, 1988, in Springfield, Ohio.

Lee located and recorded bluegrass artists who later became well known. One of those was Dave Woolum, who never went full-time as an artist and bandleader but managed to stay relevant in bluegrass circles in southwestern Ohio for the next several decades, performing only on weekends in order to keep his day job. Woolum had recorded a country record on Excellent (203) with a man named Cornelius, as Dave and Cornny.[69] His next record (Excellent 209) was full-bore bluegrass but was described in *Billboard* on January 30, 1954, as "an OK warble."[70]

Dave Woolum's next Excellent release, "I Ain't Gonna Let Her Do It Anymore" / "Single Girl, Married Girl" (Excellent 224), with Noah Crase on five-string banjo, fared much better. The *Billboard* reviewer on September 10, 1955, thought the A side was "a fine mountain style vocal" with "good banjo support," while the B side had "outstanding five-string banjo."[71] Woolum went on to record two more singles for Excellent, with Noah Crase receiving billing on both records. Noah was quoted as saying that he was never a regular member of Dave Woolum's band but that Dave always called him when he was going to record.[72]

Two other performers, Aubrey Holt and Harley Gabbard, who later helped form the Boys from Indiana, got their recording start on Excellent. In 1956 they recorded "Rock and Roll Country Style" and "Wild Rose" (279) as the Logan Valley Boys. In 1957 they recorded "Family Reunion" and "Let the Saviour In" (308) as the Logan and Laurel County Boys with Dave Woolum's band, the Laurel County Partners, minus Woolum.

Rusty York, Jewel Recording Studio, and Jewel Records

Born in Harlan County, Kentucky, Charles Edward "Rusty" York came to Cincinnati when he was seventeen years old. He could play both guitar and banjo and began working the bars in Cincinnati with another Kentucky boy, Willard Hale.[73] The duo later made some recordings on Starday Records.[74] Rusty acquired his nickname because people in the clubs assumed that the name inscribed on his secondhand guitar was his. In the bars, York played the banjo when he and Hale were doing bluegrass, and guitar when they did rockabilly and country songs. Rusty went to work for Jimmie Skinner and became his right-hand man at the Jimmie Skinner Music Center.[75] He also played banjo, Dobro, and electric lead guitar behind Skinner as the occasion demanded.

Rusty York became perhaps the only artist to have simultaneous careers in rockabilly and bluegrass music.[76] He recorded rockabilly demos in the Gateway Studio and cut rockabilly records for King.[77] "Sugaree" became a national hit on Chess Records, securing appearances for Rusty on Dick Clark's Bandstand Tour, at the Hollywood Bowl, and at many other venues.[78] He recorded an original banjo instrumental, "Banjo Strut," on Mercury Records.[79]

After the excitement of being a road musician and a rockabilly star started to wear off, Rusty wanted to stay closer to home. Since he loved country and bluegrass music and had gained sound engineering experience working at the Jimmie Skinner Music Center, he decided to open his own recording studio. It started in his garage in 1961, and he worked it part-time while also doing personal appearances and fronting Bobby Bare's country band. When York finally came off the road for good, he first rented and then purchased a building at 1594 Kinney Avenue in the Cincinnati suburb of Mount Healthy that he turned into a studio. The building became the home of Jewel Recording Studio and Jewel Records (named after Roy Acuff's song "The Precious Jewel") for the remainder of their existence.[80]

In his new studio, Rusty put together a set of gospel EPs to be sold through the Jimmie Skinner Music Center. It included recordings by local artists Roy Shepard, the Upchurch Brothers, Ted Mullins, Esco Hankins and Jackie, and Rusty with his band, the Kentucky Mountain Boys.[81] At roughly the same time, he helped put together another set of EPs, this time all bluegrass, to be sold by the Jimmie Skinner Music Center under its own label, Blue Grass Special.[82]

Rusty credited gospel singer J. D. Jarvis with helping to keep his studio and label afloat in the early years.[83] J. D. had a primitive but strong and sincere singing style that was much loved by gospel music fans.[84] Jarvis made and sold a lot of records, including singles and LPs on Jewel as well as on the California-based Rural Rhythm label, engineered and recorded by Rusty for label owner "Uncle" Jim O'Neal.

In 1969 blues singer Lonnie Mack cut an album for Elektra at Jewel, bringing credibility to the studio for more than just country and gospel. The Grateful Dead also recorded at Jewel.[85] Jewel recorded TV soundtracks, jingles, and high school bands. By 1971 Jewel was averaging fifteen sessions a week, using the latest equipment.[86]

Over nine hundred single records were issued on the Jewel label, along with several hundred LPs. Later they shifted to cassettes and CDs. In addition to the Jewel releases, thousands of recordings were engineered and recorded for others at Jewel Studio. Jewel acquired a reputation for good engineering and what some referred to as a "warm" sound. By the time Rusty York retired and closed the studio in 2008, Jewel had cemented a reputation as the "go to" place to record in the Cincinnati area.

Blue Grass Special and All Time Country Hits

Two labels were created in 1961 by the Jimmie Skinner Music Center in Cincinnati for marketing special record offers. Lou Epstein, manager of the record store, put together numerous bargain packages of records, primarily for mail-order sales. Blue Grass Special (note that "Blue Grass" is spelled with two words instead of the eventually standardized "bluegrass") must have sold really well, because a lot of them are still around today.

Blue Grass Special encompassed five EP records, each containing six songs. This set included recordings leased from King plus new recordings by Jimmie Skinner and by Rusty York and the Kentucky Mountain Boys, which included Rusty on banjo, longtime Cincinnati sideman Herman Kress on string bass, Bill Lanham on guitar, Billy Thomas on fiddle, and Curly Tuttle on mandolin. The tracks licensed from King included songs by Leon Jackson and Johnny Bryant, Grandpa Jones, J. E. and Wade Mainer, Jimmy Martin and Bob Osborne, and Don Reno and Red Smiley.

The All Time Country Hits package consisted of two six-song EPs. Twelve songs by twelve different artists, previously released on King Records, were licensed to the Jimmie Skinner Music Center for this offer.

QCA Studio and QCA Records

Edward R. Bosken started a printing business in the late 1940s; in the early '50s he began printing jackets for LP albums.[87] He called his business Queen City Album Company or QCA. In the early '70s Bosken built a recording studio at 2832 Spring Grove Avenue in Cincinnati.[88] He began issuing singles and LPs on the QCA label. Although he didn't produce a lot of bluegrass, he did issue LPs by the Easter Brothers, J. D. Jarvis, Jimmie Skinner, and the Sullivan Family. One of the most unusual LPs issued by QCA was a collaboration between bluegrass banjo player/rockabilly singer Rusty York and blues/rock guitarist and vocalist Lonnie Mack performing "Dueling Banjos" and other songs, released at the time of the *Deliverance* craze.

In 1977 Bosken hired Chuck Seitz as his chief engineer, enhancing the studio's reputation.[89] Seitz had started as an engineer at Gateway Studio in Cincinnati, moved to King Studio, and then to RCA in Nashville for fourteen years, where he engineered recordings for high-profile singers such as Eddy Arnold, Perry Como, Waylon Jennings, and Elvis Presley.

QCA added a pressing plant and began doing custom pressing in addition to its own singles and LPs. Beginning in the late 1960s and for the next several years, Rusty York used QCA to manufacture most of his Jewel singles and LPs.[90] As times changed, QCA moved into cassette manufacturing and later into CD and DVD manufacturing.

Vetco Studio and Vetco Records

In the mid-1960s Lou Ukelson purchased a controlling interest in the Jimmie Skinner Music Center. By 1965 he had moved the store to 1300 Vine Street in Cincinnati's Over-the-Rhine neighborhood. In 1966 he decided to start his own record label, Country Corner. It was probably so named because the center was selling country music and was located at the corner of Thirteenth and Vine. Records were issued in 1966 and '67 by the Barnett Brothers, Jimmie Skinner, and Susan Wheeler. By 1968 Country Corner had morphed into Vetco Records, a name that Ukelson claimed "came from out of nowhere."[91]

After being left out of the Jimmie Skinner Music Center ownership when his manager Lou Epstein passed away, Jimmie acquired some sort of interest in Country Corner and Vetco. He has been listed sometimes as a co-owner, but Lou Ukelson has also been listed as sole owner. Whatever the arrangement Jimmie made some money out of the labels because the songs went through the Jimmie Skinner Music Publishing Company. Jimmie also recorded numerous singles and albums on the Vetco label.

Vetco began issuing singles during 1968. The first was by Jim McCall, a veteran bluegrass singer and guitarist who had paid his dues in Baltimore and at the Ken-Mill Café on McMillan Street in Cincinnati playing with Earl Taylor and the Stoney Mountain Boys.[92] This was his first record as a solo artist. The second Vetco single was by the Barnett Brothers, who had previously recorded on Country Corner. "Tragedy of Silver Bridge" was one of many country and bluegrass records lamenting the collapse of the bridge over the Ohio River between Gallipolis, Ohio, and Point Pleasant, West Virginia, an accident that killed sixty-seven people. The third single was by the Easterners, a young band making some noise around the Dayton area. That group included Roy Lee Centers, Liz and Vernon McIntyre Jr., and Fred Spencer.

Jimmie Skinner had six singles on Vetco. Other local bluegrass artists who recorded singles on Vetco were Appalachian Grass, Hylo Brown, Jeff Campbell, Harley Gabbard, Katie Laur, Vernon "Boatwhistle" McIntyre Sr., Mr. Spoons (Joe Jones), and Nelson Young.

The original 3000 series of LPs began in 1968 and documented local bluegrass artists who were active in the 1970s and '80s. Appalachian Grass, Roy Lee Centers, the Easterners, Dave Evans, Harley Gabbard, J. D. Jarvis, Katie Laur, Jim McCall, Muddy River, Paul "Moon" Mullins, Jimmie Skinner, Mr. Spoons, and Earl Taylor all recorded albums at Vetco during this period. A cassette series in the 1990s featured recordings by Harley Allen, Kitty McIntyre, Vernon McIntyre Jr., Union Springs, and Wild and Blue.

The 3000 series of LPs was pretty much bluegrass, but the 500 series, which began in 1974, is a little more difficult to categorize. The first release was by a Spring Valley, Ohio, band calling itself the Hotmud Family. They combined old-time country with bluegrass and went on to record three more LPs on Vetco and back up Fiddlin' Van Kidwell on two others. Regional groups like Country Ham, the Falls City Ramblers, the Hutchison Brothers, and the Wilson Brothers recorded in this series, as well as nationally known artists Shot Jackson, Joe Meadows, and Mac Wiseman.[93]

In 1971 Vetco started a short series of old-time country reissues by artists such as Uncle Dave Macon, the Skillet Lickers, and themed LPs of railroad songs and old-time fiddlers. The 78 rpm records used on these LPs were furnished by Bob Hyland, a nationally known collector from Springfield, Ohio.

Besides Vetco, Ukelson had other labels on which he issued a few records. He used the Octev (Vetco spelled backward) label to issue a jazz album by Katie Laur, who recorded bluegrass on Vetco. He issued some off-color or party records on the Outhouse label. He also put out thirteen records on the Feathers label, featuring former Sun Records rockabilly artist Charlie Feathers. The Papa Lou label released blues and funk music.

Many of the early Vetco recordings were done at Rusty York's Jewel Studio, with Lou Ukelson producing. Around 1976 Ukelson built his own Vetco Studio in the back room of the final incarnation of the Jimmie Skinner Music Center at 5825 Vine Street, in the Elmwood Place suburb of Cincinnati.[94] There he recorded his Vetco artists and some outside custom recordings. He did the producing, with Larry Nager doing much of the engineering.[95]

In 1971 Ukelson purchased the Terrace Bar at 1207 Main Street in the Over-the-Rhine area of Cincinnati and turned it into Aunt Maudie's Country Garden. Aunt Maudie's was the Queen City's best-known bluegrass bar after the demise of the iconic Ken-Mill Café.[96]

Lou Ukelson should be remembered for his leading role in the rebirth of bluegrass music in southwestern Ohio during the 1970s and 1980s and for documenting on record the artists—both old and new—who were making the music.

Artist's Recording Studio, Pressing Plant, and Record Label

Artist's Recording was founded in 1969; owner Carrol Rawlings came on board in 1970.[97] The company was located in the Sunday school building of the one-time Landmark Baptist Temple at 210 Mill Street in the village of Lockland, a suburb of Cincinnati.[98] It was a custom recording and pressing business whose original operation was 95 percent gospel but later took on more secular customers. Engineers were Vic Clay and Rollin "Junior" Bennett.[99] The company had its own record label called Artist's Recording, but most of its artists were unknowns who stayed that way. Studio recording and record pressing for other labels and artists were the company's main sources of income. Artist's Recording closed in the early 1990s.[100]

Arvis Records

In 1959, shortly after the end of Estel Lee's Excellent record label, Lee and Bob Mooney founded the Arvis label in Cincinnati. The label only lasted through 1961. Estel Lee and Dave Woolum each made one record on Arvis. Harley Gabbard and the Burns Brothers made two. Ernest Stacey and Harlin Kazy, bluegrass artists from northern Ohio, had one joint release on Arvis.[101]

Total releases for Arvis were fewer than twenty. At the same time that Arvis was active, co-owner Bob Mooney started Rem Records in Lexington, Kentucky. Rem lasted longer, issuing around two hundred releases, including both singles and LPs by several bluegrass artists from southwestern Ohio.[102]

Acorn Records

Acorn Records was located at 7771 Cheviot Road in Cincinnati and was owned by Joe Grieshop, a longtime artist, songwriter, publisher, and artist manager. He used the label to promote artists he managed. The label operated from 1959 until the late 1960s and is best remembered for its numerous recordings by the Acorn Sisters, three siblings whose actual surname was probably the same as that of the Browns, a popular country group at the time, resulting in the change of the Acorn Sisters' professional name.[103] Their recordings were eventually leased to national label Starday, and they went on to record for Boone Records.

Adco Recording Studio and Adco Records

The Adco Studio and record label were both owned by "Hobo Jack" Adkins, who came to Cincinnati in 1960.[104] Born in Regina, Kentucky, Adkins acquired his nickname because of his rambling around the country. He was in the Civilian Conservation Corps, worked in the coal mines, was a carpenter, and eventually joined the navy. While living in Kentucky, he recorded on Acme and Starday Records and on his own labels: Ace, Big A, and Lucky. In Cincinnati he settled in at 7527 Juler Avenue in the Cincinnati suburb of Madeira. There he built a studio in his basement and started his own Adco label,[105] recording himself, Gurney Adkins and Ray Goins, Jack Dockery, Cuddles Newsome, Don McHan, Gene Sweet and Curly Tuttle, and other bluegrass, gospel, and country artists.

Jack's day job in Cincinnati was as an electrical engineer, so setting up the studio and engineering the recordings would have been within his expertise. After a religious conversion in the mid-1960s, Adkins leaned toward recording gospel songs. In 1975 he moved back to Kentucky and operated a record shop and recording studio near Elkhorn City until his death in 1977.

Ark Records

Ark Records was founded in 1961 by Roy Shepard and Bill Lanham. For part of its existence, Ark was located at 795 E. McMillan Street in Cincinnati. Shepard was a gospel singer. He and his daughter, Becky, recorded singles that were popular in Cincinnati. Lanham was a guitar player who had previously worked for Jimmie Skinner and recorded on Ruby Records in Hamilton. The label issued approximately 120 singles and a few LPs before going out of business around 1967.[106]

Their output was primarily gospel and bluegrass gospel, but they did issue straight bluegrass and country as well. In 1963 Ark started a subsidiary label, Tela-Star Records, which issued approximately ten singles. Ark records were stocked by the Jimmie Skinner Music Center. One thing set Ark apart from other local labels: a substantial number of their singles were issued with picture sleeves, including a picture of the artist and a short biography.

Local bluegrass artists who recorded for Ark included Harley Gabbard, J. D. Jarvis, Dave Woolum, and Nelson Young.[107] Notable artists from outside the area included Jack Cooke, "Old Joe" Clark, and Jimmy Murphy.[108]

King Bluegrass Records

Robert Trout operated a farm near Maysville, Kentucky. He started King Bluegrass on a part-time basis but soon sold his farm and gave full-time attention to the fledgling record company.[109] Moving to Newtown, Ohio, just east of Cincinnati, he opened a business location at 4766 Glendale-Milford Road in nearby Blue Ash. This seemed to be nothing more than a distribution center for King Bluegrass. All of the recording was done at Lemco Studios in Lexington, Kentucky, with Robert Trout producing and Cecil Jones engineering. The pressing was handled by Artist's Recording in Cincinnati. There was apparently a connection with the Lemco record label in Lexington, as some of J. D. Crowe's early Lemco LPs were reissued on King Bluegrass. Because of confusion with King Records in Cincinnati, King Bluegrass finally changed the name of the company to KBA.[110]

Southwestern Ohio artists who recorded for King Bluegrass included Red Allen, the Allen Brothers, the Boys from Indiana, and Larry Sparks. Tony Rice recorded his first LP on King Bluegrass, as did his brother Larry. Don Reno and Bill Harrell also recorded for the label. Fewer than twenty singles and fifty or sixty LPs were issued.

The label started in the late 1960s or early '70s, but by 1980 it was gone. In that short period of time, they issued several records that received national attention. Eventually, rights to some or all of the LPs on both Lemco and King Bluegrass were sold to Rebel Records, which reissued recordings by the Boys from Indiana, J. D. Crowe, Tony Rice, and Larry Sparks.

Hamilton-Middletown Studios and Labels

Melody Recording Studio, Melody, Pine Tree, and Sunrise Record Labels

Melody Recording Studio was founded by the Rev. William M. Jones (also known as W. Merle Jones), pastor of the Pentecostal Church of Hamilton, who also engineered the recordings.[111] It was located just north of Hamilton, Ohio, in a house at 1912 St. Clair Street in the village of New Miami. Jones started Melody in 1964 as an all-gospel label. Over the next fifteen years or so, he recorded well-known bluegrass gospel singers like Ernest Carter and the Hymn Trio, Joe Isaacs, J. D. Jarvis, Joe and Blanche Lewis, and Dave Woolum.[112]

In 1965 Jones formed the Sunrise label, which he used mostly for country recordings. Three local artists with recordings on Sunrise were J. D. Jarvis, Steve Lake, and Joe "Cannonball" Lewis.

The Pine Tree label had been owned by an Indianapolis bluegrass band, the Bluegrass Blackjacks. In 1970 they sold the label to Melody Records, which continued Pine Tree as an all-bluegrass label.[113] The first LP release was Larry Sparks's initial album after leaving the Clinch Mountain Boys, *Ramblin' Guitar*. By 1981 Pine Tree had issued approximately sixty bluegrass albums. Some noteworthy artists who recorded on Pine Tree include the Bluegrass Hymn Trio, the Country Gospel-Aires, Joe and Lily Isaacs, the Kentucky Gentlemen, the Nu-Grass Pickers, Carl Story, the Wilson Brothers, and Dave Woolum and Paris Decker.

Delbert Barker, Steve Lake, Central Recording Studio, and Central Records

Delbert Barker lived in Middletown, Ohio, and got his start in the music business around 1949 when he appeared on WKRC-TV in Cincinnati for six months.[114] Barker could play rhythm guitar and steel guitar. In 1951 he was appearing on Cincinnati's WCPO-TV when Carl Burkhardt hired him to do a series of soundalike records for the Big 4 Hits and Kentucky labels. These were imitations or covers of current hit records, sold at bargain prices. Many years later, European record collectors began referring to Barker as the "King of the Covers."[115]

Delbert Barker recorded for King and worked in bands in the East before coming back to Middletown in 1959. Leaving the music business to go into law enforcement, he eventually attained the rank of lieutenant of detectives. In the late 1970s he and Steve Lake founded the Central Recording Studio.

Steve Lake lived in Franklin, Ohio, where his father, Wilbur "Red" Lake, ran a jewelry and record store. Steve grew up with country music, played electric bass, and formed his own band, the Swingmasters. The band backed numerous big-name artists at local shows and traveled with Charlie Gore and with Connie Smith. For several years, until the park was sold in 1968, Steve promoted Sunday afternoon country and bluegrass music shows at Chautauqua Park, near Franklin.

In the late 1970s Delbert Barker and Steve Lake started the Central Recording Studio at 1226 Central Avenue in Middletown. Both were experienced musicians and Steve had a working band, so they could provide backup for singers who needed accompaniment; Delbert did the engineering. They started the Central Record label and issued recordings by the Dixie Ryders, Pam Gadd, the Kentucky Cut-Ups, Rex Patrick, and other local artists, as well as bands from out of state.[116] For a time, they ran the Miami Valley Opry on Saturday nights on the second floor of the building that housed the studio.[117]

Baron Recording Studio and Baron and Harp Records

The Baron Recording Studio was located at 108-110 E. State Street in Trenton, Ohio, near Middletown. It was owned and operated by Bill Harp, a well-regarded lead guitar player and recording engineer. Bill Harp built guitars for Bobby Grove, Wynona Judd, Bobby Lewis, and Kenny Price.[118] He also built steel guitars and other instruments, first with Hap Hammond and later with Terrill Scribner. Scribner may have been involved in Harp Records, as his name appears with Bill Harp's on an early Harp record.

Harp Records started in 1963, ran until 1966, and issued no further releases until 1971. Baron Records began in 1967 and ran through 1969, seeming to fill the gap while Harp was on hiatus. Most recordings on both labels were by local artists, although Claude Sweet from the Renfro Valley Barn Dance recorded a single on Harp. Bluegrass groups who recorded on these labels included Ernest Carter and the Hymn Trio, Zeke Hoskins, J. D. Jarvis, Bill Kilburn and the Bluegrass Gospel Travelers, and Raymond Robinson and the Ohio Valley Boys.

Dayton Studios and Labels

Jack Lynch and Jalyn Records

John D. "Jack" Lynch was born in eastern Kentucky and at one time lived in Richmond, Kentucky.[119] He served in the US Air Force and, after his discharge, came to Dayton, where he worked at National Cash Register and also sold insurance.[120] Lynch played guitar, banjo, fiddle, and bass with various bluegrass groups around Dayton. When name bluegrass groups came to Dayton for a show, they would often pick up Jack to help if they were short a musician. He played fill-in bass quite a bit with the Stanley Brothers and later with Ralph Stanley.

Lynch started Jalyn Records in 1963 because "[I] thought it was time for me to record."[121] When asked by *Dayton Daily News* reporter Vince Staten why he started the label, he said, "Sort of to record myself and sort of to record others."[122] Staten referred to Lynch as a "one-man walking record company."[123] Except for a short period of time, he didn't have an office. He conducted business in the living room of his apartment at 1806 Brown Street in Dayton and sold records out of the trunk of his car at bluegrass festivals or wherever he found a customer. National columnist Tom Teepen said he was once sitting in a restroom stall at a bluegrass show when from the adjoining stall came an LP under the partition and Lynch said, "Hey buddy, want to buy a record?"[124]

Jack Lynch truly was a character. I used to do a radio show on a station in Eaton, Ohio. I was looking for records to play on my show, so I thought I would try Jalyn. I went to the address I found on a Jalyn record, expecting to see a record company office or studio. What I found was Jack's apartment. Jack opened the door and invited me in. I told him what I was looking for, and he asked me to sit down and talk. After a while he wanted to know if I was hungry. I told him I could probably eat, so he whipped up a nice steak, baked potato, and tossed salad. I liked one of his Jalyn records that was done by a female singer and I asked about it. Jack said, "Oh, she works out at the field [Wright-Patterson Air Force Base]. I can fix you up with her if you want me to." That wasn't what I had in mind so I declined, but it shows that Jack always tried to please.

On another occasion, I went to an all-gospel show in Hamilton. Ralph Stanley was the headliner and Jack was filling in on bass. He was known to drink a little, and on this evening he had more than a little. Stanley introduced one of the songs and said, "I'd like to dedicate this next hymn to my good buddy Jack Lynch. It's called 'Drinking from the Fountain.'"

Jalyn recorded predominantly bluegrass, country, and gospel. The first two singles were by Ernest Carter and the Hymn Trio, a gospel group popular for years in southwestern Ohio. On the third single, Lynch recorded himself as Jack Lynch and the Lee Brothers. The Lee Brothers—Roy Lee Centers, who went on to be Ralph Stanley's lead singer, and Roy Lee's brother-in-law, Fred Spencer—eventually recorded five more Jalyn bluegrass singles and also backed several other acts for the label.

Some of the better-known local bluegrass groups that recorded singles on Jalyn include Lee Allen, the Burns Brothers, Gene Higgins, the Pelfrey Brothers, Jedd Raleigh, John Reedy, Estil Tuttle, and the Valley Ramblers. Nationally known groups who recorded there include the Goins Brothers, Frank Necessary, Reno and Harrell, and Ralph Stanley. One of Stanley's Jalyn singles (Jalyn 323) was rather strange; it was issued as by both the Stanley Brothers and Ralph Stanley. From Ralph's first Jalyn LP (1968), it was obviously Ralph and Larry Sparks performing rather than the Stanley Brothers. Ralph played three-finger-style mandolin on his other Jalyn single, "East Virginia Blues" (Jalyn 335, 1969), something he had done on personal appearances but never before on record.

There were two singles by the Kentuckians, a New Boston, Ohio (near Portsmouth), group that included Bill Monroe's future and longtime lead singer Wayne Lewis. Another interesting release was Larry Sparks's first solo single (Jalyn 502, with the Sandy Mountain Boys) shortly before he went to work for Ralph Stanley. Some of the notable sidemen who appeared on Jalyn records are David Cox, Bob Dooley, Dorsey Harvey, Buck Howard, Paul "Moon" Mullins, "Fiddlin'" Harold Staggs, and Frank Wakefield.

Jalyn began issuing LPs in 1966. One of the earliest was *Hymns from the Hills* by Paul "Moon" Mullins and the Backwoods Boys Quartet. The record's title was used by Mullins for his bluegrass gospel shows on WPFB in Middletown and later on WBZI in Xenia, and was carried on by Moon's son, Joe, for his gospel show on WBZI and for the title of a CD by Joe Mullins and the Radio Ramblers.[125]

Jack Lynch's most significant achievement may have been recording the first LP by teenagers Keith Whitley and Ricky Skaggs—an entire album of Stanley Brothers songs. There were also two LPs by Don Reno and Bill Harrell, two by Ralph Stanley, two by the Valley Ramblers, and one each by Lee Allen, Curly Ray Cline, the Goins Brothers, Jack Lynch, the Marcum Brothers, and Frank Necessary. Many of the other albums on Jalyn were gospel recordings, several of those by groups from Indiana.

Jalyn didn't have its own studio. Jack recorded in different places, including in people's basements and in recording studios. He recorded at least one of his early singles in country singer Herbie Smith's home.[126] Some of the early Jalyn albums were recorded at Commercial Sound Studio in Dayton,[127] which was apparently in engineer Leon Turner's home.[128] Others were recorded at Davis Recording Studio in Dayton,[129] in the home of engineer Howard Davis.[130] In 1969 Howard Davis went into partnership with Phil Mehaffey to open Cyberteknics Creative Recording Studio at 1953 E. Third Street in Dayton. After that, many of the Jalyn albums were recorded there, with Davis engineering until he decided to leave the partnership.[131] Phil Mehaffey then took over the engineering of the Jalyn album sessions.[132]

By 1978 Jalyn had wound down and Jack Lynch moved to Nashville, Tennessee. In the approximately fifteen Dayton years, Lynch issued around one hundred singles and close to sixty-five LPs. He later attempted to restart Jalyn and issued a few singles but nothing on the scale of what he had done in Dayton. He also started a new label called Nashville Bluegrass. In 2011 he passed away and was buried in the family cemetery in Red Lick, Kentucky; Joe Isaacs sang at the graveside service.[133]

Jack Lynch's achievements are notable for documenting the bluegrass and country music that was being played locally and nationally in the 1960s and '70s. Without him, much history of the music from this period would be lost, along with the names and talents of the musicians and bands who performed. It's unlikely that Lynch thought about historical significance when he was doing his work, but possibly that made for a more honest and credible representation of an era that is now gone.

Bodine Studio and the BMC Record Label

Musician and DJ Les Bodine owned Bodine's Music Center at 609 E. Fifth Street in Dayton. In the back room of the store, Les had a little studio that was used quite a bit for jam sessions and for recording.[134] Les started his own record label, BMC (for Bodine's Music Center), which lasted for four releases in 1959. One of those has been a much sought-after record by a group calling itself the Red Heads. They were Red Allen, Red Spurlock, and Frank Wakefield, all of whom became much better known in later years. It has also been discovered that Red Allen sang on BMC 1000 by Glenn and Vivian Watson, a husband-and-wife duo who performed in the Dayton area for many years.[135]

Megacity Recording Studio and the Top Tennessee, Master, and Pixie Labels

Megacity Recording operated in Dayton from the mid- to late 1960s. Owned by Ivan Freeman, it had three house labels. Top Tennessee was for country and bluegrass, Master for gospel, and Pixie for everything else. On Top Tennessee, Red Spurlock recorded the regional classic "Loneliness," and Larry Sparks made his unbilled recording debut playing guitar with Erwin Keith and the Slade Mountain Boys. Megacity was first located at 126 Davis Avenue and later at 38 Linden Avenue. Dayton DJ Tommy Turner did some of the engineering, as did Leon Turner (not related).

Cyberteknics Creative Recording Studio

Cyberteknics, located at 1953 E. Third Street in Dayton, was started in 1969 by Phil Mehaffey and Howard Davis;[136] in 2017 it was still being operated by Mehaffey. Mehaffey is well known in the recording industry because for four decades he has used an Electrodyne mixing board bought from Sigma Sound Studios in Philadelphia.[137] That board is legendary because it was used to make classic rock recordings in the late 1960s and early '70s.[138] The Rock and Roll Hall of Fame has tried to buy it but Mehaffey won't sell, because he really likes the sound.[139]

Although Davis and Mehaffey mostly recorded rock bands, they also did bluegrass sessions produced by Jack Lynch for Jalyn Records. They recorded local bands the Marcum Brothers and the Valley Ramblers. National bluegrass bands recorded at Cyberteknics included Ralph Stanley and Don Reno.

Record Stores

In the 1940s, recordings that would later be recognized as bluegrass were classified as "hillbilly" music (alongside old-time, cajun, honky-tonk, sacred, and other forms of rural music). Since hillbilly musicians were looked down upon by the general public, record stores didn't carry much of their music and such records were hard to find in southwestern Ohio. At the time, the best way to acquire hillbilly records was to buy them used from jukebox operators who serviced bars where the music was in demand.

Many record stores were pretty light on country and bluegrass music. Those listed below carried a significant selection of it. Today all are out of business, as the music industry has moved to selling its music digitally online, while local musicians are selling CDs at personal appearances or on websites.

Blue Note Record Shop, N. DIXIE DRIVE, DAYTON

The Blue Note operated out of a house a few blocks north of the N. Dixie/ Wagoner Ford traffic circle in Dayton. In the 1940s they were selling 78 rpm records. In the 1950s they moved into 45 rpm records and LPs. Bluegrass singer

Carlos Brock cited the Blue Note as the place he and his brother Lonnie went to purchase records for the purpose of learning songs to sing in the Dayton-area bars where they performed.[140] The Blue Note was still in business in the 1970s but did not make the transition to CDs.

Bullfrog Records, 4051 MARSHALL ROAD, KETTERING

Bullfrog was a used record store specializing in 45 rpm records from all genres in the 1970s and '80s. They sold records at collector prices, so there were few bargains to be had, but one could come up with hard-to-find records.

Collins Radio and TV—"Your Headquarters for Hillbilly and Sacred Records," 5449 W. THIRD STREET, DAYTON

Collins was located in Dayton's Drexel area, which had a heavy Appalachian population in the 1950s. Their main businesses were radio and TV repair and installing TV antennas and towers. They also maintained an inventory of 45 rpm country and bluegrass records, including those by local artists that were rarely found in big record stores of the 1950s. They also had a record club that rewarded a free record for every ten purchased.

Dixie Music Company, 363 N. SEVENTH STREET, HAMILTON

Dixie Music was named for the woman who owned it. It was primarily a jukebox and vending machine business. The jukebox operation used a lot of records. With Hamilton's significant Appalachian population, a large portion of records played on jukeboxes was country and bluegrass. When the records were removed, they would be brought back to the store, stacked in piles on counters, and sold for twenty-five cents each or six for a dollar. Some would be worn beyond use, but others might be almost brand-new. Saturday morning when the store opened, the latest rejects from jukeboxes would be put out. It was fun and exciting to be there, because one never knew what might be found.

Al Freeders Record Shop, W. MAIN STREET, NEW LEBANON

Al Freeders was a disc jockey at WBZI in Xenia and WCNW in Hamilton. He wrote a country music column for the *Dayton Daily News* as well as one for Larry Flynt's *Bachelor Beat* newspaper under the pen name "Cousin Owl." He and his wife, Rosie, who was a country singer, operated a small record store in downtown New Lebanon for a short time, specializing in country and bluegrass 45s and LPs.

Lake Jewelry, 215 S. MAIN STREET, FRANKLIN

Wilbur "Red" Lake operated a jewelry store and repaired watches. Because he was an avid fan of country and bluegrass music, and because those records were hard to find in standard record stores, Lake decided to start carrying vinyl records in addition to his jewelry inventory. Customers responded enthusiastically and spread the word to friends. Red advertised on Paul "Moon" Mullins's WPFB radio show in Middletown. His son Steve organized a country band and also began promoting Sunday country and bluegrass music shows at Chautauqua Park near Franklin. Red would take racks full of albums to the shows and sell them to concertgoers.

Lake's began carrying more and more records, eventually expanding into the largest bluegrass and country LP and 45 selection in the Dayton/Cincinnati area. They carried recordings by local as well as national artists. As times changed they not only added cassettes and CDs but also sold instruments and strings. The store became the go-to place if you were looking for hard-to-find country and bluegrass music. After Red passed away in 1987, his sons Steve and Gary and his widow, Betty, operated the store until closing it in 2007, after fifty years in business.

Jack Lynch Record Store, 1030 BROWN STREET, DAYTON

Jalyn Records owner Jack Lynch operated a record store at this address for a short period of time. He sold primarily bluegrass records, including his own Jalyn label.

Jimmie Skinner Music Center, 31 E. COURT STREET, 222 E. FIFTH STREET, 124 E. SIXTH STREET, 1300 VINE STREET, 5825 VINE STREET, CINCINNATI

In the late 1940s Ernest Tubb was one of the most popular stars in country music. His fans complained that they couldn't find his records because most record stores didn't stock much, if any, country music. So around 1948 he opened the Ernest Tubb Record Shop in downtown Nashville. The store's inventory was all country, and it sold records by mail order as well as to a walk-in trade. Record sales were promoted over WSM radio on *Ernest Tubb's Midnight Jamboree,* broadcast from the store immediately following the Grand Ole Opry.

Jimmie Skinner's manager, Lou Epstein, took note of this and reasoned that Jimmie—the most popular star in the Cincinnati area—could profit from a similar arrangement. On January 5, 1950, Lou and Jimmie, as partners, opened the Jimmie Skinner Hillbilly Record Shop at 31 E. Court Street near downtown Cincinnati.[141] Jimmie did a midnight show a few nights each week over Cincinnati's WCKY radio following the famous *WCKY Jamboree* and *Hillbilly Hit Parade*.[142]

Like many new businesses, the record shop ran into financial difficulties. In August of 1951 tax liens were filed against the business and against Epstein personally by the collector of internal revenue.[143] On March 7, 1952, a petition of bankruptcy was filed for the Jimmie Skinner Record Shop.[144] Later in 1952 a corporation was formed, probably to get an infusion of capital. Although Skinner and Epstein had apparently been partners in the original store, Jimmie didn't get any ownership interest in the corporation. Shares were distributed evenly among Lou Epstein, Lou's mother and father, and the respective owners of Royal Furniture and Bell Furniture.[145] The store was reopened as the Jimmie Skinner Music Center at 222 E. Fifth Street in the heart of downtown Cincinnati.

Lou Epstein had a reputation as a shrewd businessman, gained from operating one of Syd Nathan's King Records branch offices.[146] When the music center opened downtown, Epstein contracted with WNOP radio in Newport, Kentucky, to do a daily live remote show from its front window. This generated foot traffic and made the store an attraction for country music stars passing through town. Mail-order sales became a large part of the business. The store went from advertising that they would ship anywhere in the country to saying that they would ship anywhere in the world.[147]

Many of their sales came from promotional packages put together by Epstein. He leased recordings from King Records, Starday Records, and Carl Burkhardt's local labels and put them together as bargain sets to be advertised on WCKY radio and in *Country Song Roundup* magazine. Such packages included twenty-four all-bluegrass recordings and either eighteen or twenty-four country recordings. Each set sold for $2.98 and included words to fifteen old-time songs along with an autographed picture of Jimmie Skinner. The store also sold packages of polka records, sacred records, and a twenty-four-song set of Hank Williams numbers sung by Delbert Barker and including a picture of Hank Williams.[148]

Things were going well for the store until the US government decided to erect a brand-new federal building that would displace the music center, as well as longtime businesses such as the Bay Horse Café, the Oyster House, Skyline Chili, and others. As a result, the Jimmie Skinner Music Center moved to 124 E. Sixth Street in February 1962.[149] Newspaper advertisements later that year emphasized that they were selling pop, country, jazz, gospel, spiritual, folk, and comedy records.[150]

In May 1962 Lou Epstein began having health problems that led to his death in April 1963.[151] Jimmie Skinner had a verbal profit-sharing agreement with Lou Epstein, but when Lou died, the remaining partners apparently had no legal obligation to Jimmie, so he was left out in the cold.[152] Estel Lee managed the store for a while, but remaining partners brought in Lou Ukelson as manager in 1964 with the understanding that he could eventually purchase a controlling interest in the operation, which he did.[153]

By 1965 Ukelson had moved the store to 1300 Vine Street in the heart of the Over-the-Rhine district of Cincinnati, where many Appalachian migrants lived.[154] Ukelson eventually moved the store and the record operation much farther out, to 5825 Vine Street in Elmwood Place. Operation of the record label gradually took his attention and the store drifted into obscurity.

Stacy's Record Shop, 4228 LESTON DRIVE (HUB SHOPPING CENTER), HUBER HEIGHTS

In the late 1970s Stacy's Record Shop sold primarily country and bluegrass music. It must have seemed like a good idea to open a record store close to the Hub Club, a bar that featured country music several nights a week. It was a short-lived venture, however, because the bar was open at night and the record store was open in the daytime, so there wasn't much chance to attract bar patrons.

Syd's (Sol's, Halper's, or Sid's) Record Shop, 218 W. FIFTH STREET AND 1351 CENTRAL AVENUE, CINCINNATI

Syd Nathan, founder of King Records, got his start in the music business in 1938 by opening a record shop at 218 W. Fifth Street in downtown Cincinnati. When he moved to Florida the next year, he sold the store to his brother-in-law, Sol Halper. Halper operated the store, first as Sol's Record Shop and later as Halper's Record Shop, and continued in the retail record business for many years.

In the early 1940s Syd Nathan came back to Cincinnati and went into the used record business in a rented location at 1351 Central Avenue, next to the Cat and Fiddle Night Club. It was there he met WLW radio artists Grandpa Jones, Merle Travis, and the Delmore Brothers, who came in to look for songs they could use in their Brown's Ferry Four act on WLW. Thus was formed Nathan's idea to start what became King Records. Even after King was up and running, as late as December 1944, Syd was still operating the record store. The store's motto was "If you want hillbilly, we have 'em." Syd maintained that his mother named him "Syd" because she knew he was going to be smart. However, when he ran classified ads in the paper for his record store, he called it "Sid's."[155]

Universal Record Shop—"Hillbilly Record Center," 810 E. FIFTH STREET, DAYTON

This record shop was in operation in 1950. It was affiliated with the Universal Amusement Company, a jukebox and amusement machine operator at 7 Simpson Street in Dayton. The shop sold pop music records, but its main concentrations appeared to be hillbilly and sacred. Universal carried records by lesser-known artists such as the Drifting Pioneers, Bill Franklin, Shannon Grayson, the Lonesome Pine Fiddlers, Bud Messner, the Trace Family Trio, and Johnnie White, as well as by stars like Red Foley, Ernest Tubb, Jimmy Wakely and Margaret Whiting, and Hank Williams. They also operated a record-of-the-week club.

An Unparalleled Bluegrass Legacy

In the 1940s and '50s southwestern Ohio became a seriously important recording center for bluegrass music. During those decades, many future members of the Bluegrass Hall of Fame regularly went to Cincinnati to record. They included Red Allen; Lester Flatt and Earl Scruggs; Jim and Jesse McReynolds; Sonny Osborne and his brother, Bobby; Don Reno and Red Smiley; and Carter and Ralph Stanley. What they recorded there had a major impact on the direction of the music.

The region's recording entrepreneurs deserve credit for sustaining southwestern Ohio as a bluegrass epicenter. E. T. "Bucky" Herzog had the ambition and engineering experience to open the first recording studio in Cincinnati in 1946. Syd Nathan desperately wanted to be a success, which gave him the drive to start King Records. Carl Burkhardt faltered in several businesses until he figured out that people would be willing to buy bargain-priced records that sounded like current hits. Rusty York founded a studio that would become local artists' studio of choice for forty-seven years. Jack Lynch first saw the need for recording local Dayton and nationally famous artists in the 1960s. In the 1970s Lou Ukelson's Vetco label recorded veteran bluegrass musicians such as Jim McCall and Earl Taylor, and younger artists Dave Evans, the Hotmud Family, Katie Laur, and Vernon McIntyre Jr.

By the time Nashville songwriter Thom Schuyler's "16th Avenue" became a hit for Lacy J. Dalton in the early 1980s and polished Music City's reputation as a place to make records, local recording opportunities for aspiring southwestern Ohio bluegrass artists were starting to wane. For four previous decades the region's studios, labels, record stores, artists, and entrepreneurs had been encyclopedic in scale, rich in talent, and impressively influential. So when Xenia, Ohio–based bluegrass artist Joe Mullins rebranded his twenty-first-century network of regional bluegrass, country, and Americana radio stations as "Real Roots Radio," prominent among the sources he could draw upon were the historic recordings of southwestern Ohio.

Notes

1. John Broven, *Record Makers and Breakers: Voices of the Independent Rock 'n' Roll Pioneers* (Urbana: University of Illinois Press, 2010), 14.

2. Andre Millard, *America on Record: A History of Recorded Sound* (Cambridge: Cambridge University Press, 1995), 224.

3. "BMI's Timeline through History," *Broadcast Music Inc.*, https://www.bmi.com/about/75_years.

4. Millard, *America on Record*, 224.

5. "Cincy Recording Firm Bows," *Billboard*, June 8, 1946, 7.

6. "Young Company on Road to Success," *Cincinnati Enquirer*, December 1, 1947, 19.

7. Louis M. "Grandpa" Jones and Charles K. Wolfe, *Everybody's Grandpa: Fifty Years behind the Mike* (Knoxville: University of Tennessee Press, 1984), 98.

8. Randy McNutt, *King Records of Cincinnati* (Charleston, SC: Arcadia Publishing, 2009), 11.

9. Broven, *Record Makers and Breakers*, 11.

10. Jon Hartley Fox, *King of the Queen City: The Story of King Records* (Urbana: University of Illinois Press, 2009), 6–7.

11. Ibid.

12. See profile of Carl Burkhardt later in this chapter.

13. See discussion of Jimmie Skinner Music Center later in this chapter.

14. Walt Saunders, "Notes and Queries," *Bluegrass Unlimited* September 2008, 22.

15. *Estel Lee's Arizona Wildcats Song Favorites No. 1* (New York: Edward Schuberth & Co., 1947), inside front cover, 4; Linnell Gentry, *A History and Encyclopedia of Country, Western, and Gospel Music*, 2nd ed. (Nashville: Clairmont Corp., 1969), 466.

16. See profile of Jack Lynch later in this chapter.

17. See chapter 3, "All the Way to the Fence."

18. Dick Perry, *Not Just a Sound: The Story of WLW* (Englewood Cliffs, NJ: Prentice Hall), 1971.

19. Brian F. X. Powers, "Herzog Recording Studios—E. T. Herzog Recording Co.," https://myspace.com/herzogrecordingstudios/photos.

20. Ibid.

21. Ibid.

22. This came from a dealer at an Old-Time Radio Convention in Cincinnati when I asked him about Radio Artist Records.

23. Dave Samuelson, *Jimmie Skinner: Doin' My Time* (Hambergen, Germany: Bear Family Records box set BCD 16613, 2003), 20. Samuelson claims that Epstein launched Radio Artist Records but he gives no citation. The *Cincinnati Enquirer* article cited in note 6 clearly refutes this. It seems more likely that Epstein acquired the label around 1949, after the Herzogs had issued approximately forty records, mostly by WLW artists. This is borne out in an article by Ivan Tribe, "Jimmie Skinner: Country Singer, Bluegrass Composer, Record Retailer," *Bluegrass Unlimited*, March 1977, 36. Tribe states that Epstein and Skinner "took control of the Radio Artist Record Label, a local company that had recorded local country performers such as Roy Lanham, Barefoot Brownie Reynolds

and female radio personality Ruth Lyons. Henceforth, Radio Artist became an exclusive Jimmie Skinner label."

24. Mac McDivitt, *Tentative Radio Artist Label Discography*, unpublished.

25. Murray Nash, quoted in Powers, "Herzog Recording Studios."

26. Flatt and Scruggs's first Mercury session at Herzog studio took place in April or May of 1949, according to Neil V. Rosenberg's liner notes for *Flatt & Scruggs: 1948–1959* (Bear Family Records, 1990).

27. Fox, *King of the Queen City*, from an interview with Earl Herzog, 54.

28. Ibid.

29. Powers, "Herzog Recording Studios."

30. Fox, *King of the Queen City*, from an interview with Grandpa Jones, 10.

31. Nathan had a record shop at 1351 Central Avenue that is profiled in the "Record Stores" section of this chapter. He called it "Syd's," but the ads he ran in the *Cincinnati Enquirer* referred to it as "Sid's." See ad in *Cincinnati Enquirer*, October 18, 1942, 3.

32. Jones and Wolfe, *Everybody's Grandpa*, 237; Rich Kienzle, *Merle Travis* (Hambergen, Germany: Bear Family Records box set 15637, 1994), 13; Mark Humphrey, "Interview: Merle Travis, London," *Old Time Music*, Autumn 1981–Spring 1982, 22. The first two sources bear out the 1943 date. However, in the Humphrey interview with Travis, Merle gives the date as "1940 or '41, before the War." Everyone seems to agree that the recordings were done in a "makeshift" studio over the Wurlitzer Piano Company in Dayton. Dayton city directories show Wurlitzer at 126 S. Ludlow Street in 1938, 1939, and 1940, with studios on the fourth and fifth floors above the street-level store. The 1941 directory lists 126 S. Ludlow as vacant. Wurlitzer was probably gone, because the company was downsizing and closing stores all over the country. The directories for 1942 and 1943 show the occupants at 126 S. Ludlow to be Zinner's Carpet and American Engineering Company. This would seem to make the 1943 recording date unlikely, so the story of those first King recordings remains as murky as ever.

33. Gary B. Reid, liner notes to *The Best of King and Starday Bluegrass* (King Records box set KG-0952-4-2, 2004), 4–11. Reid gives a nice, concise history of pre-bluegrass on King plus the early groundbreaking bluegrass groups who recorded on the label.

34. Fox, *King of the Queen City*, 163.

35. Ibid., 182–84.

36. "Shaw Diskery in Cincy Bow," *Billboard*, October 1, 1949, 20.

37. Dan DeClark, "How to Identify Shaw Record Pressings," in *45 RPM Records of the Ohio River Valley*, http://www.45rpmrecords.com.

38. Neil V. Rosenberg, "Osborne Brothers Discography," *Bluegrass Unlimited*, June 1967, 3.

39. Ibid., 4.

40. Sonny Osborne, email to Brian Powers, March 15, 2016.

41. Neil V. Rosenberg and Edward Stubbs, *The Osborne Brothers, 1956–1968* (Hambergen, Germany: Bear Family Records, 1995), 4.

42. Rosenberg, "Osborne Brothers Discography," 4.

43. Ibid., 4–5.

44. Carl Burkhardt, liner notes to *The Early Recordings of Jim and Jesse McReynolds with Larry Roll* (Gateway 38121/2, 1978).

45. See chapter 6, "Using My Bible for a Roadmap."

46. Dennis Satterlee, *Teardrops in My Eyes: The Music of Harley "Red" Allen* (Kensington, MD: Plucked String Foundation, 2007), 23–24.

47. The Cincinnati area seemed to be a hotbed for party records. A pianist named Larry Vincent entertained at the Lookout House nightclub, across the river (or, as they say in Cincinnati, "over the river") in Covington, Kentucky. He started Pearl Records to market live and studio versions of his nightclub act. Although the records were issued under various names, most were by Larry Vincent himself. By today's standards these records were only mildly suggestive. Rusty York, owner of Jewel Records in Mt. Healthy, was reputed to have put out a handful of party records on the Fun record label. Lou Ukelson of Vetco Records in Cincinnati issued a short series of records on the Outhouse label, some of which were sung by bluegrass artist Roy Lee Centers under the pseudonym Homer Hinkledink. In the early days of Burkhardt's Kentucky label, he issued three records by Louisville DJ Jimmie Ballard that were obviously double entendre: "Birthday Cake Boogie," "Tain't Big Enough," and "Chicken Plucker." During the same period, Ballard was also recording sacred songs for the label to use in its radio offers.

48. "Year's Sentence Is Penalty on Obscene Record Charge; National Cleanup Is Hinted," *Cincinnati Enquirer*, June 17, 1950, 14.

49. *Cincinnati Enquirer*, April 13, 1950, 14.

50. "Fined on Morals Count," *Cincinnati Enquirer*, Kentucky Edition, May 30, 1953, 19.

51. "Records Firm in Court on Fair Labor Charge," *Cincinnati Enquirer*, July 7, 1955, 9.

52. Phillip M. Swatek, "Local Record Maker Served Counterfeiters," *Cincinnati Enquirer*, Kentucky Edition, February 25, 1959, 19.

53. Anonymous comment to the author, March 28, 2017.

54. Mac McDivitt, "Tentative Label Discographies for Kentucky, Alcar, Gateway, Tunes for Tots, and ARC," unpublished.

55. Dan DeClark, "How to Date Rite Pressings," http://www.45rpmrecords.com/date_rite.php.

56. Ibid.

57. Dan DeClark, "Rite Custom Pressing Discography," http://www.45rpmrecords.com/press/RITE.php.

58. DeClark, "How to Date Rite Pressings."

59. *Estel Lee's Arizona Wildcats* (New York: Edward Schuberth, 1942), inside front cover.

60. Ibid., 4.

61. Nat Green, "American Folk Tunes," *Billboard*, November 11, 1944, 63.

62. Ibid.

63. Nat Green, "Folk Talent and Tunes," *Billboard*, April 28, 1945, 67.

64. Ibid.

65. Johnny Sippel, “Folk Talent and Tunes,” *Billboard*, August 9, 1952, 38.

66. “Folk Record Reviews,” *Billboard*, August 23, 1952, 36.

67. “Country and Western Record Reviews,” *Billboard*, January 30, 1954, 47.

68. Johnny Sippel, “Folk Talent and Tunes,” *Billboard*, September 6, 1952, 64.

69. The spelling “Cornny” is correct.

70. “Country and Western Record Reviews,” *Billboard*, January 30, 1954, 46–47.

71. “Reviews of New C & W Records,” *Billboard*, September 18, 1955, 46.

72. Fred Bartenstein, “Noah Crase: It’s Not Easy Done, Part II,” *Bluegrass Unlimited*, July 1985, 27.

73. Colin Escott, liner notes to Rusty York, *Rusty Rocks* (Bear Family Records BCD 16543, 2004), 6.

74. Ibid., 10.

75. Ibid.

76. Fred Bartenstein, personal communication, March 28, 2017.

77. Escott, *Rusty Rocks*, 6, 8.

78. Rusty York, “Rusty York: Bluegrass Meets Rockabilly,” http://www.rockabillyhall.com/RustyYork1.html.

79. Ibid.

80. Cliff Radel, “Cincinnati May Become Record Mecca No. 4,” *Cincinnati Enquirer*, September 25, 1977, 111.

81. Jewel 400–403, 1961.

82. Blue Grass Special 600–604, 1961.

83. York, “Bluegrass Meets Rockabilly.”

84. See chapter 6, “Using My Bible for a Roadmap.”

85. Cliff Radel, “Jewel Recording Studio Contents for Sale,” *Cincinnati Enquirer*, October 29, 2008.

86. “From the Music Capitals of the World,” *Billboard*, April 10, 1971, 21.

87. “Welcome to QCA,” http://www.go-qca.com/about_htm/history.html.

88. Cliff Radel, “California Best Market for Bluegrass Records,” *Cincinnati Enquirer*, September 25, 1977, 112.

89. Ibid.

90. Mac McDivitt, “Tentative Jewel Label Discography,” unpublished.

91. Radel, “California Best Market,” 112.

92. See chapter 5, “Sing Me Back Home.”

93. See chapter 8, “Buckeyes in the Briar Patch.”

94. Radel, “California Best Market,” 112.

95. Larry Nager, telephone conversation, May 4, 2017.

96. See chapters 5, “Sing Me Back Home,” and 8, “Buckeyes in the Briar Patch.”

97. Radel, “California Best Market,” 112.

98. Ibid.

99. Randy McNutt, *Too Hot to Handle: An Illustrated Encyclopedia of American Recording Studios of the Twentieth Century* (Hamilton, OH: HHP Books, 2001), 27.

100. Ibid.

101. Mac McDivitt, “Tentative Arvis Label Discography,” unpublished.

102. Mac McDivitt, "Tentative Rem Label Discography," unpublished.

103. "The Acorn Sisters," *Hillbilly-Music dawt com*, http://www.hillbilly-music.com/groups/story/index.php?groupid=16516.

104. Walt Saunders, "Notes and Queries," *Bluegrass Unlimited*, September 2008, 24.

105. Ibid.

106. Mac McDivitt, "Tentative Ark Label Discography," unpublished.

107. Ibid.

108. Ibid.

109. Radel, "Cincinnati May Become Record Mecca No. 4."

110. Ibid.

111. See chapter 6, "Using My Bible for a Roadmap."

112. Joe Lewis was also known as Joe "Cannonball" Lewis.

113. Frank Overstreet, letter to *Bluegrass Unlimited*, June 1970.

114. Walt Saunders, "Notes and Queries," *Bluegrass Unlimited*, May 1997, 20.

115. Kent Heineman and Delbert Barker, *Delbert Barker, Kentucky Hillbilly Rockabilly Man: King of the Covers*, Stomper Time STCD 28, 2011, compact disc.

116. Mac McDivitt, "Partial Central Records Label Discography," unpublished.

117. Miami Valley Opry, undated flyer.

118. David Zornes, posting online at https://bb.steelguitarforum.com, November 19, 2013.

119. "Find a Grave Memorial," https://www.findagrave.com.

120. Ibid.

121. Vince Staten, "Moving: Jack Lynch Gets Set for Nashville," *Dayton Daily News*, February 19, 1978.

122. Ibid.

123. Ibid.

124. Fred Bartenstein, personal communication, March 28, 2017.

125. See chapter 3, "All the Way to the Fence."

126. Herbie Smith, comment to the author, date unknown.

127. Notations on LPs 106, 108, and 110.

128. John Wright, *Ralph Stanley and the Clinch Mountain Boys: A Discography*, 1983, unnumbered 4.

129. Notation on LP 107.

130. Wright, *Ralph Stanley and the Clinch Mountain Boys*, 5, 9.

131. Ibid., 10; Don Thrasher, "Owner of Cyberteknics Savors Sound of History," *Dayton Daily News*, January 23, 2015.

132. Notations on LPs 139–41, 146, 151–54.

133. "John D. 'Jack' Lynch," Find a Grave Memorial, https://www.findagrave.com.

134. Herbie Smith, discussion, late 2016.

135. Dennis Satterlee, "'Keep on Going': The Unknown Red Allen Recording," *Bluegrass Unlimited*, June 2016, 42–43.

136. Thrasher, "Owner of Cyberteknics."

137. Ibid.

138. Ibid.

139. Ibid.

140. Robert Leach, "Carlos Brock," *Bluegrass Unlimited*, April 2000, 71.

141. "Bankruptcy Petition Filed for Record Shop," *Cincinnati Enquirer*, Kentucky Edition, March 8, 1952, 14.

142. See chapter 3, "All the Way to the Fence."

143. "Collector Files Tax Liens against Two Concerns," *Cincinnati Enquirer*, Kentucky Edition, August 15, 1951, 15; "Tax Liens Filed," *Cincinnati Enquirer*, Kentucky Edition, August 15, 1951, 15.

144. "Bankruptcy Petition Filed for Record Shop."

145. Samuelson, *Jimmie Skinner: Doin' My Time*, 54.

146. Ibid., 20.

147. Future bluegrass great Roland White, of the Kentucky Colonels and the Nashville Bluegrass Band, remembers buying his first bluegrass records by mail from Cincinnati when he and his brother Clarence were still living at home in Maine. Another member of the Bluegrass Hall of Fame, Peter Kuykendall, bought Lou and Sonny Osborne's 1951 Kitty-label 78, "New Freedom Bell," at the Jimmie Skinner Music Center while changing trains in Cincinnati as a boy. He later took the song to Washington, DC's Country Gentlemen, who recorded it for Starday in 1959.

148. Undated flier from the Jimmie Skinner Music Center that details these offers plus others.

149. "Core Area Plans Force Business Veterans Out," *Cincinnati Enquirer*, Kentucky Edition, February 25, 1962, 6.

150. Advertisement, *Cincinnati Enquirer*, Kentucky Edition, December 12, 1962, 2.

151. "Louis Epstein, 39; Rural Music Judge," *Cincinnati Enquirer*, April 15, 1963, 30.

152. Samuelson, *Jimmie Skinner: Doin' My Time*, 54.

153. Ibid.

154. Grand Ole Opry at Taft Theatre advertisement, *Cincinnati Enquirer*, May 1, 1969, 65.

155. Sid's Record Shop advertisement, *Cincinnati Enquirer*, October 18, 1942, 3.

Built in 1963 and spanning the Ohio River at Cincinnati, the Brent Spence Bridge was the crossing point for hundreds of thousands of migrants from Appalachia. (www.nkyviews.com)

Dixie Highway: US 25 was the east branch of an automobile highway system planned in 1914 to connect Chattanooga, Lexington, Cincinnati, Dayton, and points north. (Photographer unknown; https://www.pinterest.com/pin/526921225124087569)

Price Hill neighborhood of Cincinnati, early 1970s. (Urban Appalachian Council Records, Berea College Special Collections and Archives, Berea, Kentucky)

Armco Steel Corporation, Middletown, Ohio, reached its peak local employment of 8,000 in 1966. (Middletown Historical Society Collection, Middletown, Ohio)

As late as 1990, five General Motors plants in the Dayton region employed 20,000 workers, even after massive layoffs in the previous two decades. (Special Collections and Archives, Wright State University, Dayton, Ohio)

In 1961 the Champion Coated Paper Company employed 3,300 workers in Hamilton, Ohio. Many were recruited from Appalachia because founder Peter G. Thomson found them to be loyal and adaptable hard workers who were ingenious at fixing machinery problems. (Courtesy of the George C. Cummins "Remember When" Collection at the Hamilton Lane Library, Hamilton, Ohio)

NCR (National Cash Register) Corporation employed 18,000 workers in Dayton as of 1966. (Special Collections and Archives, Wright State University, Dayton, Ohio)

Kentucky native Pete Steele migrated to Hamilton, Ohio, in 1937 to work for the Champion Paper Company. The following year, he and his family recorded for the Library of Congress Folk Music Archives. (Photo by Alan Lomax; Courtesy of the Library of Congress, ID LC-DIG-ppmsc-00650)

First broadcast in 1938 from Cincinnati, the *Boone County Jamboree* (later renamed *Midwestern Hayride*) achieved nationwide appeal and was a staple of WLW's Saturday night schedule for decades. (*Cincinnati Enquirer*, December 30, 1942; Mac McDivitt Private Collection)

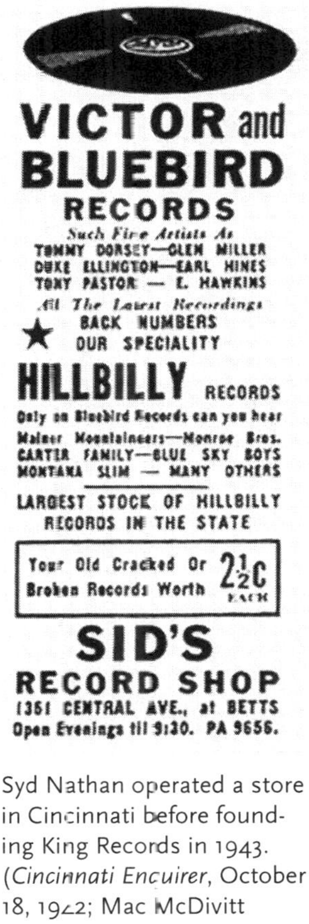

Syd Nathan operated a store in Cincinnati before founding King Records in 1943. (*Cincinnati Enquirer*, October 18, 1942; Mac McDivitt Private Collection)

Cincinnati DJ Nelson King initiated and hosted the *WCKY Jamboree* from 1946 to 1957, doing much to popularize bluegrass music in its early years. (Mac McDivitt Private Collection)

Wayne Raney, an ace harmonica player who recorded for King Records, hosted the *WCKY Jamboree* from 1957 to 1961. (Randy McNutt Private Collection)

Starting in 1950, country singer and songwriter Jimmie Skinner and his partner, Lou Epstein, sold records from a series of Cincinnati storefronts while nationally advertising mail order sales. (Mac McDivitt Private Collection)

Lester Flatt (left) and Earl Scruggs (right) were members of Bill Monroe's Blue Grass Boys when they played two sold-out shows at Dayton's Memorial Hall in February 1947. Twenty-two months later, now heading their own Foggy Mountain Boys, their recordings at Cincinnati's Herzog Studio included "Foggy Mountain Breakdown." (Richard Weize, . . . and more bears Records)

A mandolin and guitar duo on Cincinnati's WLW, the Turner Brothers recorded "Kentucky" at Herzog Studio in 1947. (Mac McDivitt Private Collection)

(Mac McDivitt Private Collection)

Telephone directory advertisement, summer 1951. (Brian Powers Private Collection)

In 1946 Earl T. "Bucky" Herzog, an engineer at WLW, built a nearby studio where numerous hits were recorded, including Hank Williams's "Lovesick Blues." (Brian Powers Private Collection)

The Barrelhead Gang at WPFB in Middletown, Ohio, early 1950s; left to right, Jim and Jesse McReynolds, Little Eller, Smokey Ward, Larry Roll, and Fairley Holden. (Middletown Historical Society Collection, Middletown, Ohio)

Pioneering country disc jockey Tommy Sutton on the air at WPFB, middle 1950s. (Middletown Historical Society Collection, Middletown, Ohio)

WPFB Radio, Middletown, Ohio, first went on the air in 1947, catering to the large regional market of transplanted Appalachians. (Middletown Historical Society Collection, Middletown Ohio)

Sixteen-year-old banjo player J. D. Crowe's first appearance with Jimmy Martin and the Sunny Mountain Boys, *WPFB Jamboree*, Middletown, Ohio, 1954; left to right, Bobby Simpson, Bill Price, Jimmy Martin, Vivian Watson, J. D. Crowe. (Fred Bartenstein Private Collection)

WPFB erected a large tent near the station's studios (housed in a farmhouse) for live Saturday night broadcasts of the *WPFB Jamboree*. (Middletown Historical Society Collection, Middletown, Ohio)

Bill Monroe and His Blue Grass Boys, guests at the *WPFB Jamboree*, early 1950s; left to right, Jimmy Martin, Joel Price, Rudy Lyle, Bill Monroe. (Middletown Historical Society Collection, Middletown, Ohio)

Dayton Daily News, May 4, 1951. (Mac McDivitt Private Collection)

Cast of the *WPFB Jamboree*, including a teenage Bobby Osborne (left of microphone) in the late 1940s. (Middletown Historical Society Collection, Middletown, Ohio)

Sydney "Syd" Nathan, founder and proprietor of King Records, Cincinnati, 1946. (Photo by Ran Cochran; Courtesy of the *Cincinnati Enquirer*)

Packaging King records at 1540 Brewster Avenue, Cincinnati, in the 1950s. (Steven D. Halper Private Collection)

King Records trade magazine advertisement, 1949. (Randy McNutt Private Collection)

King Records' first bluegrass releases were singles by Jimmy Martin and Bob Osborne, recorded August 27, 1951. (Richard Weize, . . . and more bears Records; Record label image, Mac McDivitt Private Collection)

Don Reno, Red Smiley, and the Tennessee Cut-Ups recorded for Cincinnati's King Records from 1952 until 1964; left to right, Red Smiley, Mack Magaha, John Palmer, Don Reno. "Charlotte Breakdown" was recorded in 1954 and released in 1955. (Courtesy of Gusto Records Inc.)

The Stanley Brothers recorded for King between 1958 and 1965; left to right, Ralph Stanley, Carter Stanley. "I'll Just Go Away" was recorded in 1961 and released by King in 1968, two years after Carter Stanley's death. (Photo courtesy of Gusto Records Inc.; Record image, Mac McDivitt Private Collection)

Charlie Moore and Bill Napier recorded for King between 1962 and 1966. "Long White Line," a single from a 1966 album of truck driving songs, was revived by Sturgill Simpson in 2014. (LP cover, Fred Bartenstein Private Collection; Record label image, Mac McDivitt Private Collection)

Locally produced 78 rpm records from the 1950s. (Mac McDivitt Private Collection)

In the early 1950s, Red Allen, Sonny Osborne, and Jim and Jesse McReynolds recorded at Carl Burkhardt's Northside Cincinnati studio. (Brian Powers Private Collection)

Between 1955 and 1984, Carl Burkhardt operated his studio and custom pressing business as Rite Record Productions Inc. in Lockland, just north of Cincinnati. (Brian Powers Private Collection)

Promotional sleeve from Cincinnati's Jimmie Skinner Music Center. (Brian Powers Private Collection)

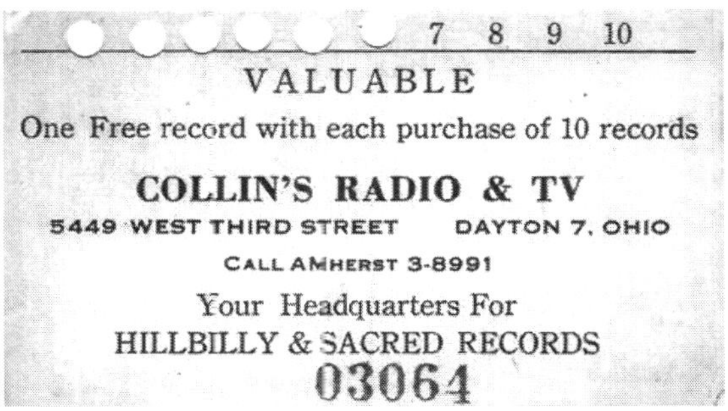

Discount card from Collins Radio & TV in Dayton's Drexel neighborhood, which sold country and bluegrass records by local artists rarely found in larger 1950s record stores. (Mac McDivitt Private Collection)

Promotional photo from 1957 highlighting the use of double banjos on "Ruby, Are You Mad?"; left to right, Bobby Osborne, Ray Anderson, Sonny Osborne, Red Allen. (Richard Weize, . . . and more bears Records)

Entertaining—Exciting
OSBORN BROS. & RED ALLEN
WITH ART STAMPER
RCA Victor Recording Stars
ENGLE'S BAR
400 Cincinnati St. AD-0563

Dayton Daily News, March 9, 1956. (Fred Bartenstein Private Collection)

The Country Pardners, RCA recording artists; left to right, Bobby Simpson, Bill Price, Carlos Brock, mid-1950s. (Courtesy of Bill Nowlin)

COUNTRY MUSIC
Thurs., Fri. and Sun.
OSBORNE BROS.
with Benny Birchfield
Sat. Nite
BROCK BROS.
with Red Spurlock
Charley's Nite Club
401 Wayne Ave.

Dayton Daily News, May 18, 1963. (Mac McDivitt Private Collection)

The Circle Bar in downtown Dayton, Ohio; left to right, Johnnie McKee, Frank Wakefield, Noah Crase, early 1950s. (Courtesy of Bill Nowlin)

HILLBILLY MUSIC
AT ITS BEST

KEG No. 1

1725 W. 3rd St. at Western Ave.

RED ALLEN AND HIS BLUE RIDGE
MOUNTAIN BOYS

MUSIC and DANCING

Friday and Saturday nights
8:00 p.m. to 1:00 a.m.

Popular prices
COMPLETE BAR SERVICE

Dayton Daily News, July 15, 1953. (Mac McDivitt Private Collection)

Location and date unknown. Left to right, Curley Tuttle, Virgil Joseph, Noah Crase, Dave Woolum. (Courtesy of Bill Nowlin)

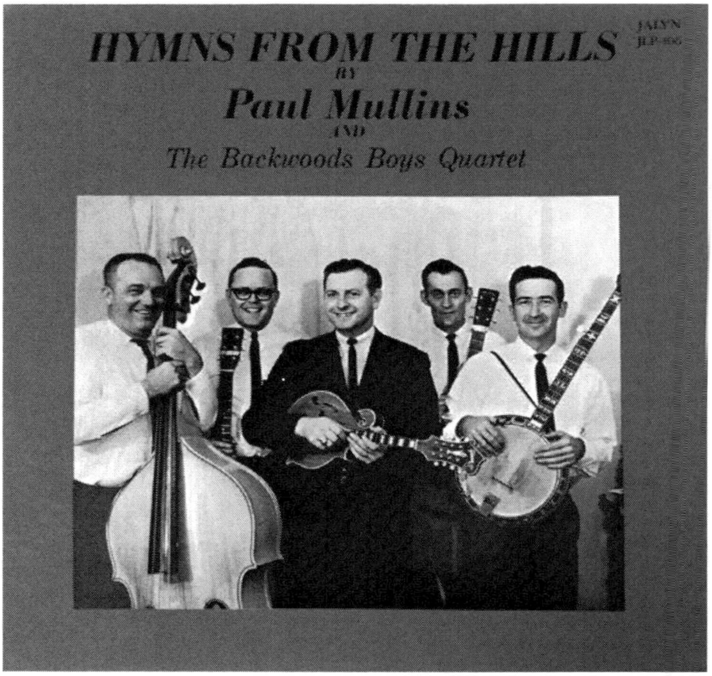

Dayton-based Jalyn LP; left to right, June Thompson, Paul Morris, Paul Mullins, Walter Adams, R. C. Meade, 1966. (Fred Bartenstein Private Collection)

Hamilton-based Pine Tree LP; left to right, front row: Donald Ballenger, Bradley Howard; back row: Paris Decker, Ruby Decker, Judy Decker, Dave Woolum, 1970. (Sherrill Jennings Private Collection)

John Reedy and the Stone Mountain Gang; left to right, Julian Ramey, Glenn Ramey, John Reedy, Frances Reedy. Residents of Dayton from 1953 through the mid-'60s, the Reedys brought "Somebody Touched Me" and "Oh Death" to the Stanley Brothers. (Courtesy of Bill Nowlin)

Current photo of the building that housed the Ken-Mill Café, at the corner of Kenton and McMillan Streets in Cincinnati. Earl Taylor and Jim McCall played there six nights a week starting in 1960. (Brian Powers Private Collection)

Ken-Mill Café; left to right, Paul Mullins (hidden), Vernon McIntyre Jr., Robby Robinson, Benny Birchfield, Jim McCall. (Photo by Marlene Hobbs; Frank Godbey Private Collection)

Joe "Cannonball" Lewis was a Kentuckian who eventually landed in Hamilton, Ohio. He made eight singles for MGM, many with a strong bluegrass flavor. "Before I Met You," which he cowrote and recorded on Gateway, later became a standard for Lester Flatt and Earl Scruggs. (Ivan M. Tribe Private Collection)

The Osborne Brothers were the first bluegrass act to play at a college, Antioch College, Yellow Springs, Ohio, March 5, 1960; left to right, Bobby Osborne, Sonny Osborne, Jimmy Brown Jr. (Photo by Ann Milovsoroff)

The Stanley Brothers and the Country Gentlemen soon followed with concerts in Kelly Hall, on the second floor of the historic Main Building. (Courtesy of Antiochiana, Antioch College, Yellow Springs, Ohio)

ADVERTISEMENT

Local Boys Make Good—Record

The Osborne Brothers have a new Decca recording, "Take This Hammer" b/w "Don't Even Look At Me." Nationwide reports show that it has a lot of promise.

In addition to personal appearance tours, The Osborne Bros. are a guest act on The Grand Ole Opry whenever their schedule permits. They make their homes in Dayton, and when in town, appear at The Bitter End, 401 Wayne Ave.

If you enjoy outstanding music and vocal harmony, we urge you to give our boys a boost.

The record may be pur-[illegible]chased at Collins Radio, 5149 W. Third St., and Xenia Avenue Music Center, 719 Xenia Ave. Also, listen for it on Les Bodine's dj show over WING, 5 to 6 A. M.

THE OSBORNE BROTHERS

The Osborne Brothers promote their new record and local appearances in the *Dayton Journal Herald*, November 8, 1963. (Mac McDivitt Private Collection)

5. Sing Me Back Home

Early Bluegrass Venues in Southwestern Ohio

LARRY NAGER

IT WAS MY FIRST TIME in downtown Cincinnati, but it felt like Mars. It was 1975, and my college bluegrass group, Red Mountain String Band, was playing its first night at legendary Aunt Maudie's Country Garden on Main Street in Over-the-Rhine. It was hallowed ground, a designated stop on the Ohio bluegrass trail. We were from Columbus, home of bluegrass havens like the Astro Inn and the Bluegrass Palace. But southwestern Ohio spots like Aunt Maudie's and Sam's Bar and Grill in Dayton were well known to all Ohio bluegrass fans and pickers.

Maudie's, as everybody called it, had everything you'd expect from an old-school bluegrass bar. Mr. Spoons was the colorful doorman, entertaining folks with percussive flatware and selling bouquets of artificial flowers. Doug Bailey was Maudie's gruff, gun-toting owner/bartender, and the crowd was a mix of middle-age and older transplanted Kentuckians and younger, more affluent suburban bluegrass fans, ex-folkies who'd probably been converted hearing Flatt and Scruggs on *The Beverly Hillbillies* or Earl Scruggs and John McEuen picking banjo on *Will the Circle Be Unbroken*.

We played our opening set, all six of us cramming onto the tiny stage, which made up in height what it lacked in width. It was so high, you could lose a bass headstock or fiddle bow to the ceiling fan if you weren't vigilant. On break, I stepped outside to escape the noise and smoke. Leaving that raucous, crowded bar was like stepping through a wormhole. It was Saturday night, but Main Street in downtown Cincinnati was a silent, darkened wasteland. There wasn't another business open on the entire block, not a single car rolling down the street. I expected tumbleweeds to blow by. Inside Maudie's, the party raged on.

I didn't realize it then, but I was standing at the end of an era. The inner-city bluegrass bars that had thrived since the 1950s in southwestern Ohio, from Cincinnati to Dayton, were just about all gone. Maudie's was one of the last holdouts. Years earlier, the white Appalachian population that had filled the rundown apartments and rooming houses in the Over-the-Rhine neighborhood where Maudie's was located—and throughout the city core in general—had headed for the suburbs. Many had moved to Norwood, an industrial community north of downtown, where there were still plenty of well-paying union factory jobs.

The population shifted after the Cincinnati powers that be converted many downtown apartment buildings into Section 8 housing, serving a Black population displaced from the city's West End by urban development and the construction of I-75. Some called it "white flight," a population shift that was occurring in thousands of cities across America. Anyone who could afford to do so was leaving downtown Cincinnati. Businesses closed, apartments deteriorated into tenements, and the city core sank into a morass of neglect that, despite repeated attempts at revival, never truly came back until the new millennium, after long efforts by downtown activists, private developers, and city government.[1]

In the 1970s bluegrass in Cincinnati moved uptown to the University of Cincinnati area, to spots like King's Row in Clifton and, later, to Dixie's on Short Vine. In the 1980s the Village Tavern in Elmwood Place served the tristate's growing bluegrass audience, regularly featuring national touring bluegrass bands like Del McCoury and His Dixie Pals. Downtown revivalist and bluegrass fan Jim Tarbell, later a Cincinnati city councilman and vice mayor, often booked bluegrass into his eclectic bar/restaurant, Arnold's, on Eighth Street. But on that night in 1975, Maudie's was downtown Cincinnati's lone survivor, alive and kickin' to the end, the last of a long line of tough, seedy, inner-city southwestern Ohio bluegrass bars.

The Great American Musical Migration

Just about every folklorist and roots music fan knows the great American musical migration story. Jazz was born in the saloons and whorehouses of New Orleans and exported to the rest of the country on riverboats. The blues came out of Mississippi cotton fields and turpentine camps and the rough juke joints that serviced them, heading north out of the Delta on Highway 61 through the hill country south of Memphis and straight onto Beale Street. The story of bluegrass in southwestern Ohio is a mirror image of that blues odyssey.

The parallels between blues and bluegrass were explored in Jim Rooney's groundbreaking book *Bossmen: Bill Monroe and Muddy Waters*, which profiled leading bandleaders of both genres.[2] Just as homesick Southern Blacks flocked to hear the blues in the juke joints of Memphis, St. Louis, and especially Chicago, displaced white Appalachians came to their own neighborhood bars to be sung back home by local bluegrass bands. The experience of rural Southerners in the

North became grist for hundreds of country and bluegrass songs, from Bobby Bare's "Detroit City" and "The Streets of Baltimore," to Skeeter Davis's "Bus Fare to Kentucky," to "John Deere Tractor," recorded by Larry Sparks, who started playing those southern Ohio bluegrass bars when barely a teenager.

As Northern industrialization grew dramatically in the mid-twentieth century, factory owners actively enlisted Southern workforces, running ads in newspapers or even sending recruiters down South. Harley "Red" Allen, later to become one of the finest lead singers in bluegrass history, grew up in Pigeon Roost outside Hazard, Kentucky. He remembered a foundry sending buses to Hazard to hire workers and bring them to Indiana, an offer he himself took up for a few months.[3]

The heavy industry and population booms of the first three-quarters of the twentieth century fueled a secondary boom to serve all those new urbanites, providing jobs for truck drivers, cab drivers, deliverymen, construction workers, day laborers, cooks, waitresses, and bartenders. Northern Kentucky became Cincinnati's Tijuana after Prohibition was repealed, as rich ex-bootleggers invested in huge casino and prostitution operations under direction of the Cleveland Syndicate. There was plenty of work there—from dealers, to waiters, to busboys, to more dangerous employment for country boys handy with fists, knives, and guns. It was the perfect location for such an operation, with Cincinnati's large customer base just across the river, yet remote enough from the Kentucky capitol in Frankfort to provide plausible deniability to corrupt state officials.[4]

Before World War II, Bobby and Sonny Osborne's father, Robert Osborne Sr., taught school to miners' kids in Hyden, Kentucky.[5] The Osbornes were better off than most families in the area, and Bobby even had a horse of his own. But with the war industries ramping up, Robert Sr. moved north to Dayton to take a job on the assembly line at National Cash Register. It paid better than teaching, but it was also in his mind to save his sons, Bobby and Sonny, from the coal mines, and his daughter, Louise, from the hard life of a miner's wife. Robert Sr. had bigger dreams for his kids, hoping that Bobby, the eldest, would become a doctor.[6]

If African Americans moving north sometimes found less prejudice and overt racism, white "hillbillies" and "briarhoppers," as they were sometimes derisively called, could find the opposite. Immigrants within their own country, they could be suspiciously viewed as virtual foreigners, with different religious beliefs, strange foods, and, with their mountain dialects and heavy accents, even a different and sometimes undecipherable language. When treated like other unwelcome immigrants, they kept to themselves as much as possible.

In Cincinnati, the biggest city in the area, newcomers could more easily assimilate in some situations, such as going to baseball games to see the Cincinnati Reds play at Crosley Field, or to the *Boone County Jamboree* and its later incarnation, the *Midwestern Hayride*.[7] It's not that they were naturally more accepted in Cincinnati; it was just easier to lose your past in a large city milieu. Even in cities, however, migrants tended to band together in communities. And for those whose original home ties remained strong, Kentucky was right across the Ohio River. On any given Friday they could head out of town in their old cars or take a Greyhound bus at the downtown terminal and spend the weekend down home. Even into the 1970s, Cincinnatians could count on two weekly traffic jams on I-75, the first heading south on Friday nights after the five o'clock whistle, the second northbound on Sunday nights. Dayton was fifty miles farther north, so that meant at least an extra hour each way for homesick Kentuckians.

A Thriving Bluegrass Bar Scene

The grand brewing tradition of the German Catholics who had founded Cincinnati meant plenty of beer gardens and taverns all over town, many featuring local country artists as well as the new acoustic banjo-driven sounds modeled by Flatt and Scruggs, the Stanley Brothers, and Bill Monroe and His Blue Grass Boys ("bluegrass" as the name of the genre would not become popular until the early 1960s).

We don't know exactly why—perhaps because it was a bigger, more lively and diverse city with many other entertainment options—but Cincinnati's bluegrass bar scene didn't develop until the late 1950s. Up the road a piece, in Hamilton and Dayton, bluegrass bars were in evidence a decade earlier, and the bluegrass acts spawned there had a far greater impact both locally and nationally.

In his essay "Industrial Strength Bluegrass," written for the program accompanying the Dayton Bluegrass Reunion, an event produced in 1989 by the Cityfolk organization,[8] bluegrass historian Neil V. Rosenberg listed some of the bars featuring bluegrass in southwestern Ohio in the 1950s and '60s: "Ruby's White Sands, the Hilltop Inn/Tavern, Keg #1, Keg #2, the Mecca Bar, the Mermaid, Johnnie's, the Blazing Stump, Little Mickey's, Babe's Place, the Horseshoe Bar, Tom's Tavern, the Friendly Inn, the Circle Bar, the Family Room, [and] the Golden Fly." Little Mickey's was owned by little person Milton "Little Mickey" Friedman, perhaps better known for wrestling and baseball promotion and his chain of adult bookstores.

The business model for those places was a lot like the dystopian honky-tonk in Frank Capra's *It's a Wonderful Life*, where bartender Nick (Sheldon Leonard), annoyed by Clarence the Angel's request for a mulled wine, angrily responds, "Listen, mister, we serve hard drinks in here for men who want to get drunk fast."[9] Like Nick's, and jukes in Mississippi, Memphis, St. Louis, and Chicago, the first bars presenting bluegrass in Ohio were short on atmosphere or anything else that might get in the way of the speedy and efficient consumption of alcohol. They were usually just storefronts with a bar against one wall, a cigarette machine and a jukebox on the opposite wall, and a few wooden tables and chairs scattered in between. Butting up against the back wall was a tiny dance floor and an even tinier stage, sometimes just a corner of the makeshift dance floor.

In the early 1950s there was little musical difference between country music and bluegrass. Both used upright basses and no drums (even the Grand Ole Opry didn't allow drums back then). Instrumentally, a country band usually had an electric "take-off" guitar or a non-pedal steel; a bluegrass band would have a banjo and a mandolin. Both styles used fiddles, and many fiddlers worked both country and bluegrass gigs.

Back then there were no firewalls between the musical styles, no purists deciding what was correct and what wasn't. All of it was just country music for country people, and most bars would have either country or bluegrass, depending on the musicians they could get. Being purely acoustic, bluegrass was the easiest type of live music for a bar owner to present. A guitar amplifier required an electrical outlet; a banjo did not.

Most bluegrass bands could only afford to play as a trio, without the upright bass. "Three pieces is all they'd pay for back then. You never saw a four-piece bluegrass band in Dayton," said Red Allen in Dennis Satterlee's biography, *Teardrops in My Eyes*.[10] Even a three-piece bluegrass band playing in a bar for around a hundred people might be able to perform without a costly sound system: microphones, stands, cables, amplifiers, or speakers. One microphone for the band was the industry standard. Vernon McIntyre Jr. remembers the sound system at the Ken-Mill Café, Cincinnati's most important bluegrass bar of the late 1950s and '60s: "It had this little old thirty-five-watt Bogen amplifier, and one of them big silver mics, and Earl [Taylor] had gotten some of those little speakers from the jukebox, man, and it was the best sound we all ever heard."[11]

In the same competitive bar business that once offered free lunches, live music was a draw, setting a place apart from the pack, and the musicians worked cheap. There was no cover charge in the early days, and for displaced mountain people bluegrass was the perfect attraction, an alternative to going to the movies or sitting at home listening to the radio (in the 1950s televisions were a luxury few could afford). So they headed to the local bars, playing the jukebox and drinking on the cheap.

Live or on the Wurlitzer, bluegrass was the ideal soundtrack for homesick country folks. The songs offered a nostalgic look back at the life they left behind, the memories becoming sweeter the farther away they got. After a few beers, their run-down shack in a sooty coal town was romanticized into that "Little Cabin Home on the Hill." Bluegrass used the old themes and the old instruments, the banjos and the fiddles from the barn dances, and the mandolin and guitars from the parlor serenades of sweet-voiced brother duets. But the music was brand-new, with all the drive and frenetic pace of big-city lives, thanks to that newfangled Scruggs-style banjo and the bluesy edginess of Bill Monroe's high lonesome singing, 180 degrees from the laconic, reassuring baritones of Grand Ole Opry superstars Red Foley and Ernest Tubb.

The Blue Grass Boys Inspire Young Ohio Musicians

The biggest difference between the blues and bluegrass was their origins. Where the blues began was murky, lost in time, but bluegrass had a very prominent "patient zero," Bill Monroe. In the first seven years of the 1940s, Bill Monroe's band, the Blue Grass Boys, established the musical style, the repertoire, and even the look—Stetson hats, jodhpurs, and riding boots—for other early bluegrass bands. In the days before rock and roll took over, bluegrass was a young person's music. It was new, it was thrilling, and no one was immune.[12]

The "Big Bang" for bluegrass in southwestern Ohio was Bill Monroe's February 9, 1947, appearance at Memorial Hall in Dayton. Bobby Osborne was at that show and still considers it the defining musical event of his life. He saw how Earl Scruggs managed to get all that sound out of a banjo (until then, he thought Earl was using a flat-pick, like the hyperactive Dixieland banjo players of the day). That was the classic bluegrass band: Monroe, Scruggs, Lester Flatt, Chubby Wise, and Howard Watts.

Osborne wasn't alone in that epiphany, and within a few years other young Appalachian transplants in southwestern Ohio were forming bands modeled on Bill Monroe's. Like a virus, the spread of bluegrass was aided by former Blue Grass Boys themselves. Osborne said:

> Bill didn't want nobody playing the music. He just wanted to play the music with the people that played with him, but he forgot to remember that nobody stayed very long who played with him, temperamental type person that he was. So when that person left, he knew Bill Monroe's music. And if somebody found out you played with Bill Monroe, you were the star of the night. And when that person went with somebody else, that band wanted to know how Bill did this, how he did that.[13]

Osborne played with ex–Blue Grass Boy Jimmy Martin before joining the marines and fighting in the Korean War. While he was gone, his little brother, Sonny, spent a summer playing banjo with Monroe. Just fourteen, Sonny recorded nine sides with the Blue Grass Boys, including "Pike County Breakdown."

In the early 1950s, before the rock and roll revolution, audiences experienced bluegrass as a kind of proto-rock. The music was fast and loud. The Scruggs-style banjo, played with metal fingerpicks, had much more volume than Uncle Dave

Macon's or Stringbean's hand-strummed styles. The crowds at appearances by Monroe and His Blue Grass Boys went into Elvis/Beatles–level hysteria whenever Scruggs took a solo or Monroe went into a high lonesome falsetto. The bass was often slapped and heavily syncopated, a precursor to Bill Black's sound with Elvis. (Even before Scruggs, Monroe was rocking. Listen to the original 1940 recording of the Blue Grass Boys' "Mule Skinner Blues," with Monroe playing syncopated blues-style rhythm guitar and "Cousin Wilbur" Wesbrooks slapping the bass.)

One of the teenagers enthralled by Bill Monroe, Earl Scruggs, and the hot new sound of the Blue Grass Boys was Noah Crase, who started playing the banjo in high school after migrating with his family from eastern Kentucky to Middletown, Ohio. "Unless you knew someone who played, you had to figure everything out yourself," he told Fred Bartenstein in a 1983 interview. "When I started playing three-finger style, there wasn't anybody to come over and give you a little hint. I remember I didn't know how to hold my fingers on the banjo. . . . When I finally got it, I had my own style."[14]

In southwestern Ohio, bluegrass's dynamic combination of the familiar and the strikingly new found a ready audience and a new generation of musicians as young men like Crase and the Osbornes started performing. But when they had honed their skills enough to "play out," there weren't many options for those early musicians. Only top, nationally visible stars could play at a venue as large as Dayton's Memorial Hall. For everyone else, the best start was a spot on the radio, usually unpaid, where you could make a name, then book a gig and promote it over the air. It's what B. B. King did in Memphis, and it worked for bluegrass pickers in Dayton, where fewer than a dozen musicians created a music scene downtown. "There was a lot of bars around then, and you could just take your choice of jobs," Crase told Bartenstein. He elaborated:

> We were playing for seven or eight bucks a night. Sometimes you'd get ten, and when you got up to twelve-fifty you were in heaven. If you could get four or five nights, you were in pretty good shape. We'd play like Thursday, Friday, Saturday, Sunday afternoon for a jam session from three to six, and then back again Sunday night, then Monday we'd play and get off Tuesday and Wednesday.
>
> I had a little sleeping room on the fourth floor of this place downtown. It wasn't very big, but it was big enough for me. In five minutes I could walk over to the bars. Maybe one week I'd be playing with Red [Allen] and Frank [Wakefield]. The next week maybe they didn't have a job, so I played with Carlos and Lonnie Brock. At that time there wasn't that many banjo players around. Sonny Osborne lived in Dayton; he came in a few places I played. And there was another banjo picker or two. But that was about it. Some of the other pickers were Johnny McKee, a fiddle player from up in Fairborn [Ohio], and another fiddler that used to work with us quite a bit, Bob Dooley.

> A mandolin player I always thought was good is David [Dorsey] Harvey. I worked a lot with both him and Frank. With bars on both sides of the street, we'd even switch during the night, trade banjo pickers and everything.[15]

Everyone played with everyone else, making up bands as the gigs demanded, but the team that really clicked for Dayton bluegrass was formed when Bobby and Sonny Osborne got together with another former Kentuckian, Harley "Red" Allen. Red had had a rough life back in Pigeon Roost Hollow. His mother, Sally, died when he was nine. Faced with an alcoholic, abusive father, he ran away at fifteen to join the army in the final days of World War II, but his age was discovered before he could ship out, and he was discharged. Red made his way to Dayton a few years later, working jobs for short periods of time and playing music when he could. Able to sing any part, he was the perfect front man for the Osborne Brothers, and they were soon playing clubs like the Circle Bar and the Ring Bar.

A Soundtrack for Drinking and Fighting

These were rough places, where music was usually just a soundtrack for drinking and fighting. The Osbornes steered clear of the latter, but Red was known to take on just about anybody after he'd had a few. Bobby recalled one night in particular at the Ring Bar:

> He [Red] and I both worked at National Cash Register and played there seven nights a week and had to get up at five o'clock in the morning. Sonny [six years Bobby's junior], he slept in all day. It was a huge place and, man, they had some ruckuses in that place.
>
> Red was kind of a hot-tempered person. We'd take breaks through the night [each set was forty-five minutes on stage, fifteen minutes off] and they had a big pinball machine in the back. One Sunday night the place was crowded with people and we took a break, and I went back and played the pinball machine. I knew Red had got himself a beer and went over to sit at a table with these guys that he knew. And everything was going along fine, and all of a sudden I heard [bangs fist down loudly on the table], and I looked and Red was right in the middle of a big brawl.
>
> Somebody said something and this guy called Red a son of a bitch. And he [Red] told me later, "I was just sitting there figuring out what I was gonna do right there." And when he figured out what he was gonna do, he put his beer bottle in his left hand and he caught that guy right through there [Bobby mimes holding a bottle by the neck, tipping it back as if taking a drink but instead stabbing it like a knife, driving the bottle right between the man's eyes]. And blood started flying everywhere and that started it. The bartender came around and picked up a chair and hit Red right over the back of the head with it. Red

never left his feet but he was out of it, staggering all over the place, falling over the chairs and blood was coming out from him. I figured I better get him to the hospital. I got him in the car and took him to Good Samaritan Hospital and they patched him up. Afterwards, we were standing around and he said, "Let's go back to work." So we went right back there and started singing again.[16]

Red could hold his own, but he didn't often take part in the fights that regularly occurred in the bluegrass bars. Fists and bottles were the usual weapons, but many of the patrons carried knives and, almost as often, pistols. Dorsey Harvey was a prominent Dayton mandolin player who often played with Red. His son, David, a skilled mandolin and fiddle player who now heads Gibson's mandolin division, remembers his father telling him about a particularly rough gig with Red:

> They were playing one night, I think it was the Circle Bar, and it was one of those places that had chicken wire in front of the stage, and I asked him, "Why do they have chicken wire in front of the stage?" And he said, "So the beer bottles wouldn't hit you when they got in a fight." And he said, "We were playing in there one night and these two guys, they were sitting together with this woman and they'd all come in there together, and they just sat there all night arguing over this woman. And finally one of them jumps up and pulls out a pocketknife—a switchblade—and just cuts that other dude's ear completely off." And when that guy's ear hit the floor, my dad said he looked at Red Allen and said, "What are we gonna do?" And Red said, "Keep playin'. We don't wanna make 'em mad."[17]

"I'd rather play in a bar than anywhere else," said Noah Crase:

> Most of the people that came in the bar, back in that time especially, knew who was there and what to expect. They were great to you. There were fights and everything else, but I felt just as safe there as I do sitting here, because I knew a lot of the guys. One night I played a tune for thirty or forty minutes because they were fighting. What wasn't fighting was standing up on the tables watching them. I didn't pay any attention to it. We got off the stage and they got through and that was it. We'd get back up and start picking again. It's just a way of life.[18]

Like Sonny Osborne with Bill Monroe, J. D. Crowe got his start with Jimmy Martin at the age of fourteen, playing the *WPFB Jamboree* in Middletown. Martin didn't play many clubs, which was just fine with Crowe:

> I remember we played a little old club in Hamilton, just a regular bar, played there Friday and Saturday night for about a month—nine to one a.m., four sets of music, forty on, twenty off. We didn't play a lot of clubs. I remember going to Dayton. There was a bar up there called the Circle Bar. It was a wild

place and across the street from it, about a block, was the Friendly Inn, and a block up from there was the country music bar, the Ring Bar.

I didn't want to be part of the club scene. They were rough. They had a fight about every night. Sometimes it would get pretty bad; sometimes it would just be a scuffle, and sometimes the proprietor would start more trouble than the patrons. They were mostly old country rednecks, I call 'em. They'd work those factories, steel mills, whatever, around there. The jobs were opened up and people were getting a lot of work. Kentucky and Tennessee were empty after all those people left.

It was just a typical bar scene back then. They'd pay attention till they got about half drunk. Then they'd try to talk louder than you're playing. We never had any problems. Fights would break out and they'd start throwing bottles and, when a fight breaks out, they get mad and don't look where they're throwing and it might get past the guy they're throwing at and hit somebody on stage. But they wouldn't throw at us deliberately. They'd protect us. If people would hassle us, they'd say, "Don't bother these guys."[19]

Every musician who played those bars, whether it was Cincinnati, Dayton, or the towns in between, describes them the same way. "The work brought people in there, and after work they'd come out to fight and listen to the music," remembers Larry Sparks, who grew up in Lebanon, Ohio, and started playing the bluegrass clubs when he was barely a teenager. "We didn't have many places to play unless you played in bars and nightclubs," he said. "There was not a whole lot going on."[20]

Incubator of Industrial Strength Bluegrass

Despite the long hours, low pay, and audiences that ranged from apathetic to violent, the bluegrass bars were the incubator for the rich southwestern Ohio scene. Playing on the radio made you a name, and getting a record deal meant better gigs and higher pay. But like the audience it served, bluegrass was working music for working people. Four sets of music a night for four, five, or seven nights a week was hard physical labor. But like boot camp, once a musician did that for a year or two, they were playing at a level that part-time players could not imagine. They kept to the template forged by Monroe, Flatt and Scruggs, and the Stanleys, but night after night in those Ohio bars the music got tougher, more urban, and more muscular. "It makes you a lot better picker," J. D. Crowe asserted. "Because you did things in those clubs that you didn't ordinarily do. For me, I always wanted to expand my catalog of music and do different stuff, not playing the same numbers all the time. You can't survive in the clubs doing that."[21]

The apathetic crowds actually helped musicians try new things. Bobby Osborne remembered: "Until our records came out, it was the only place there was to play. Ain't nobody knew us until our records started coming out. That's where I really learned how to play the mandolin was in a nightclub. A bunch of drunks setting out there, they don't care; as long as there's noise, they don't care."[22]

Bobby's original mandolin style came out of those bars. He didn't follow the Monroe style of heavy downstrokes and bluesy licks. Bobby's playing was bouncy and melodic, more like a fiddle than a mandolin, which made sense, since Bobby, a frustrated fiddle player, modeled his playing on the bluegrass fiddle pantheon: "Benny Martin, Tommy Jackson, Howdy Forrester, Chubby Wise—just great players. My dad had a fiddle at home, and I got to foolin' with that fiddle before I ever seen a mandolin. I loved the fiddle so much, but I was just too busy trying to sing and play the mandolin."[23]

In keeping with author Malcolm Gladwell's "10,000 hours to greatness" rule,[24] all that time and work paid off, as J. D. Crowe, Bobby Osborne, Larry Sparks, and others from the scene forged powerful, unique styles that have stood the test of time for more than fifty years. Playing every night, four sets a night, the musicians in the bars of southwestern Ohio had plenty of room to experiment, take chances, and stretch out. They challenged themselves and one another.

While their audiences were fighting physically, the musicians would sometimes have musical battles on stage. Red Allen was competitive in both arenas. Bobby Osborne recalls:

> I've never told this story before. He [Red] challenged me all the time on the tenor part. We were playing one time at the Royal Crest Restaurant in Dayton, and he said, "If I can sing tenor higher than you, could I do the tenor and you do my part?" And I said, "Yeah, if you can sing higher than me, you're welcome to do it. What song do you want to do?" And he said, "I want to do 'Ruby'; I think I can do 'Ruby' higher than you do."
>
> We were standing on the stage there in that little ol' club, all those drunks watching. (I hate to call 'em drunks, but everybody drank back then.) And we started singing "Ruby" in D and I'd bring it up a fret, and we started singing it in E-flat. And I said, "Red, can you sing any higher than that?" And he said, "Yeah." He had just enough beer in him that he could, I guess, and I think we went as high as F.
>
> And those people out there, they sobered up, they knew what we was doin'. And I said, "If you can't get the intro on the start of it—Ru-BEE! [he does that famous vocal leap]—that's part of the song, and if you can't get that, you lose." He said, "OK, buddy, I can do it." I said, "I know I can do it." So he went first, and he tried four or five times at it—Ru-BEE!—and he couldn't do it. I said, "I've got all these people as witnesses. You're gonna sing your part and I'm gonna sing my part on everything from now on."[25]

"Ruby, Are You Mad?" was a remake of an old Cousin Emmy song that Sonny Osborne had worked up in a twin-banjo arrangement with Noah Crase, another example of Dayton bluegrass innovation. Not long after, Crase, reliably undependable, disappeared. For the group's MGM Records audition, Bobby learned the part in G tuning, capoed to D, while Sonny played in D tuning. The first bluegrass record featuring twin banjos, topped by Bobby's stratospheric vocals, "Ruby, Are You Mad?" was a high lonesome tsunami. Released in 1956, it was their first hit, a certified bluegrass classic. It didn't free them completely from the clubs, but it landed them on WWVA's *Wheeling Jamboree*, where they heard another song that would change everything for them.[26]

Another performer on the Jamboree, Dusty Owens, had written a song called "Once More." Featuring Owens and Donna Darlene, it sounded like a Kitty Wells knockoff. But it caught Bobby's ear, and one night on the show he asked Owens's permission to record it for MGM. Bobby recalled, "We tried regular three-part harmony: tenor on top, lead in the middle, and baritone underneath. But it was a ballad, and that just wasn't sounding good. We stopped the car in Cambridge to get the guitar out of the trunk or something, and I just all of a sudden started singing the lead to it.[27]

Red Allen told me his version of the story when I was playing bass with him in the 1980s, saying that when Bobby started singing the high lead, Sonny came in with the baritone as usual, and though Red had challenged Bobby's tenor singing before, he wasn't up to it that night. Red said he "was layin' in the backseat, drunk, and I wasn't going to sing that high tenor, so I just lifted my head and came in with the low part." Bobby doesn't dispute that, adding with a laugh, "Course, he was drunk all the time." Accident or not, when Bobby's lead soared over Sonny's baritone and Red's low tenor, they realized they'd split the bluegrass harmony atom. "We just sat there and stared at each other," Bobby said. "We ain't never heard anything like that. So we just sung that all the way to Dayton, just sat in the car and sung it over and over again, so we wouldn't forget it. There wasn't anybody singing like that, they were still doing the old Flatt and Scruggs and Bill Monroe–type harmony."[28]

Back in Dayton, even though they needed new material for their club appearances, they kept their discovery secret: "We didn't sing that in front of anybody. We wanted to put that on record before anybody else." When they polished "Once More" to where they wanted it, the excited young musicians met with Wesley Rose in Nashville. "And we said, 'Wesley, we got a new song. See if you like it.' And we did 'Once More' with that high lead."[29]

Rose argued that they shouldn't change their successful formula. But Bobby, Sonny, and Red knew they had something special: "So we went round and round, and he said, 'If I let you do that, you'll probably lose your recording contract. MGM's got you signed to do bluegrass and that ain't bluegrass. It's too slow. Can you speed it up?'" They refused, and then began the argument over putting snare drum and Dobro on the record. They won again. Bobby remembers

Rose had a final warning: "'You may not have a contract after this.' So we said, 'We're just gonna take a chance.' And back then, they had the Top 40 stations. And 'Once More,' when it came out, it went to number thirteen. And we never heard nothing more from Wesley after that."[30]

Red Allen: Genetically Engineered to Play Bluegrass Bars

With his revolutionary low-tenor harmony part, Red Allen had innovated himself right out of a job. The Osbornes had found their signature sound, one that allowed Bobby to become the lead singer, freeing them from having a singer/guitarist front the band and become the de facto star. In many ways Red Allen was the perfect front man: prodigiously talented, charismatic, and very funny on stage. He was also an alcoholic plagued by wild mood swings, an erratic performer who could be incredible on the night's first set and barely able to perform the second. When they parted ways, soon after the success of "Once More," Bobby took over as primary lead singer, and from then on all they needed was a solid rhythm guitarist who could sing low tenor. From 1958, when they split with Red, to 2005, when Sonny retired, they never gave co-billing to anyone again.

The Osbornes/Allen group's tenure with MGM gave Red Allen a higher profile as well. He came home to Dayton and took some time off, but Red was a man genetically engineered to play bluegrass bars. He complained about the apathetic crowds, but he loved the spotlight, making the crowds laugh (often at jokes more fitting for a stag party than a bluegrass club). And he loved playing with the Dayton scene's world-class musicians: mandolinists Frank Wakefield (Red's longtime partner) and Dorsey Harvey; multi-instrumentalist Red Spurlock; banjo man Noah Crase; Dobro player Gene Sweet; and, in later years, Red's sons, Ronnie, Neal, Greg, and Harley. Red also had a well-known weakness for whiskey and women, both readily available in the bluegrass bars. (That's one more way in which the Osborne Brothers and Red Allen personified the southwestern Ohio club scene. Some of the musicians, like Bobby and Sonny, had ambitious, long-range plans and focused on the music and their careers. Others, like Red, settled for the immediate gratification of the night, living for the moment, enjoying the party.)

Red Allen had enough pure talent and raw bluegrass power in his voice and guitar playing that he could party and still perform at a very high level. Red relocated to Washington, DC, in 1959, performing and recording with Wakefield, calling his band the Kentuckians.[31] The duo recorded the classic 1963 Folkways album *Bluegrass*, produced by a young David Grisman. Featuring Bill Keith's melodic banjo, it was one of the first bluegrass albums to fully showcase that influential style.

Red went on to record excellent albums for County and Melodeon in the mid-'60s and a series of great singles for Starday and Rebel. In 1967 he briefly replaced Lester Flatt with Earl Scruggs while Flatt recuperated from a heart attack. Then it was back to the barrooms again as Red took an ongoing gig in Kentucky with J. D. Crowe, Doyle Lawson, and Bobby Slone at the Red Slipper Lounge in the Lexington Holiday Inn—the last great bluegrass house band run of the 1960s. In the '70s Red returned to Dayton, formed a group with his sons, and hit the burgeoning bluegrass festival circuit.

In 1972, in an interview with the *Dayton Daily News*, Red reminisced about his days in the rough bluegrass bars, telling the reporter he was paid only ten dollars a night "and all I could drink. . . . People were cut and shot, and I just went on singing." But he said those days were over. "I won't play any more dives. You don't graduate from something then go back to it."[32]

Despite his vow, Red always seemed happiest on stage in a Dayton nightspot after he'd had a few. I first played with Red in 1978, and for the last time in 1989 at the Dayton Bluegrass Reunion. But the night I'll never forget was in tiny Arnold's in Cincinnati, on a winter night in the early '80s. It was a gig for Red's son Harley's band with Mike Lilly, and Red was just sitting in. With no stage, we were packed into a corner when Red, with just a few dozen people in front of him, spontaneously swapped parts with Harley, who sang lead as Red unleashed that powerful tenor voice on a duet of the old Bill Monroe number "The First Whippoorwill." I've never heard better bluegrass anywhere in my life.

A New Generation of Pickers

With the Osborne Brothers in Nashville and Red Allen on the road for much of the 1960s, southwestern Ohio produced a new generation of pickers, people like Joe Isaacs (whose children are today's popular gospel group the Isaacs) and Roy Lee Centers (who would later sing lead with Ralph Stanley, perhaps the closest vocalist to Carter of all Ralph's lead singers). Noah Crase joined forces with fiddler/disc jockey/songwriter Paul "Moon" Mullins after recording his legendary "Noah's Breakdown" with Dave Woolum.[33]

The biggest name in bluegrass to emerge from the southwestern Ohio bluegrass bar scene of the 1960s was Larry Sparks. Born in 1947 in Lebanon, Ohio, he began playing the bars when he was a young teenager and landed his first major gig as lead guitarist with the Stanley Brothers at age sixteen. A few years later, after Carter died at the end of 1966, Sparks became Ralph's first lead singer. He recalls:

> I took the job with Ralph in Dayton. He asked me to come and sing with him. The band was Ralph and Curly Ray [Cline] and Melvin Goins. It was at Tom's

Tavern. Ralph came in to play a weekend in there. Jack Lynch [owner of Jalyn Records, one of the great Ohio bluegrass record companies] told me he was going to be there. The house band was Roy Lee Centers and Fred Spencer. I had sung a couple songs that night with him and I guess Ralph liked what he heard.[34]

Sparks remains one of the great singers, guitarists, and bandleaders in bluegrass, and he knows that his years in the Ohio bluegrass bars made him the artist he is today. But he's seen so many of his fellow pickers who never made it out of the bars, who wound up like the fallen angel in the Stanley Brothers' "She's More to Be Pitied," where "the lure of the honky-tonks wrecked her young life." Sparks said of the club grind:

> It'll tighten you up for sure. It will give you some good practice, and if you stay sober, you'll know what's going on. I just really don't want to go anymore. It takes me back to when I had to be there, just trying to make a buck. It's a tough way to go. They're no good for you. I'm just glad I don't have to play 'em no more. When I was young, I had a pretty good run of it. If you live your songs or live the bar life, you've had it. You can't live these songs . . . some of these songs you just have to get rid of. Don't sing 'em.[35]

Despite his reservations, the bluegrass bars of southwestern Ohio were very good to Sparks. In Dayton he landed gigs with the Stanley Brothers and, later, Ralph Stanley. In Cincinnati he found his trademark 1954 D-28 Martin guitar hanging on the wall of the Queen City's renowned bluegrass venue, the Ken-Mill Café.

The Ken-Mill Café: Legendary Cincinnati Bluegrass Venue

In Cincinnati, bluegrass could be heard on the *Midwestern Hayride* and DJ country shows on WLW and WCKY, on the records coming out of King and Gateway (which featured a series of bluegrass cover records by area musicians, including Sonny Osborne), and on tiny custom labels. Jim Tarbell cited an array of beer joints along Vine Street in Over-the-Rhine that had country and bluegrass in the 1950s: the Swing Bar, the Arrow Café, the Silver Dollar, Jeanne's, and Pappy's. The one that really left a mark on him, said Tarbell, was the Ken-Mill, located at the corner of Kenton and McMillan Streets in Walnut Hills.[36]

The house band there didn't come from Kentucky. Earl Taylor and the Stoney Mountain Boys had arrived from Baltimore, seeking work in what was then a broadcasting and recording mecca. They played briefly at the Walnut Café at Thirteenth Street, but soon found their way to the Ken-Mill. The classic lineup of that band was Earl Taylor on tenor and mandolin, Jim McCall on guitar and lead vocals, Walter Hensley on banjo, and Vernon "Boatwhistle" McIntyre Sr. on bass and comedy. They arrived with a pretty good résumé, including the distinction of being the first bluegrass band to play Carnegie Hall, a show produced in 1959 by eminent folklorist Alan Lomax.

The Ken-Mill was a long way from Carnegie Hall. Owned by Stewart Salmons, it was a standard-issue storefront bar, with enough of a sound system to amplify a bluegrass band, with that 35-watt Bogen amplifier powering jukebox speakers that Earl Taylor had MacGyvered into a sound system.

The early 1960s saw enormous interest in bluegrass, as country music met the folk revival. It was before the Beatles, Elvis was just getting out of the army, and the record business was open to suggestion. The Carnegie Hall show had helped the Stoney Mountain Boys land a contract with Capitol Records. But where a few years earlier the Osborne Brothers and Red Allen could tinker with the bluegrass formula and land on the mainstream country charts, Taylor's album stiffed.

In Cincinnati the Stoney Mountain Boys played dyed-in-the-wool bluegrass for Kentucky expats and urban folk fans. They were the match for any traditional bluegrass band going. Taylor, a powerful tenor-singing mandolinist resolutely in the Bill Monroe mold, had played and recorded with Jimmy Martin and would later do a stint with Flatt and Scruggs. He was matched by the powerful voice of McCall, a barrel-chested lead singer, who sometimes doubled as the Ken-Mill bouncer. Hensley was a dynamic, inventive banjo picker who had earned his own Capitol contract. When Hensley moved back to Baltimore, he would be replaced by Vernon "Junior" McIntyre Jr., who had been playing in New York City after appearing on the *Ted Mack Amateur Hour* (the *America's Got Talent* of its day). Junior remembers getting to Cincinnati in 1960 and replacing Hensley. "That's where it started," McIntyre said. "Six nights a week for about six and a half years."[37]

Junior remembers other artists playing bluegrass and country around town, including Nelson Young, Jimmy Fee, and George Robinson. But the group at the Ken-Mill had the steadiest gig in town. And, though it didn't pay much, it paid every night. Together with the tip jar, it was a living.

"You could make a living, you know. Barely," said Junior McIntyre. "I made a hundred dollars a week, tips and everything." The group would make occasional appearances on the *Midwestern Hayride* and on local TV variety shows, including the one hosted by Maysville, Kentucky, native and Cincinnati TV personality Nick Clooney, whose son, George, is also in show business. But even if it wasn't much, dependable income was rare in bluegrass. That's one reason Josh Graves, the great Dobro player with Flatt and Scruggs, would come play the Ken-Mill during breaks from the Foggy Mountain Boys. "He'd come up and play two weeks with us on his vacation," Junior said. "He first did it when Walt

[Hensley] was there and then we became pretty good friends. He'd come up on his vacation and the way he was talking, he was gonna leave Flatt and Scruggs if they [Earl Taylor and Jim McCall] would come to Nashville. He loved playing with them; it was some of the best stuff I ever heard. As good or better than Flatt and Scruggs."[38]

Josh Graves agreed, and he fondly recalled the club in his *Bluegrass Bluesman: A Memoir*:

> I left Flatt and Scruggs for another short time in about '63. I was just looking around to see if I could find something. Benny Martin told me to call this club in Cincinnati called the Ken-Mill and they'd hire me, and they did, for a heck of a lot more money than Flatt and Scruggs was paying me. So I went in and worked five nights a week with Earl Taylor, Boatwhistle McIntyre, Walter Hensley, and Jim McCall. Man, they had a tough outfit![39]

He meant that in more ways than one. The bluegrass scene was changing in the '60s, with a lot more younger folks there for the music, but some customers still liked a brawl as much as a beer or a banjo breakdown. As Graves remembered:

> This one cat come in there . . . he didn't dig me too much, and he thought I was a smart aleck or something . . . you know how a drunk will do. And I said, "Well, if you don't appreciate what I'm doing, maybe somebody else does, and if you've got something to say to me after I get through, just bring it outside." Well, he had two or three others there with him. I went out and I had that Dobro bar in my hand, you know. I didn't ask nobody to go out there with me, but I looked around and there was Boatwhistle. He said, "Well, that'll even the odds a little bit." Here come Earl Taylor. Here come Walter Hensley. Jim McCall didn't come out.
>
> But there was a boy there—he'd been learning Dobro—and you talk about a tough little dude. He had a chain, and he knew karate and all this. He said, "All of you just go back in. I'll take care of this situation myself." And, bud, he run them off, and I never was so glad. I wasn't about to run, but, you know, a guy like that, you could get killed. But I'll never forget Boatwhistle. He come right in there. He was a true ol' showman."[40]

"There were always fights," said Junior. "And you never knew who would walk in there. We had lots and lots of famous country people would come by. Janis Joplin came by when she was playing the Cincinnati Gardens."[41]

Paul "Moon" Mullins is best-known as part of the Middletown scene, presenting bands at the Horseshoe Café or broadcasting over WPFB, but his son, Joe, leader of the Radio Ramblers, remembers Paul's affection for the Ken-Mill: "He had more fond memories about playing the Ken-Mill Café than just about anything else he ever did. He was in the house band for a big chunk of the '60s. It was Dad, Jim McCall, Benny Birchfield, and Junior McIntyre. And on the weekends they had the Stanley Brothers, or Reno and Smiley, or Reno and Harrell. They all dropped in and out of there."[42]

Harry Sparks Remembers the Cincinnati Bar Scene

Harry Sparks (no relation to Larry Sparks) may have been the Stoney Mountain Boys' number-one fan. The Kentucky-born singer/guitarist/luthier/architect/entrepreneur would play a huge role in the spread of bluegrass in Cincinnati, starting the music store Famous Old Time Music Company in Pleasant Ridge and playing in Cincinnati's first revivalist bluegrass band. His introduction to bluegrass came when he heard Flatt and Scruggs by accident at a Kentucky drive-in theater but had no idea who or what that music was. He came to Cincinnati for college in 1961 and, not long after, was at a party with a bunch of young folkies: "We were all trying to learn to play some kind of music, and at that party somebody put on a Flatt and Scruggs album and I spun around and said, 'That's what I heard that night!'"[43]

He asked where he could hear more and soon found the Stoney Mountain Boys playing the Walnut Café. He followed them when they moved to the Ken-Mill. By 1964 Sparks was a Ken-Mill regular, learning bluegrass rhythm guitar from McCall and sitting in whenever he had the chance: "I was there many nights. . . . I'm sort of an insomniac. They'd start about 8:30 or 9:00 and quit at 12:00 or 1:00." He remembers the Stanley Brothers playing there when they would come to town to record for King, as did other King artists. Junior McIntyre would play with Charlie Moore and Bill Napier. Reno and Smiley would come in, as would the Osborne Brothers, with Benny Birchfield on guitar. Despite the occasional big-name acts, Sparks said the Ken-Mill almost never charged a cover.[44]

There was nothing glamorous about the place. Even as adventurous folkies started to trickle in, the audience was mostly local people, Kentuckians who had come north to find work. Sparks remembers some ladies who found work right at the Ken-Mill:

> There were an awful lot of floozies, as we called them in those days, who hung out and serviced the band and various clientele. But the music was always amazing. And Boatwhistle did the comedy kind of things. He got up and told some jokes, and we'd just listen to these wonderful stupid jokes night after night and everybody would laugh and everybody would tip the band. It was fun. But it was definitely a knife and gun club.[45]

Sparks remembers one night when that was literally true:

> One night I was in there and I stayed till closing time. I liked to bullshit with everybody, and the Osborne Brothers just happened to be there that night.

Sonny came off the stage and said, "Bobby has just traded for the most lovely little pearl-handled, engraved automatic .22 you've ever seen." And everybody said, "Wow, let's have a look." Bobby just reached into his pocket and pulled this pistol out. He'd had it in his pocket all night. And he pulled the clip out and opened the chamber, and there was a bullet in the chamber and it fell out on the bar, and so, with the gun open and safe, he hands it around. And there were like fifteen people in the bar that night at this time, and so Sonny said, "I've got this stupid thing. I've got a .38 automatic." And it was all black, not fancy at all. And he took the clip and took the bullet out of the chamber. And so Jim McCall took a revolver out of *his* pocket. It was fairly good size and then he dumped all the bullets out of the cylinder. And then Earl Taylor pulled out a revolver and dumped the bullets. And this went on until everybody in the bar looked at me to get my pistol out and show them what I had. And so I said, "I don't have a pistol." And they said, "You don't have a pistol? What's the matter with you?" And I said, "With friends like you, I don't need one." And we laughed about it.

And then Stew said, "Let me show you something." And he went over to the cash register. He said, "Harry, point your finger at me and say, 'This is a stickup.'" So we're all standing around watching Stew, and he was kind of a showman. So I point my finger at him and I say, "This is a stickup." He reaches over and hits the button on the cash register without the drawer buffer, so the drawer flew out really fast. All the money flew out all over the floor and we all watched it fall, and when we looked up, he was holding a gun on us, a big .44. And he said, "They always watch the money."

And then he walked to the cooler and he said, "And if anybody comes in at this end . . ." And in between the top of the cooler and the bottom of the bar there was a little three- or four-inch space, and he reached in there and came up with a sawed-off shotgun, and of course it was loaded. And it was highly illegal. He had sawed the stock off to where it was just like a pistol, this side-by-side shotgun. Definitely a knife and gun club.[46]

The weaponry wasn't just for show. Owning a bluegrass bar could be hazardous to your health. In 1974 Charles Engle, owner of Engle's Bar, a popular Dayton bluegrass venue in the 1950s and '60s, was shot and killed in a late-night robbery attempt at his nightspot.[47]

Along with swapping guns, they'd swap instruments in the Ken-Mill. (These were days when there were no such things as vintage guitar dealers, eBay, or Craigslist, and it was seen as a radical idea when Harry Sparks opened his Famous Old Time Music Company to serve the bluegrass and folk community.) Salmons kept an old Martin guitar in the bar for people to play when they sat in with the band. Larry Sparks was one of the people who would come in and borrow it. "He kept it on stage," Larry remembers. "And he wanted to sell it. 'Let me take it,' I said. And next year it'll be fifty years I've been playing it. Hap Hammond made the pickguard; he did Jimmie Skinner's pickguard."[48] Larry paid three hundred dollars for that 1954 D-28, and it's been on every one of the dozens of classic bluegrass recordings he's made in the half century since he picked it off the wall.

Clubs Keep the Bluegrass Flame Burning

Larry Sparks's old boss Ralph Stanley had even more reason to fondly remember the Ken-Mill. That's where he met his wife, Jimmi, a story he told in his autobiography, *Man of Constant Sorrow*. She was a transplanted Kentuckian, her family members were all Stanley Brothers fans, and she came to a Stanley Brothers show at the Ken-Mill with her older sister, Louise, and Louise's husband, Duane. Ralph was transfixed, but Jimmi was playing hard to get. "I figured that was that," he wrote. "I was wondering if there were any other girls like her in Cincinnati. Sure wasn't none like her in Dickenson County or Bristol [both Virginia] or anywhere else I'd been." In 1968, seven-and-a-half-years later, he finally convinced her to marry him and they were together until Ralph died.[49]

The bars of southwestern Ohio were an important vector for the spread of bluegrass music in the 1950s and '60s. In today's media-saturated world, where a few taps on your smart phone can get you thousands of rare and classic bluegrass songs and video clips, it's hard to realize how difficult it was in earlier eras to find out anything about the music. Records were hard to find, there was no International Bluegrass Music Association, no big network of festivals every weekend, no *Bluegrass Unlimited* magazine or *Bluegrass Today* or *Bluegrass Situation*, no Facebook pages, no YouTube. In 1965, in Fincastle, Virginia, promoter Carlton Haney started bluegrass festivals as we know them today, but they took a while to catch on. And even though there were sporadic outdoor bluegrass shows or a major Opry star might come to town, it was the clubs that kept the flame burning, with live bluegrass just about every night of the week. That's what created the southwestern Ohio bluegrass community from the ground up, uniting the urban bluegrass fans with the folks for whom it really was folk music, the songs of their parents and grandparents.

Although the bars were run by locals for locals, adventurous urban bluegrass fans would travel to check out other cities' club scenes. In 1964 two banjo pickers made a national pilgrimage in search of bluegrass. One of them, Sandy Rothman, wrote to Cityfolk director Phyllis Brzozowska after attending the Dayton Bluegrass Reunion: "In 1964 Jerry Garcia and I took a cross-country driving trip, during which time Neil Rosenberg pointed us towards an Osborne Brothers club date one night at the White Sands [in Dayton]." After the journey, Garcia returned to San Francisco and started the band that would become the Grateful Dead. Rothman was a dedicated bluegrasser, and having found the richest scene in Ohio he returned a few years later. As he wrote in the letter, "I spent five years in Ohio (1969–1973), learning the essence of bluegrass by working with bandleaders such as Earl Taylor (Cincinnati), Sid Campbell (Columbus), and Red Allen (Dayton)."[50]

During those years the bluegrass revival had begun in earnest. Harry Sparks and his mandolin-playing friend Bill Lawarre had learned their Ken-Mill lessons well and soon formed their own band and started doing gigs, notably at the Black Stallion, a Cincinnati nightclub northeast of downtown on Kellogg Avenue that presented mainstream country recording artists and hired bluegrass bands as cheap, low-maintenance openers.

The day they were scheduled to play one of those shows, Lawarre developed the flu. Earl Taylor didn't have a telephone, so Sparks rushed over to Taylor's house to ask him to sub that night. That was when Sparks realized just how little his idols had been making. "Earl asked me, 'How much does it pay?' and I told him thirty-five dollars. And then he asked, 'And how much of that do I get?' When I told him it was thirty-five dollars apiece, he wouldn't let me out of his sight for the rest of the day; he just followed me around like a little puppy dog."[51]

The Bluegrass Scene Changes and Endures

In the late 1960s, when race riots tore apart America's cities following the assassination of Martin Luther King, the Ken-Mill was caught in the crossfire. Harry Sparks tells of Stew Salmons guarding his bar with a few of his guns, even tossing back a Molotov cocktail that landed inside the bar but hadn't exploded on impact.[52]

When the Ken-Mill hit hard times, Jim McCall and Junior McIntyre and their band, the Appalachian Grass, moved over to Aunt Maudie's Country Garden on Main Street in Over-the-Rhine. Aunt Maudie's owner, Lou Ukelson, was an important figure in Cincinnati bluegrass who also took over the Jimmie Skinner Music Center and founded the bluegrass label Vetco Records. He bought the old Terrace Gardens and changed the name after he heard a Jerry Reed song called "Aunt Maudie's Fun Garden," about a woman who grew a different kind of grass. The times indeed were a-changin'.

Aunt Maudie's was where pioneering female bandleader Katie Laur discovered bluegrass music. She said some girlfriends had told her, "'There's a place you might like downtown.' And I got outside the door of Aunt Maudie's, and Jim and Junior and whoever else was there were playing 'Salty Dog Blues,' and I was just mesmerized."[53] She became a regular and was soon getting up to sing harmony and do her specialty number, a high energy "T for Texas" that featured her powerful, soulful voice and amazing ability to hold a note. She was an immediate hit.

"I just got up and sang for free and didn't think anything about it," she said. "And the people were lined up outside Aunt Maudie's. And I would get up and sing 'T for Texas' and it would start a riot. And this guy came in one night and said to them [Jim McCall and Junior McIntyre], 'If you come in and play at my bar in Clifton, five nights a week, the pay would be such and such, but the only thing is, you have to bring the girl.'" They accepted, despite the fact that a woman in the band was a pretty radical departure for bluegrass bars. It was definitely a man's world on that stage. But Katie hadn't quite cut all the way through the grass ceiling. "They were paid eighty-five dollars a week and I was paid eighty," she said, still sounding angry at the inequity. "I couldn't understand why, and they explained it's 'cause I didn't have a family to support. As if any of them supported their families." So Katie went on strike. "I felt really awful, but I just stuck to my guns and I just laid off one night, and I got the five-dollar raise the next night to come back to work."[54]

The scene was changing.[55] It was the 1970s and bluegrass and acoustic music were hip, thanks to a perfect storm that included Crosby, Stills, and Nash; "Dueling Banjos"; the early Eagles (who covered the Osborne Brothers' "Midnight Flyer"); James Taylor; John Denver; and especially the Nitty Gritty Dirt Band's hit album *Will the Circle Be Unbroken*. What had been the music of a desperate, displaced people had become a signature sound for the entire region, indeed, the entire country.

Generations later, it has never really "got above its raisin." The down-home, distinctly Kentucky sound of southwestern Ohio bluegrass lives on today in such bands as the Comet Bluegrass All-Stars, with its standing Sunday night gig at the Comet in Cincinnati's Northside neighborhood, as well as in groups like the all-female Ma Crow and the Lady Slippers, and even jamgrassers (progressive bluegrass bands that play extended improvisations, as in rock and jazz) like the Rumpke Mountain Boys. Those first migrant Appalachians had come north for work in the factories, and though they and those factories are long gone, the music and the community they helped create and nurture—and, yes, even fight over—lives on, inspiring musicians and bluegrass fans the world over.

Notes

1. Larry Nager, "Over-the Rhine: Reviving Cincinnati's Endangered Heart," *Cincinnati Gentlemen*, November/December 2006, 53–57.

2. James Rooney, *Bossmen: Bill Monroe and Muddy Waters* (New York: Dial Press, 1971).

3. Dennis Satterlee, *Teardrops in My Eyes: The Music of Harley "Red" Allen* (Kensington, MD: Plucked String Foundation, 2007), 14. Quoted by Satterlee from anonymous liner notes to the album *Collectors Classics 21*.

4. Larry Nager, "Saul's Things Considered," *Cincinnati Magazine*, August 2007, 90. See

also interviews with longtime Northern Kentucky haberdasher Marv Polinsky, *Cincinnati Magazine*, August 2007, 90, and with confessed Northern Kentucky hitman, pimp, and armed robber Wayne Anthony Stuart Stratton, aka "Tony the Barber," *Cincinnati Magazine*, April 2007, 82.

5. See chapter 2, "Bobby Osborne Remembers How It Was."

6. Bobby Osborne, interview by author, June 2017.

7. See chapter 3, "All the Way to the Fence."

8. Neil V. Rosenberg, "Industrial Strength Bluegrass," *The Dayton Bluegrass Reunion: An All-Star Salute to Dayton's 40-year Bluegrass Legacy* (Dayton, OH: Cityfolk, April 22, 1989), 3–6. An updated version of the article appears as the foreword to this volume.

9. RKO Pictures, *It's a Wonderful Life*, Frank Capra, director, 1946.

10. Satterlee, *Teardrops in My Eyes*, 14.

11. Vernon McIntyre Jr., interview by author, spring 2017.

12. There was plenty of "billy" in the first generation of rockers, and the sound was fueled as much by bluegrass as by R&B. Elvis's first Sun single, recorded in 1954, was the quintessential yin and yang of rock and roll: Mississippi bluesman Arthur "Big Boy" Crudup's "That's All Right (Mama)" was the A side; Bill Monroe's "Blue Moon of Kentucky" was the flip, done in a 4/4 arrangement that the Stanley Brothers would copy for Mercury (and that Ralph continued performing until his death in 2016). The impact that bluegrass was having on the younger generation could be heard even more clearly in the informal recording session held at Sam Phillips's Memphis Recording Service on December 4, 1956, when Elvis, after signing with RCA, revisited his Sun stomping grounds. The legendary Million Dollar Quartet sessions with Elvis, Johnny Cash, Carl Perkins, and Jerry Lee Lewis featured four of Monroe's bluegrass songs: "Little Cabin Home on the Hill," "Summertime Is Past and Gone," "I Hear a Sweet Voice Calling," and "Sweetheart You Done Me Wrong."

13. Bobby Osborne interview, June 2017.

14. Fred Bartenstein, "Noah Crase: It's Not Easy Done, Part I," *Bluegrass Unlimited*, June 1985, 50.

15. Ibid.

16. Bobby Osborne interview, June 2017.

17. David Harvey, interview by author, spring 2017.

18. Bartenstein, "Noah Crase," 51.

19. J. D. Crowe interview, spring 2017.

20. Larry Sparks, interview by author for liner notes, *Almost Home* (Rounder, 2011), and Sparks, interview by author, spring 2017.

21. J. D. Crowe interview, spring 2017.

22. Bobby Osborne interview, June 2017.

23. Ibid.

24. "In his book *Outliers* [*Outliers: The Story of Success* (Boston: Little, Brown, 2008)], Malcolm Gladwell, citing the work of Anders Ericsson, popularized the 10,000-hour rule, which states that it takes 10,000 hours of practice to become an expert in a given field. Gladwell writes: 'Ten thousand hours is the magic number of greatness.'" Nils Salzgeber, "Malcolm Gladwell's 10,000-Hour Rule & What Really Separates the Best

from the Rest," *NJ Life Hacks*, November 5, 2019. https://www.njlifehacks.com/malcolm-gladwell-10000-hour-rule/.

25. Bobby Osborne interview, June 2017.

26. See chapter 2, "Bobby Osborne Remembers How It Was."

27. Bobby Osborne interview, June 2017.

28. Ibid.

29. Ibid.

30. Ibid.

31. There were two bands named the Kentuckians: Red Allen's and a group based in New Boston, Ohio, who recorded under their own name and with Paul "Moon" Mullins.

32. Dave Allbaugh, "Red Allen Has Edge on Future," *Dayton Daily News*, November 10, 1972, 45.

33. For more about Paul Mullins, see chapter 3, "All the Way to the Fence." For more about "Noah's Breakdown" see chapter 11, "Distinctive Qualities of Southwestern Ohio Bluegrass."

34. Larry Sparks, interview by author, spring 2017.

35. Ibid.

36. Jim Tarbell, interviews by author, spring 2017.

37. Vernon McIntyre interview, spring 2017.

38. Ibid.

39. Josh Graves, *Bluegrass Bluesman: Josh Graves, A Memoir*, ed. Fred Bartenstein (Urbana: University of Illinois Press, 2012), 40.

40. Ibid.

41. Vernon McIntyre interview, spring 2017.

42. Joe Mullins, interview by author, spring 2017.

43. Harry Sparks interview, spring 2017.

44. Ibid.

45. Ibid.

46. Ibid.

47. "Beavercreek Woman Shot," *Xenia Daily Gazette*, September 23, 1974, 5.

48. Larry Sparks interview, spring 2017.

49. Ralph Stanley with Eddie Dean, *Man of Constant Sorrow: My Life and Times* (New York: Gotham, 2009), 260–74.

50. Sandy Rothman, letter to Phyllis Brzozowska, May 1989.

51. Harry Sparks interview, spring 2017.

52. Ibid.

53. Katie Laur, interview by author, spring 2017.

54. Ibid.

55. The proliferation of bluegrass festivals was a big part of the changing scene from the mid-1960s to the present. These are addressed in more detail in other chapters.

6. Using My Bible for a Roadmap

Sacred Bluegrass Music in the Miami Valley

FRED BARTENSTEIN

I'm using my Bible for a roadmap
Ten Commandments they tell me what to do
The twelve disciples are my road signs
And Jesus will take me safely through.
—RENO AND SMILEY, "I'm Using My Bible for a Roadmap"[1]

BLUEGRASS MUSIC WAS first made and enjoyed by people steeped in evangelical Protestant Christianity, so it should be no surprise that sacred musical expressions took place alongside the secular. This was particularly true in southwestern Ohio between 1947 and 1989, years when the region played a key role in the nationwide development and popularization of bluegrass. This chapter chronicles how bluegrass music that was influenced by religion—and practiced as part of personal and group worship—differed from purely secular bluegrass phenomena.

Background of Southern Gospel Music

The Second Great Awakening (1790–1840) spread evangelical Protestant Christianity throughout the rural South. In contrast to earlier beliefs that humans are born sinful and their fates predestined, evangelical Protestantism emphasized the freedom and obligation of individuals to personally choose salvation. Baptist, Methodist, and new denominations proliferated, as did well-attended revivals and camp meetings. Missionary preachers traveled on horseback into the most isolated communities. Thousands of small churches were founded and grew rapidly. Religion took on a much greater role than it had before in personal, family, and community life. Rural Southerners in the late eighteenth and early nineteenth centuries desired a more traditional, primitive, and Bible-based Christianity than was commonly found in cities.[2]

The family and community practice of religion—and sacred music in both settings—supported courage to face a rough pioneer life and, much later, the often socially hostile environment of the industrial North. It also helped people cope with the grief of losing loved ones to disease, accidents, childbirth, and violence, and offered the promise of an afterlife where conditions would be far more pleasant than those of the present. Communal singing was also an escape from the constant toil involved in supporting and maintaining a family.

In rural areas the advent of shape-note singing sparked a wave of recreational, communal music making that included singing schools, singing conventions, all-day singings with dinner on the grounds, and a proliferation of inexpensive paperback songbooks containing newly composed gospel songs.[3] Invented around 1800 in Philadelphia, shape notation was a tool that helped individuals to learn and read sacred vocal music. It replaced the familiar ovals on a musical staff with simple shapes (triangles, squares, diamonds, etc.), each representing a pitch associated with the syllables *do, re, mi, fa, sol, la, ti,* [*do*]. Itinerant instructors visited rural areas, typically teaching their pupils the new system over ten evenings.

Gospel songs, a new style of sacred musical expression, began to emerge in the late nineteenth century, and shape-note songbooks became a key conduit for their spread. The term "gospel songs" first appeared in print in 1874 as the title of a collection published by the John Church Company of Cincinnati.[4] Their musical composition drew more upon popular marches, dances, and parlor songs than traditional hymnody. Lyrics were uncomplicated, often including repeated phrases and call-and-response features characteristic of African American music. Most gospel song lyrics were organized into verses and choruses, although some songs contained only verses.[5]

By the early twentieth century, shape-note gospel conventions and all-day singings were bringing people together from multiple congregations and across geographic regions to sing from the latest gospel songbooks. Hartford Music Company (Arkansas), James D. Vaughan (Tennessee), Stamps-Baxter (Texas) and other major publishers issued scores of paperback songbooks every year replete with new material. One of the most influential collections of these songs was the *Church Hymnal*, popularly known as "the red book." First published by the Church of God in 1951 but widely used in many other denominations, it sold more than six million copies.[6] According to Stephen Shearon, "So many evangelical Christians have sung [gospel songs] regularly that they are, arguably, among the most frequently sung songs in human culture, even today."[7]

Sacred Country and Bluegrass Music

Scores of published gospel songs were well known to the men and women who established commercial country music in the 1920s and 1930s. Most country performers included a healthy share in their record, radio, and concert repertoire. Among them were the Carter Family from Virginia, the Chuck Wagon Gang from Texas, the Monroe Brothers from Kentucky, Mainer's Mountaineers and the Blue Sky Boys from North Carolina, and Roy Acuff from Tennessee. The very familiarity of their gospel song repertoire did much to endear such acts to their listeners, and they heavily influenced later generations of artists.

Gospel singing and performance styles helped to shape bluegrass, the still-unnamed branch of country music that evolved from older string-band musical forms in the 1940s. Bill Monroe, Lester Flatt, Earl Scruggs, Carter and Ralph Stanley, Don Reno and Red Smiley, and the scores of bluegrass musicians who followed them were steeped in gospel songs and evangelical Protestant Christianity. Many had attended singing schools, sung the repertoire at home and at church, and absorbed harmony-singing conventions of the gospel style, such as voicing the melody in tenor rather than soprano range. The country acts they emulated typically performed a healthy dose of sacred music alongside their secular repertoire.[8] Neil V. Rosenberg has calculated that the bluegrass patriarchs named above included, on average, 30 percent religious material in their recordings and songbooks.[9]

Bluegrass vocal music is typically arranged at the higher limits of a singer's range (whether male or female), and bluegrass rarely uses quartets except in religious songs; thus there is little call for bass singers in most traveling ensembles.[10] Resonant-voiced low bass singers are sometimes imported from the Southern gospel field for recording sessions of bluegrass quartets.

In the late 1940s, while bluegrass was still new and considered part of country music, the phenomenon of all-gospel bluegrass groups began to emerge in the South. Three were prominent among professional acts. Carl Story (a North Carolinian) and the Rambling Mountaineers had their first hit with "My Lord Keeps a Record" in 1949 and recorded mostly sacred music during the next four decades. Alabama's Sullivan Family began performing in 1949. Georgia's Lewis Family began in 1951 and started radio broadcasts and recordings in 1954.[11] Many amateur and semiprofessional bands specializing in gospel bluegrass also played in community and church settings.

From the beginning, it was common for bluegrass artists to release all-sacred recordings, and few successful bands have failed to do so at some point in their careers. On two-sided singles, six-song extended-play records, and the LP albums that replaced them in the 1960s, gospel was rarely combined with secular music.[12] Such market segmentation is both a contributor to and a result of increasing divergence in the secular and sacred forms of bluegrass.[13]

Bluegrass Gospel Comes to the Miami Valley

Between 1900 and the 1970s, 20 million Southerners migrated north and west, including 1.4 million Blacks and 2.6 million whites during the 1940s alone.[14] Bluegrass was just getting started as war industries accelerated the flow of migrants from eastern Kentucky, southwestern Virginia, eastern Tennessee, Appalachian (southeastern) Ohio, and West Virginia to southwestern Ohio.

Appalachian migrants, initially concentrated in inner-city neighborhoods within walking or streetcar distance from their jobs, soon spread to many urban communities, small towns, and rural areas between the Cincinnati metropolis on the south and the Dayton and Springfield metropolitan areas on the north ends of the Great Miami and Little Miami River valleys.[15] While relatively integrated into workplaces and dwelling areas, Appalachian people tended to form and join churches populated with other Appalachians. These numerous churches and their tens of thousands of congregants provided a rich and eagerly welcoming environment for the growth of sacred bluegrass music.

Bluegrass was often used in regular worship services as well as in revivals, homecomings, and special concerts sponsored by churches. Musicians who were already members of a congregation volunteered their services, while touring bands played for a freewill offering, a travel stipend as well as a freewill offering, or—for popular national artists—a contracted fee not dissimilar from what they could receive in secular settings. Record sales, sometimes banned from the sanctuary and vestibule, also helped to defray expenses for those offering their musical ministry in church settings. Sacred bluegrass bands regularly played for an informal circuit of churches within a three-hundred-mile radius encompassing Ohio, Indiana, Kentucky, Michigan, and West Virginia (similar circuits operated in the Mid-Atlantic states, the Mid-South, the Deep South, and the West).[16]

Practicing members of the stricter denominations preferred to avoid the alcohol, dancing, smoking, and immodest clothing and behaviors found in bluegrass nightclubs and bars of the time.[17] And they mostly preferred the religious themes of gospel bluegrass to the songs of murder, violence, rambling, and "low life" often heard at secular venues alongside songs about mother, home, and nostalgia for the mountains.[18] Gospel songs represented a common vocabulary for anyone raised in Southern evangelical Protestantism, across a wide variety of sects and home regions. Even the unchurched found the bluegrass gospel repertoire familiar and appealing. Musicians themselves moved freely between secular and sacred bluegrass bands.

Sacred bluegrass could be heard daily on Miami Valley radio stations: live broadcasts from Appalachian churches on Sunday mornings, bluegrass gospel record programs like WPFB's *Hymns from the Hills* or WYSO's *Rise When the*

Rooster Crows, and, in time, twenty-four-hour Christian stations in Cincinnati, Columbus, Dayton, Fairfield, Hamilton, Norwood, Springfield, Troy, and Wilmington.[19] Bluegrass gospel records were sold at personal appearances by artists and alongside secular albums, singles, and cassette tapes at record stores,[20] flea markets, and truck stops.

Sacred bluegrass live performances, radio, and records appealed to three audiences: the devout, the homesick, and those who loved the sound of bluegrass music in any form. Sacred bluegrass music was widely played in, imported into, and exported from southwestern Ohio, a region that became highly significant to the development of bluegrass music in its earliest decades. Prominent national artists who traveled to southwestern Ohio to record bluegrass gospel are profiled below, followed by a summary of the region's own sacred-bluegrass figures.

The Brown's Ferry Four, King's Sacred Quartet, Shannon Grayson

Although not a bluegrass act, the Brown's Ferry Four had an important influence on bluegrass gospel repertoire and performance style. Organized in 1943 as a replacement for a gospel quartet that had left a thirty-minute daily radio slot in Cincinnati, the group's original members included WLW country artists Alton and Rabon Delmore, Grandpa Jones, and Merle Travis. The group was named for "Brown's Ferry Blues," a popular and decidedly secular Delmore Brothers song. They were strictly a broadcast and recording ensemble and did not tour. As did later bluegrass bands seeking sacred material, the Brown's Ferry Four mined the shape-note paperback hymnals still in widespread use at the time, as well as 78 rpm recordings by Black gospel groups.[21] These they found at a Cincinnati used record shop operated by Syd Nathan, who began King Records in 1943 with a release by Travis and Jones.[22]

Several members passed through the Brown's Ferry Four during the war years, and then the original group reunited to make its first recordings in 1946. "Will the Circle Be Unbroken" backed with "Just a Little Talk with Jesus" was a two-sided hit; both songs became staples of the bluegrass repertoire, as did many of the group's twenty single releases for King. Four of its seven recording sessions were conducted in Cincinnati. Alton and Rabon Delmore appeared on all of them, but Grandpa Jones and Merle Travis were replaced on some of the later sessions (the last in 1952) by Red Foley, Ulysses "Red" Turner, and Clyde Moody. Simple accompaniment was limited to one or two guitars and instrumental turnaround introductions and breaks,[23] an arrangement style duplicated two decades later by the Hee Haw Gospel Quartet with Grandpa Jones, Buck Owens, Roy Clark, and Kenny Price (the latter a native of Florence, Kentucky, across the Ohio River from Cincinnati).

Another recording gospel "supergroup," King's Sacred Quartet, was assembled by Clyde Moody for one six-song King Records session in August of 1947 at Herzog Studio in Cincinnati. Its records were almost as influential as those of the Brown's Ferry Four. Featured were three members of the Tennessee Mountain Boys: Johnnie Wright (lead vocal), Jack Anglin (tenor vocal), and Raymond "Duck" Atkins (baritone vocal). The group also included a former member of the Tennessee Mountain Boys, Ernest Ferguson (mandolin), and a recent alumnus of Bill Monroe and the Blue Grass Boys, Clyde Moody (guitar and bass vocal). All were important figures in the acoustic style of country music that was popular when bluegrass arose, and fans at the time would have made no genre distinction. Indeed, the records of King's Sacred Quartet—"I'll Be Listening," "This World Can't Stand Long," "The Old Country Church," "I Heard My Name on the Radio," "Turn Your Radio On," and "He Will Set Your Fields on Fire"—feature the same sparse guitar and mandolin brother-duet-style accompaniment used on Bill Monroe and Carl Story's sacred recordings of that era.[24]

Another act, Shannon Grayson and the Golden Valley Boys, came the closest to bluegrass of any of the early King gospel quartets. On their four-song Cincinnati session of May 1950, Grayson sang lead vocals and played a primitive three-finger-style banjo; Millard Presley sang baritone and played mandolin; Dewey Price sang tenor and played guitar; and Harvey Raborn sang bass. Unidentified string bass and steel guitar players were also included. "I Like the Old Time Way," "Let Me Travel Alone," and "Since His Sweet Love Rescued Me" were either borrowed or rearranged from earlier paperback hymnal songs. "I'm Gonna Walk On" was an original. Grayson, a North Carolinian, was a longtime member of the WBT Briarhoppers, based in Charlotte.[25]

Flatt and Scruggs, Jim and Jesse

> Are you going to be a saint on that shore
> Or a sinner left far behind?
> Don't you think of your soul and want to be saved
> Don't you want to go to Heaven sometime?
> —FLATT AND SCRUGGS, "I'll Be Going to Heaven Sometime"[26]

In 1949 Lester Flatt, Earl Scruggs, and the Foggy Mountain Boys made the first true bluegrass recordings produced in the Miami Valley. Their Cincinnati sessions for Mercury Records—three at Herzog Studio—waxed twelve sides.[27] Two songs dealt with explicitly religious themes: "I'll Be Going to Heaven Sometime" and "So Happy I'll Be." Two more—"Bouquet in Heaven" and "No Mother or Dad"—concerned the death of loved ones, a theme that bluegrass fans typically subsume within the sacred category.

In 1951 and early 1952, Jim and Jesse McReynolds, natives of southwestern Virginia's coalfields, were appearing on Middletown's WPFB with "Smokey" Ward, Little Eller, Fairley Holden, "Old Joe" Clark, and Larry Roll.[28] As the Virginia Trio, Jim, Jesse, and Larry recorded ten gospel songs for Carl Burkhardt's Kentucky label in Cincinnati.[29] Accompaniment included two guitars (Jim and Larry), mandolin (Jesse), and string bass (Dave Woolum). Gorgeous harmonies and cross-picked mandolin distinguish these first commercial recordings by the Bluegrass Hall of Fame inductees later known simply by their first names as Jim and Jesse. Included were some of the earliest bluegrass-style versions of "I'll Fly Away" and "God Put a Rainbow in the Clouds."[30]

After an unsuccessful audition with King Records in Cincinnati, Jim and Jesse heard on their car radio that Capitol Records executive Ken Nelson was visiting Jimmie Skinner's record shop in the same city. They introduced themselves to Nelson, played their audition demo discs, and were signed for a Nashville session in June of 1952.[31] Unlike other early bluegrass artists, Jim and Jesse recorded mostly secular material during the Capitol years, with only an occasional sacred song.[32]

Ironically, the Louvin Brothers—friends with the McReynolds, who had their first hit with the Louvin-penned "Are You Missing Me?"—were signed to Capitol later that year. Ken Nelson told Ira and Charlie Louvin he already had a secular brother-style act in Jim and Jesse and restricted the Louvins to gospel recordings until 1955, the year Jim and Jesse left Capitol Records.[33]

Reno and Smiley

In March of 1951 Don Reno came to Cincinnati with Tommy Magness and the Tennessee Buddies to record four gospel songs he had written. King Records owner Syd Nathan wanted them released under Don Reno's name on King's Federal subsidiary, but Reno deferred and his employer's name was used instead. Tommy Magness—formerly a fiddler for Bill Monroe, Roy Hall, and Roy Acuff—played bass. Reno, his future partner Red Smiley, Remus Bell, and Jackie Phelps made up the vocal quartet.[34]

Reno and Smiley soon formed their own group, the Tennessee Cut-Ups, and contacted Nathan about recording for King. They arrived in Cincinnati in mid-January 1952 and waxed sixteen songs in one day, half of them gospel and all written or cowritten by Don Reno. In order to ensure airplay on Cincinnati's clear-channel powerhouse WCKY, Reno initially gave DJ Nelson King half the credit for "I'm Using My Bible for a Roadmap." This became a signature song for Reno and Smiley and provided a needed financial infusion for King Records.[35] The next day, the band of Red Smiley (guitar), Don Reno (tenor vocal and mandolin), Gopher Addis (fiddle), and Jay Haney (string bass) accompanied King artist Mac O'Dell (Odell McLeod) on four gospel recordings.[36]

The economic realities facing a new full-time touring group forced Reno and Smiley to disband before their first release, "I'm Using My Bible for a Roadmap" and "Hear Jerusalem Mourn," hit the market in June of 1952. They nevertheless returned to Cincinnati for three more King sessions, which produced forty-four masters and twenty-two single releases between 1953 and 1954. Sacred songs, secular songs, and instrumentals each composed approximately a third of the repertoire, and almost all were original compositions. The duo reunited to form a touring act in early 1955, and Reno and Smiley remained successful King artists until splitting again in 1964.[37]

Long-play, 33 1/3 rpm vinyl albums (LPs) were first marketed to bluegrass fans in 1957, about when the term "bluegrass" entered popular parlance and a decade after the long-play format was first introduced. Cincinnati-based King was among the first labels to release bluegrass LPs; Reno and Smiley's *Sacred Songs* (King 550) and *Instrumentals* (King 552) were both issued in February 1958.[38]

Reno and Smiley completed their partnership with a flurry of seventeen album releases on King between 1959 and 1965. While the occasional single achieved radio and jukebox popularity, the consumer market was shifting to LP albums. During this period there was a significant reduction in the proportion of religious material; only four of the albums were entirely sacred, and the first-ever bluegrass Christmas album mixed sacred and secular repertoire.[39] Following Red Smiley's departure for health reasons that restricted his touring, Don Reno teamed with Bill Harrell. Their reformed Tennessee Cut-Ups continued to travel to Cincinnati's King studios, releasing one secular and two sacred albums in 1968 and 1969.[40]

Sonny Osborne, Red Allen

Cincinnati's Carl Burkhardt recognized a strong market for bluegrass-style music and enlisted banjoist Sonny Osborne, a Dayton-area high school student who was already a veteran of Bill Monroe's Blue Grass Boys, to record a number of sessions with area musicians. These were released on the Kentucky and Gateway labels between 1952 and 1955 under Sonny Osborne's own name, that of Enos Johnson, and as the Queen City Sacred Quartet. About 10 percent was gospel material, mostly covering popular sacred releases by Bill Monroe and Flatt and Scruggs.[41]

Sonny and Bobby Osborne's later partner Red Allen appeared regularly with his band, the Kentuckians, in the rollicking Dayton bar scene.[42] Uncharacteristically, Allen arranged an all-gospel session with Carl Burkhardt that resulted in three singles on the Kentucky label in 1953. Fiddler Johnny McKee sang most of the lead vocals. Other musicians included Red Allen (guitar), Claude Stewart (mandolin), Noah Crase (banjo), and Smokey Tinkerson (string bass). Among otherwise familiar covers was the first bluegrass-style recording of "Paul and Silas"; it had been recorded by African American singer Josh White in 1935 and was later popularized by bluegrass artists Carl Story, Flatt and Scruggs, and the Stanley Brothers.[43]

The Stanley Brothers, Moore and Napier

> I heard about a man one day who wasted not his time away
> He prayed to God every morning noon and night
> He cared not for the things of Baal, he trusted one who would not fail
> Oh, Daniel prayed every morning, noon, and night.
> —THE STANLEY BROTHERS, "Old Daniel Prayed"[44]

The LP era was already under way when the Stanley Brothers, Carter and Ralph, moved from Mercury to the King label. Their first Cincinnati sessions, September 30 and October 1, 1958, produced a self-titled debut secular album. Their next, *Hymns and Sacred Songs*, resulted from back-to-back February 1959 sessions with Al Elliott (mandolin), Chubby Anthony (fiddle), and George Shuffler (string bass). This album's repertoire was a 60/40 mix of originals and material from other sources.[45] The quartet arrangements of "Old Daniel Prayed" and "He Said If I Be Lifted Up" have stood the test of time, reprised by numerous later bluegrass artists.

King Records released thirteen more Stanley Brothers albums between 1960 and Carter Stanley's death in 1966, five of them entirely sacred. Ralph Stanley continued recording in Cincinnati for King through 1969, releasing one sacred and two secular albums under his own name.[46]

Charlie Moore, Bill Napier, and the Dixie Partners followed Reno and Smiley and the Stanleys as King's next bluegrass act. Moore and Napier recorded nine albums in Cincinnati between 1963 and 1968. Two of them were entirely sacred, and a 1966 patriotic album invoked God on the side of US forces.[47] Charlie Moore continued recording in the Miami Valley after partnerships with King and Bill Napier dissolved; a pair of his albums, one sacred and one secular, was released by Cincinnati's Vetco label in 1972.

J. D. Jarvis, Lillimae Whitaker

John Dill "J. D." Jarvis (1924–2010) was born near Manchester in Clay County, Kentucky. He began playing guitar and clawhammer banjo and composing rhymes while still in elementary school. After his father was murdered, he joined the Civilian Conservation Corps at sixteen and then moved to Cincinnati with his mother and stepfather. Enlisting in the army, Jarvis participated in the 1944 Normandy invasion and was badly wounded in combat a month later.

He married in 1946 and then worked in heavy industry and played in hillbilly bars. After almost killing his family while driving intoxicated, he quit drinking and gave his life to Christ at a 1953 tent revival.

For the rest of his life Jarvis worked mainly as a painting contractor while devoting his musical talents almost entirely to sacred performance and composition. He played mandolin and tambourine with Pentecostal legend Brother Claude Ely at sessions for King (1953–1954) and Jewel Records (1967). Permanently locating in Hamilton in 1959, Jarvis played widely with gospel groups in church and radio performances, where his primitive vocal style made him a favorite with many transplanted Appalachians. The foremost exponent of bluegrass gospel music in southwestern Ohio during the 1960s and early '70s, Jarvis recorded at least nineteen singles, five EPs, and twenty-four LP albums for Ambrosia, ARC, Ark, Artist, Down Home, Gospel Gems, Harp, Heartwarming, Jessup, Jewel, King, Log Cabin, Melody, Old Homestead, Polymax, QCA, Rural Rhythm, Sagegrass, Sunrise, Table Rock, Vetco, and his own Nation Wide label.[48] Accompanying him on these releases was a "who's who" of local and national bluegrass artists. J. D. Jarvis's best-known compositions include "Take Your Shoes Off, Moses," "I Am the Man, Thomas," "Come On Little Children," and "The Hyden Miners' Tragedy."[49]

Lillimae Haney Whitaker (1939–2014), a daughter of Magoffin County, Kentucky, natives, was born and spent most of her life in rural Hardin County, Ohio, seventy-five miles north of Dayton. By the age of eight she was playing guitar and mandolin and singing with her sister, Wilma Jean, at churches and camp meetings, emulating Bill Monroe and Molly O'Day. After Wilma Jean married and left the duo, Lillimae and her father, Leroy Haney, continued with a band that included Kentucky-born Charlie Whitaker and Noah Hollon on mandolin and banjo. Lillimae married Whitaker in 1955. They made church and radio appearances as the Southern Gospel Singers, recording a few singles and a successful 1966 album with J. D. Jarvis.

Deciding to become more serious about their sideline performing (Lillimae was a real estate broker; Charlie ran a scrap yard and later drove Bill Monroe's bus), they adopted the band name Lillimae and the Dixie Gospel-Aires and were booked by the Monroe Talent Agency. Lillimae thus became one of the first female bandleaders in bluegrass history. The Dixie Gospel-Aires Quartet was an all-male group within a group. The Whitakers lived in the western Ohio area, recording on Arco, Down Home, Gloryland, Jewel, Old Homestead, Raindrop, Rome, and Rural Rhythm labels and performing throughout the United States and in Canada. Some notables who passed through the Dixie Gospel-Aires include Tommy Boyd, Dave Evans, Joe Isaacs, Wayne Lewis, and Curnie Wilson. Lillimae's sons, Jeff, Rick, and Ron, later played in the band, which lasted more than fifty years.[50]

Paul "Moon" Mullins, the Boys from Indiana

> There'll be no sorrow in our new home
> No funeral train in the sky
> No rents to pay, no taxes come due
> And he tells me no burdens pass through.
>
> —PAUL MULLINS AND THE BACKWOOD BOYS QUARTET, "No Burdens Pass Through"[51]

Paul "Moon" Mullins (1936–2008), a native of Frenchburg (Menifee County), Kentucky, a radio personality, fiddler, and alumnus of the Stanley Brothers' Clinch Mountain Boys and the Bluegrass Playboys, arrived at WPFB Middletown in 1964.[52] Aware of the popularity of bluegrass gospel music in the region, he initiated in 1965 a daily one-hour, all-gospel radio program dubbed *Hymns from the Hills*. Including both musical recordings and church announcements, the program continues to this day on his son Joe Mullins's Real Roots Radio network of stations in Xenia, Wilmington, Eaton, and on the internet. In 1966 Paul Mullins assembled two former bandmates from the Bluegrass Playboys (Walter Adams and June Thompson) and two members of the New Boston, Ohio–based Kentuckians (Paul Morris and R. C. Meade) to record the LP album *Hymns from the Hills* on Dayton's Jalyn label.

Mullins performed, recorded, and organized concerts with a number of regional and national bluegrass acts. He was instrumental in the formation of the Boys from Indiana in the early 1970s.[53] Their first album, for Cincinnati's Jewel label, was the all-gospel *We Missed You in Church Last Sunday* (1973). Included were brothers Aubrey Holt on guitar and Jerry Holt on bass, as well as their uncle Harley Gabbard on Dobro, Noah Crase on banjo, and Paul Mullins on fiddle. Four of the twelve songs were originals by Aubrey Holt: the title track, "The Kingdom of Heaven Is at Hand," "Stairway of Gold," and "Family Reunion." "Family Reunion," cowritten with Harley Gabbard, was already well known from Harley and Aubrey's original 1957 version on Excellent and from Carl Story's cover later that year.[54]

Larry Sparks, Joe Isaacs

Although he had recorded one secular Jalyn single in 1966, Lebanon, Ohio, native Larry Sparks (1947–) came to fame as Ralph Stanley's first guitar-playing lead singer after Carter Stanley's death. With Stanley (1967–1969) and later with his own Lonesome Ramblers, Sparks had a particular aptitude for performing and writing sacred material. He wrote or cowrote numerous well-known bluegrass gospel songs, including "Jesus Is the Rock," "Thank You, Lord," and "The Testing Times." During the 1970s he recorded the album *New Gospel Songs* (on

Hamilton's Pine Tree label) and *Christmas in the Hills* (on Cincinnati's King Bluegrass label), along with twelve secular albums. During the 1980s he recorded the sacred albums *Green Pastures in the Sky*, *The Testing Times*, and *Gonna Be Movin'*, as well as eleven secular albums.

Joe Isaacs (1947–), a native of Jackson County, Kentucky, came to the Miami Valley in 1964. He began his professional career as a singer and multi-instrumentalist in Dayton bars, first touring and recording with southwestern Ohio legends Frank Wakefield and Larry Sparks. From 1970 until 2000 he recorded only sacred music.[55] Under his own name and with various band names and configurations that often included members of his talented family, he released eleven LPs, including four on his own Sacred Sounds label, three for Hamilton's Pine Tree, two for Michigan-based Old Homestead, and one each for Hamilton's Melody and Dayton's Gospel Shore. Joe Isaacs became a prolific songwriter. Among his best-known gospel songs are "Cast the First Stone," "Garden Tomb," "He's Everything to Me," "I Pressed through the Crowd," "Man on the Mule," "Reaping in the Spirit," and "Ye Men of Galilee."

Three Colorful Pastors: Kash Amburgy, Norm Livingston, and Lawrence Bishop

Many ministers supported the growth and development of the gospel bluegrass scene in southwestern Ohio. Three who particularly deserve to be remembered are Kash Amburgy, Norman Livingston, and Lawrence Bishop.

Kash D. Amburgy (1922–2002) was born in Lerose (Owsley County), Kentucky, and preached for more than sixty years. From 1950 through the mid-'70s he pastored the Bible Church of God at 500 W. Mulberry Street in Lebanon, Ohio. His WPFB broadcasts from Middletown were reportedly carried by more than one hundred radio stations. Starting his career as a Bible salesman (he boasted of once selling 170 Bibles in a single day), Amburgy was also a home builder and operated Kash's Big Bargain Barn, a successful carpet and appliance store in South Lebanon. Styling himself "the Old Country Boy," he made legendary TV and radio commercials in the raspy, shouting manner of a Pentecostal preacher. With his wife, Mary Lou, he organized numerous tours of "the Holy Lands," some co-led by Joe Isaacs.[56]

A possibly apocryphal incident from Amburgy's pre-Ohio ministries suggests his colorful character:

> [He] apparently was a snake-handler early on. A story circulated about a couple of boys at one of his backwoods churches deciding to get some rattlesnakes or copperheads who weren't de-fanged (as "de-fanged" was the rumored practice for ol' Kash) for Kash to handle up at the pulpit, because they wanted to see if he really believed God would protect him. Kash was apparently rather

surprised when he was bit by one! Anyway, I was told he lost part of a finger, but survived the bite. I guess the boys believed him after that.[57]

Norman L. "Norm" Livingston (1932–2011) was born in Livingston (Overton County), Tennessee. At the age of seventeen he married Velma Looper and moved to Dayton a year later. A Free Will Baptist pastor and evangelist beginning in 1954, he also worked in a public school transportation department, in a factory, and was a door-to-door salesman of vacuum cleaners, Rawleigh Products, and Bibles. He founded a mission in a West Dayton garage in 1958, built two churches, pastored the Greenview Calvary Temple at 8010 N. Main Street in Dayton for more than fifty years, led preaching revivals and tent meetings in several states, syndicated *Norm's Gospel Sing* on radio and television, and owned WGNZ Radio and Gospel Shore Records. For twenty-four years he booked concerts into Dayton's twenty-five-hundred-seat Memorial Hall. These were consistently the venue's best-selling events, featuring the top Southern gospel acts in the nation and including bluegrass gospel artists.[58]

Lawrence Bishop Sr. (1942–2011) was born in Zag (Morgan County), Kentucky. A great lover of bluegrass music, he played the mandolin, sang, and wrote songs. At nineteen he married his seventeen-year-old neighbor Darlene. Known as "the king of the Christian cowboys," Bishop achieved early success as a horse auctioneer and breeder in Ohio, establishing LB Ranch as a private company in 1962. From a hundred-acre property on the west side of Interstate 75 in Butler County, he exported quarter horses nationally and internationally, producing several world champions. Three years after giving his life to Christ in 1975 at a local church service, he and Darlene began co-pastoring a congregation of twelve members at a firehouse in Middletown. According to the church's website, "In 1980 they purchased a building on Grand Avenue and adopted the name Middletown Evangelistic Center [MEC] with the vision of becoming a 'soul-saving station' to touch the lives of people in the surrounding community." MEC eventually became Solid Rock Church and relocated to Monroe, on the east side of I-75, a short distance north of the LB Ranch. There a racially mixed membership has subsequently grown to three thousand plus, and a sixty-two-foot statue of Jesus in front of the church once attracted the attention of millions of highway travelers.[59] After Lawrence Sr.'s death, Darlene and their son, Lawrence II, continue Solid Rock's ministries, including gospel bluegrass concerts and an orphanage in São Paulo, Brazil.[60]

An Extended Cast of Characters

The following biographical sketches profile other individuals and organizations connected with bluegrass gospel music in the region between the 1940s and the 1980s.[61] Researched by Mac McDivitt for the Southwestern Ohio Bluegrass

Music Heritage Project, they appear along with numerous secular entries at swohiobluegrass.com.

The **Acorn Sisters**, whose family name was probably Brown, were discovered by Joe Grieshop and were presumably renamed to avoid confusion with country singers the Browns, who were popular at the time. Grieshop became their manager and used his Cincinnati record company, Acorn Records, to promote them. The sisters—Goldie, Rosemarie, and Evelyn—were from near Corbin, Kentucky. In 1963 they appeared regularly on the *WWVA Jamboree*. They recorded bluegrass gospel, country, and rockabilly. Their most popular sacred numbers included "Where Will I Shelter My Sheep?" and "Alpha and Omega."

Ray (Raymond L.) Anderson (1924–2010) was a musician, DJ, songwriter, minister, and label owner. In his early days he recorded on Dixie Jamboree and Cozy Records before coming to Cincinnati and cutting a local hit on Kentucky Records with "Stalin Kicked the Bucket." He also recorded sacred songs on Kentucky and its sister label Big 6. He worked as a DJ at WCHO in Washington Court House, where he recorded on the Mountaineer label. He moved to WWVA in Wheeling and joined the Osborne Brothers. After leaving them he became a minister and eventually founded GRS Records in Richmond Dale, Ohio. His label specialized in gospel recordings, including some bluegrass. At the time of his death he was living in Camden, broadcasting the radio show *Country Camp Meeting* over WCNW in Fairfield, and pastoring a church in Cincinnati.

Born in Mount Vernon, Kentucky, **John Lee Burke** (1931–2006) settled in Miamisburg. In the early 1970s he founded the popular Dayton-area bluegrass gospel group John Burke and the Layman Trio. He recorded LPs on Jack Lynch's Jalyn label in 1971, 1972, and 1973; on his own Layman label in 1977 and 1979; and on Artist's Recording in 1977.

Ernest Carter played both guitar and mandolin. With his brothers Frank and Cliff and cousin Denzil Ferguson, he formed the Hymn Trio in the early 1960s. It was a country gospel band that recorded on several area record labels. The group recorded perhaps the first single issued on Jalyn and the second single issued by Melody. They also recorded on Ark, Harp, and Starday. Ernest had a show on WPFB in Middletown and owned a music store in Germantown. In 1970 he moved to Kentucky to work as a farmer, but eventually he reformed his band as Ernest Carter and the Bluegrass Hymn Trio. In 1973 he recorded an album with Zeke Hoskins.

The **Corny Four Quartet** was a group within a group. When Smokey Ward was at WPFB in Middletown from 1949 to 1954, his group of entertainers was called the Barrelhead Gang. When it was time for a gospel song, Smokey would call for the "Corny Four Quartet" to gather around the microphone. It consisted of Smokey, Bobby and Sonny Osborne, and either Jimmy Martin or Fairley Holden, depending on who was in the Barrelhead Gang at the time. They never recorded but performed at all of the Gang's personal appearances. They regularly sang "Gone Home," "A Beautiful Life," and songs recorded by Shannon Grayson, whom Smokey admired.

Born in McKee, Kentucky, **William Thomas "Tommy" Crank** (1926–2007) was serious about religion and eventually became a minister. As a young man he moved to Ohio, where he preached and sang both church music and bluegrass. Later he moved to Jackson, Michigan, and began releasing records on his Irma label. He produced LPs and singles for Hylo Brown, Wade Mainer, Ralph Stanley, Carl Story, Lowell Varney, and Jimmy Williams and Red Ellis. Crank came back to Ohio and worked as a DJ at WPFB in Middletown, where he renewed an old friendship with Joe and Lily Isaacs, who backed him on an LP. He recorded four albums for Pine Tree Records in Hamilton and others for Golden Eagle, Irma, and Old Homestead.

Southwestern Ohio mandolin player and bluegrass gospel pioneer **Paris Decker** (1925–2008) partnered with Dave Woolum to cut two bluegrass gospel albums on Hamilton's Pine Tree label in the early 1970s. Decker's daughter Judy, a bass player and singer, is married to Sherrill Jennings, a bluegrass banjo player and gospel songwriter.[62]

Born into a Pentecostal Holiness family in rural Puckett's Gap, Virginia, **Claude Daniel "Brother Claude" Ely** (1922–1978) was to become a legend as a traveling evangelist and recording artist. He lived through a near-fatal bout with tuberculosis at the age of twelve, giving him time to learn and practice the guitar and other musical instruments. At the age of eighteen Claude enlisted in the army, where he stayed until 1945. Upon his discharge he, like many in the region, went into the coal mines. A miraculous rescue from a mine-wall collapse led him to leave that occupation and become a minister. For more than twenty years he pastored, conducted revivals, and made guest appearances at little mountain churches across eastern Kentucky, eastern Tennessee, and southwestern Virginia. In 1954 King Records released five of his live performances, including "There Ain't No Grave Gonna Hold My Body Down," his signature song. Label owner Syd Nathan felt that Brother Claude combined hillbilly gospel with the energy of rhythm and blues, much as Elvis Presley was doing at the time with rock and roll. More recordings followed on King, Jewel, and Jordan Records. Brother Claude Ely's final ministry, from 1965 to 1978, was at the Charity Tabernacle in Newport, Kentucky, across the Ohio River from Cincinnati. He passed away there from a heart attack during a service, while singing "Where Could I Go but to the Lord?"

The **Harlan County Four** consisted of Alton and Rabon Delmore, Red Turner, and Zeke Turner (whose real name was James Grishaw). They recorded one eight-song session for King Records in October 1951 that produced four single records released in 1951 and 1952. Although the Delmore Brothers are included, the quartet sound is different from that of the Brown's Ferry Four. The tone is not quite as somber, and the instrumental breaks feature mandolin (probably played by Red Turner) and two different guitar styles, one in the Delmore style and the other probably by Zeke Turner. "John Three Sixteen," "The Atomic Telephone," and "I Cried Holy" were among the group's releases.

Dennis Hensley has had a long and varied career in the music business. His father, the Rev. Harley Hensley, was an evangelist, and Dennis played lead guitar in his church services as well as for some EPs on Jewel Records in the 1960s. He traveled with and played lead guitar for evangelist Brother Claude Ely and played banjo and mandolin with the Bluegrass Flyers and Old North. He played guitar on numerous gospel recording sessions in the Cincinnati and northern Kentucky area, eventually moving into producing and engineering. This led him to found Jordan Recording Studio at 5358 Taylor Mill Road in Covington, Kentucky, where he has produced or engineered gospel, bluegrass, and country records for more than forty-two years. In the late 1970s he founded Sagegrass Records in the same location. Some of the artists recorded at Jordan Studio include Clarence Kelly, Marty Raybon, and Larry Sparks.

Zeke Hoskins (ca. 1927–2014) was a well-known gospel singer and bandleader in the Dayton-Middletown area for many years with his band the Country Gospel-Aires, later known as the Bluegrass Gospel-Aires. His early band consisted of Hoskins on lead vocals and guitar, Jake Bowling playing banjo, and Richard Lewis on mandolin. Eventually Zeke's sons, Mike and Rick, became regular band members. Other members included Charlie Hager, Ronald Jackson, Perry Kuhn, and Dave Tackett. Zeke, who eventually became a minister recorded extensively. He made albums for Ark, Baron, Crusade, Golden Shield Gospel Gems, GRS, Jalyn, MGMA, Pine Tree, Prism, Rite, and Rose, and singles for Ark, Prism, and Sulkie.

Rev. Carl I. Howard (ca. 1935–2011) was born in Kentucky and was pastor of the W. Seventh Street First Church of God in Newport, Kentucky, a church he and his wife, Mary, founded in 1967. He was also a guitar player and singer who played bluegrass gospel in his church and on the road for many years. He played at churches and family reunions in the Cincinnati and Northern Kentucky area, as well as at cemetery gatherings, funerals, and reunions in Kentucky's Harlan, Jackson, and Knott Counties. Howard fronted groups that included the Kentucky Gospel Trio and the Kentucky Bluegrass Gospel Singers.

The Isaacs are a family gospel group that originally consisted of Joe and Lily Isaacs and their three children: Becky, Ben, and Sonya. Joe and Lily Isaacs lived in Morrow and, from 1975 to 1986, had a band called Joe Isaacs and Sacred Bluegrass. As the children got older and began appearing more and more, they decided in 1986 to name the family band the Isaacs. Now based in Hendersonville, Tennessee, and consisting of Becky, Ben, Lily, and Sonya, the group has been accepted by both bluegrass and Southern gospel audiences.[63]

Cincinnati-area singer and guitar player **Joseph Louis "Jay" Johnson** (1934–1987) performed country, bluegrass, and gospel music. He recorded with the Sandy Valley Boys for Briar, for Bobby Grove's Oak label, for Big 6, and recorded two bluegrass singles in the 1960s backed by Earl Taylor and the Stoney Mountain Boys. One of these was on Cincinnati's Rocket label and the other on Nashville, a subsidiary of Starday.

The **Kentucky Bluegrass Gospel Singers** began as the Kentucky Gospel Trio, consisting of Rev. Carl Howard playing guitar and singing lead; his daughter, Rosemary Howard, playing bass and singing tenor; and Bill Beavers on banjo and singing bass. After cutting a single record and an album at Rusty York's Jewel Studio in Cincinnati they expanded into the Kentucky Bluegrass Gospel Singers, which included the three original members plus Bessie Combs as a solo singer and Charles Watts on mandolin. The group appeared in the Cincinnati and Northern Kentucky area and traveled into other parts of Kentucky.

Born in Laurel County, Kentucky, **Jesse E. "Joe" "Cannonball" Lewis** (1924–2001) grew up in Connersville and Lawrenceburg, Indiana, and eventually made his home in Hamilton, Ohio. An excellent country singer with a strong and expressive voice, he made eight singles for MGM. Many of them had a strong bluegrass flavor, with instrumental leads taken by fiddle and mandolin and a five-string banjo in the background. "Before I Met You," which he cowrote and recorded for Gateway, became a bluegrass standard when Lester Flatt and Earl Scruggs cut it. He had singles on other local labels—Kentucky, Lucky, Lunar, and Sunrise—but these were much more country in style, using electric lead and steel guitar. He and his wife also recorded gospel music for Hamilton's Melody label.

The Marshall Family, a sensation on the bluegrass gospel circuit in the mid- to late 1970s, was based in the Columbus metropolitan area but played frequently in the Miami Valley. The five siblings—Ben, Danny, Dave, Donna, and Judy—had been drilled on harmonies by their father, Chester, who had once been part of a gospel act with his brother. Their performing career began in 1967 in the five-state area surrounding their Canal Winchester home. They recorded for Gloryland (1969, 1971) and Rebel (1974, 1975, and 1977). Their music was distinctive for gentle close harmonies, Judy's beautiful solo voice, and David and Judy's gospel compositions. Some of their best-known songs are "Come Springtime," "I Just Want to Thank You, Lord," and "When I Wake Up to Sleep No More." They were an important influence on the Forbes Family, the Isaacs, Ralph Stanley, and other bluegrass gospel performers.

The three **Pelfrey Brothers**—Chester (1933–1990), Ellis (1930–2014), and Forest (1932–2016)—were originally from eastern Kentucky. As early as 1954 Forest was living in Fairborn and fronting a group called the Pelfrey Quartet. At some point he joined brothers Ellis and Chester to form the Pelfrey Brothers and the Bluegrass Partners. They recorded two singles on the Ark label in Cincinnati in

1962, three EPs on Jalyn in Dayton in 1964, and an LP titled *Songs That Never Grow Old* on Jalyn in 1967. On the LP, Forest sang lead and tenor and played mandolin, Chester sang lead and baritone and played banjo, and Ellis sang bass. The Bluegrass Partners at that time included Jack Austin, Bootie Burgess, Vic Hurst, and Paul Provence.

John William Reedy (1918–1983) was born in Tennessee. His wife, **Frances Williebob Ridner Reedy** (1922–2006), was born in Bell County, Kentucky. They were married in 1936 in Harlan, Kentucky, where they appeared on radio for seventeen and a half years. In 1939 John wrote his most famous song, now a gospel standard, "Somebody Touched Me." Around 1953 they moved to Dayton and John went to work in one of the General Motors plants. They recorded an EP for Cincinnati's Ark label, three singles for Jalyn, one for Rusty York's Jewel label in Cincinnati, and four self-produced singles for their own label at 5180 Wolf Creek Pike in Dayton. One of John Reedy's self-produced singles was "Oh Death." Although he didn't write it, this recording was highly influential. In the early 1960s the Reedys cut six EPs on Starday, with Dayton's Dorsey Harvey the probable mandolin player. They moved back to Kentucky in the mid-1960s, went through a divorce and remarriage, and started recording again in the mid-1970s.

Lawrence "Larry" Roll was the third member of the Virginia Trio with Jim and Jesse McReynolds when they were at WPFB in Middletown and when they recorded for Kentucky Records. He was born in South Dakota and later moved to Cincinnati, where he worked on WKRC, WCPO, and WZIP, with a short detour to Renfro Valley, Kentucky, before going to WPFB. He played guitar and had a wonderful mellow voice.

Roy Shepard (?–1981) was a part of the Cincinnati country and bluegrass music scene from the 1950s into the '70s. He named his group the Tri-State Singers to reflect Cincinnati's location on the border of Ohio, Kentucky, and Indiana. In 1960 Shepard recorded several gospel EPs for Starday and in 1961 a gospel EP for Rusty York's brand-new Jewel label. In 1961 he founded his own label, Ark, which he operated through 1967.[64]

Fred Spencer Sr. (?–2000), Roy Lee Centers's brother-in-law, worked a lot around Dayton with Roy Lee in the Easterners and as the Lee Brothers. Later on he formed his own bluegrass gospel group, the Spencer Family, which included his wife, son, daughter, and nephew Lennie Centers (Roy Lee's son). They lived and performed in the West Portsmouth, Ohio, area.

From 1959 to 1963 **Cecil Surratt** (1926–2006) and **Smitty Smith** (1929–198[illegible]) recorded for King Records in Cincinnati, releasing two LPs for King and one for the King subsidiary Audio-Lab, plus several singles. Some of their recordings were unusual in that they paired a five-string banjo and a tenor banjo. Their sacred recordings for King included "The Last Mile of the Way," "Never Grow Old," "All Because of Calvary," and "Read the Bible Every Day."

The **Trace Family Trio** consisted of mother, Sylvia (1915–1989), and daughters Darlene (1932–) and Teena (1934–), all natives of Scioto County, Ohio. They recorded three singles for their own Trace label, the best known of them "The Lord Will Make a Way Somehow." They got the record to Dayton DJ Tommy Sutton, who promoted it on his radio shows and was instrumental in securing a recording contract for the trio with King Records in Cincinnati. Between 1953 and 1959 they released sixteen King sides, including "The Lord Will Make a Way Somehow," "I'll Be No Stranger There," and "My Title to Heaven," which Ralph Stanley recorded as "I Hold a Clear Title" in 1971. They had a lasting influence on other gospel groups.

Ulysses "Red" Turner (1916–) played mandolin in the Turner Brothers duet. He and his brother, Lige, performed together on WLW from 1945 until 1950, when Lige left the music business. After that parting, Red teamed up with Zeke Turner (James Grishaw) as Red and Zeke, the Kentucky Boys. They released two singles on RCA's "X" label. In 1954 Red left WLW to go into evangelical work. He eventually became a Baptist minister in Covington, Kentucky, and started his own Turner record label that issued gospel records, mostly his own.

Clyde "Curly" Tuttle (?–2011) was a mandolin player in the Hamilton-Cincinnati area, active from the 1950s through at least the 1980s. He played with Dave Woolum, worked with Jimmie Skinner, recorded for Hamilton's Melody Records with a group called the Good News Trio, recorded for Adco with Gene Sweet, and played and recorded with Joe "Cannonball" Lewis.

The **Wilson Brothers** performed together from the late 1960s into the early '80s. Curnie (1943–), born in Jackson, Kentucky, played guitar and sang lead. Russell (1945–2013), born in Dayton, played bass and sang tenor. They got their start playing in churches with J. D. Jarvis, and formed their own group in 1970 to play Ralph Stanley's festival in McClure, Virginia. They issued their first LP in 1971 for the Pine Tree label. Five more albums followed, three for Old Homestead and two for Vetco. In 1979 they were calling their band the Bluegrass Harvesters. Its members over the years included Lonnie Bolin, Denver Jones, Larry Polley, and Scotty Sparks. In 1984 the group disbanded because of health problems. Curnie never returned to active performing, but Russell did in 1998. The Wilson Brothers had a sound eerily similar to that of the Stanley Brothers. They wrote the music and Ed Hamilton wrote the words to "Lonesome Old Home," a perennial bluegrass favorite. Curnie's son, Curnie Lee Wilson, became an accomplished acoustic lead-guitar player.

David Emon "Dave" Woolum (ca. 1913–1986) was born in Laurel County, Kentucky, but came to Ohio in his teens. In 1954 the Laurel County Partners organized, with Dave playing guitar and singing lead. Dave and the band played on various radio and TV stations around southwestern Ohio, including WHBD in Mt. Orab, WPFB in Middletown, WCKY and WKRC-TV in Cincinnati, and

WHIO and WHIO-TV in Dayton. Although he never became a full-time musician, Woolum did open for a number of country acts around the Cincinnati area in the 1950s, when there were very few professional bluegrass bands. In 1960 he became a regular on the *Renfro Valley Barn Dance*. Later he teamed with Paris Decker; Decker's wife, Ruby; and the Deckers' daughter, Judy. He recorded for Ark, Arvis, Excellent, Melody, Pine Tree, Rem, Sage and Sand, and Starday. In 1974 he retired to Florida.

* * *

These dedicated artists, ministers, and music promoters—and the churches, recording studios, and radio programs they frequented—made southwestern Ohio fertile ground for sacred bluegrass music. Many famous artists who lived elsewhere recorded and frequently performed in the Miami Valley. Scores of additional gospel bluegrass practitioners resided in the region. Some became nationally prominent full-time professionals and others worked non-musical day jobs while performing locally. Many are still active today. Their legacy of joyful noise from the Miami Valley is etched deeply into bluegrass history.[65]

Notes

1. "I'm Using My Bible for a Roadmap" by Don Reno (Fort Knox Music, Trio Music), as recorded by Don Reno and Red Smiley at their first session for King in Cincinnati, January 15, 1952.

2. *UShistory.org*, "Religious Transformation and the Second Great Awakening," http://www.ushistory.org/us/22c.asp.

3. Wayne Daniel, "Making a Joyful Noise unto the Lord: The Gospel Roots of Bluegrass," in *Bluegrass and Old Time Country Music: Buried Roots of Early Days, International Country Music Journal* (Winter 2016): 55.

4. Stephen Shearon, "The Sacred in Country Music," in *The Oxford Handbook of Country Music* (New York: Oxford University Press, 2017), 399.

5. Ibid., 397–400.

6. Kevin Donald Kehrberg, "I'll Fly Away: The Music and Career of Albert E. Brumley," PhD diss., University of Kentucky, 2010.

7. Shearon, "Sacred in Country Music," 395. Kevin Kehrberg, PhD, Professor of Music and Chair, Department of Music at Warren Wilson College, provided helpful guidance on this section of the chapter.

8. Jimmie Rodgers (1897–1933) and Bob Wills (1905–1975) were notable exceptions. Both rarely, if ever, performed gospel songs, although they did include sentimental songs with family themes from the Victorian parlor era; country music audiences often conflate that repertoire with sacred music.

9. Neil V. Rosenberg, *Bluegrass: A History* (Urbana: University of Illinois Press, 1985, 2005), 231.

10. Fred Bartenstein, "Bluegrass Vocals," unpublished paper, *Bartenstein & Bluegrass*, 2010, http://www.fredbartenstein.com/bgvocals.html.

11. *Encyclopedia of American Gospel Music* (New York: Taylor & Francis Group, 2005), 229–30, 378, 380–81.

12. Ten-inch 78 rpm format singles progressively gave way to the seven-inch 45 rpm format between 1950 and 1958. Extended-play 45 and 33 1/3 rpm releases (EPs) contained two or three songs on each side. Typically featuring cardboard picture sleeves, EPs were a forerunner of the album format but had mostly disappeared by the mid-1960s.

13. Dr. Richard C. Stern, professor emeritus of Homiletics at Saint Meinrad Seminary and School of Theology, explored the theology of bluegrass gospel music in "Bluegrass Gospel: The Music of Exiles," *International Country Music Journal* (2013): 51–75.

14. James N. Gregory, *The Southern Diaspora: How the Great Migrations of Black and White Southerners Transformed America* (Chapel Hill: University of North Carolina Press, 2005), 32.

15. See chapter 1, "Appalachian Migration."

16. Much of the information in this and the next two paragraphs is drawn from the author's interview with Joe Mullins, December 30, 2018.

17. See chapter 5, "Sing Me Back Home." The Church of Christ, Missionary Baptist, and a few other congregations did not allow mechanical instruments of any kind, holding that they were not used for worship described in the Bible or in early Christian practice. See, for example, Wayne Jackson, "What about Use of Mechanical Instruments of Music in Christian Worship?," *Christian Courier*, https://www.christiancourier.com/articles/615.

18. In the bars a request from an inebriated patron for a gospel song would usually be met, because that might be the very person who most needed the message of available salvation.

19. "Ohio Christian Radio," *ChristArt*, https://www.christart.com/radio/ohio.

20. See chapter 4, "Taking the Music Home."

21. Kevin Kehrberg, personal communication, January 6, 2019: "Alton Delmore had worked as a singing-school teacher and reportedly taught the rest of the Brown's Ferry Four how to read shaped notes. He was also a gospel songwriter with published songs in Stamps-Baxter, Winsett, and Hartford books during the 1940s and 1950s."

22. Gary B. Reid, liner notes to *Brown's Ferry Four: Rockin' on the Waves* (King Records, 1997). See chapter 4, "Taking the Music Home."

23. A mandolin was added in some of the group's later recordings.

24. Eddie Stubbs, liner notes to *Johnnie & Jack & the Tennessee Mountain Boys* (King Records, 1992), 12–13.

25. Gary B. Reid, liner notes to *The Best of King and Starday Bluegrass* (King Records, 2004), 4–5.

26. "I'll Be Going to Heaven Sometime" by Howard Watts (Peer International), as recorded by Lester Flatt and Earl Scruggs at their third Cincinnati session, Herzog Studio, December 11, 1949.

27. Neil V. Rosenberg, discography in liner notes to *Flatt & Scruggs: 1948–1959* (Bear Family Records, 1991).

28. See chapter 3, "All the Way to the Fence."

29. See chapter 4, "Taking the Music Home."

30. Dale Vinicur, liner notes to *Jim & Jesse: Bluegrass and More* (Bear Family Records,

1993), 8. The mandolin style Jesse McReynolds introduced on the Virginia Trio recordings is discussed at greater length in chapter 11, "Distinctive Qualities of Southwestern Ohio Bluegrass."

31. Dale Vinicur, liner notes to *Jim & Jesse: 1952–1955* (Bear Family Records, 1992).

32. Jim and Jesse released an all-gospel EP for Starday in 1959, but their first all-gospel LP wasn't issued until 1964.

33. Colin Escott, liner notes to *Love and Wealth: The Lost Recordings of the Louvin Brothers* (Modern Harmonic Records, 2018), 7–8.

34. Gary B. Reid, liner notes to *Don Reno, Red Smiley, and the Tennessee Cut-Ups, 1951–1955* (King Records, 1993), 4–5.

35. Ibid., 6.

36. "Mac Odell," Praguefrank's Country Discographies, http://countrydiscoghraphy2.blogspot.com/2015/01/mac-odell.html.

37. Reid, liner notes to *Don Reno, Red Smiley and the Tennessee Cut-Ups, 1951–1955*.

38. Charley Pennell, Bluegrass Discography, http://www.ibiblio.org/hillwilliam/BG-discography.

39. David Edwards, Mike Callahan, and Patrice Eyries, King Discography, parts 2–6, http://www.bsnpubs.com/king.

40. Ibid., part 7.

41. *The Early Recordings of Sonny Osborne: 1952–1953, Volumes One, Two, and Three* (Crosscut Records, undated).

42. See chapter 5, "Sing Me Back Home."

43. Dennis Satterlee, *Teardrops in My Eyes: The Music of Harley "Red" Allen* (Kensington, MD: Plucked String Foundation, 2007), 23.

44. "Old Daniel Prayed" by G. T. Speer (James D. Vaughan Publishing Company), as recorded by the Stanley Brothers at King Studio, Cincinnati, February 10, 1959.

45. Gary B. Reid, liner notes to *The Stanley Brothers: The Early Starday King Years, 1958–1961* (King Records, 2003), 4–5.

46. Edwards, Callahan, and Eyries, King Discography, parts 4–6.

47. Ibid., parts 5–7.

48. "J. D. Jarvis," Praguefrank's Country Discographies, http://countrydiscoghraphy2.blogspot.com/2017/12/j-d-jarvis.html; Mac McDivitt, personal communication, January 6, 2019.

49. Mac McDivitt, "J. D. Jarvis," *Southwestern Ohio Bluegrass Music Heritage*, swohiobluegrass.com; Ivan M. Tribe, *Folk Music in Overdrive: A Primer of Traditional Country and Bluegrass Artists* (Knoxville: University of Tennessee Press, 2018), 19–26.

50. Mac McDivitt, "Lillimae Whitaker," *Southwestern Ohio Bluegrass Music Heritage*, swohiobluegrass.com; Tribe, *Folk Music in Overdrive*, 99–104; Jeff Whitaker, personal communication, September 12, 2019.

51. "No Burdens Pass Through" by Paul Mullins and Carter Stanley (Fort Knox Music Trio Music), as recorded by Paul Mullins and the Backwoods Boys Quartet for Jalyn Records, Dayton, Ohio, 1966.

52. Paul Mullins's important roles in the Miami Valley bluegrass scene are detailed in chapter 3, "All the Way to the Fence."

53. See chapter 8, "Buckeyes in the Briar Patch."

54. The 1957 version of "Family Reunion" was released under the name of the Logan and Laurel County Boys.

55. See chapter 7, "Green to Bluegrass."

56. "Kash D. Amburgy," *Cincinnati Enquirer*, October 25, 2002; "Historic Lebanon, Ohio," https://www.facebook.com/164041409065/photos/a.10150359471919066/10153263309829066/?type=1&theater.

57. "William Branham and Snake Handling," *Seek the Truth, William Branham Historical Research*, September 4, 2015, https://www.facebook.com/WilliamBranhamOrg/posts/william-branham-and-snake-handlingin-the-few-years-that-we-have-been-writing-art/670110876423646.

58. "Norman L. Livingston," *Dayton Daily News*, April 17, 2011.

59. The original statue of Jesus, constructed in 2004 of Styrofoam and fiberglass on a metal frame, was hit by lightning and destroyed in 2010. A fifty-two-foot replacement statue, of different design, was built in 2012. "King of Kings (statue)," Wikipedia, https://en.wikipedia.org/wiki/King_of_Kings_(statue).

60. "Lawrence Bishop," October 2011, Brown-Dawson-Flick Funeral Home, http://browndawsonflick.com/obituaries/1875/lawrence-bishop; Rick McCrabb, "Solid Rock Still Growing, Winning Souls a Year after Founder's Death," *Dayton Daily News*, December 2, 2012; Solid Rock Church, http://www.solidrockchurch.org/who-we-are.

61. Birth and death dates are included where known.

62. See chapter 1, "Appalachian Migration," for more information on Paris Decker's daughter, Judy Jennings, and her husband, Sherrill.

63. See chapter 7, "Green to Bluegrass."

64. See chapter 4, "Taking the Music Home."

65. See additional information on the topic of sacred bluegrass in chapters 1, 3, 4, and 8.

7. Green to Bluegrass

Reflections on an Unlikely Musical Career

LILY ISAACS

Lily Isaacs, matriarch of the Isaacs—a currently popular family gospel act—offers a unique outsider/insider perspective on the southwestern Ohio bluegrass gospel experience of the 1970s and '80s. Portions of this chapter are adapted from You Don't Cry Out Loud: The Lily Isaacs Story *(New Leaf Press, 2014), used by permission.*

I WAS BORN IN MUNICH, Germany. My mother and father were Polish Jewish Holocaust survivors. My parents survived one of the most horrific times in history. My little family of three came to New York City in 1949. It was hard, but my parents were determined to make a new life here in our new home. I'm grateful for every opportunity that life has given me. We always dream of how our lives will turn out. My life has certainly not turned out the way I had planned. But I wouldn't change it for anything.

Growing up in a Jewish home, my mother would always sing Yiddish lullabies to me. I loved acting and wanted to be a star in the Jewish theater. I took an apprenticeship at the Woodstock Playhouse while attending Queens College. I also got a part in an off-Broadway production of *Antigone*. My dreams of being a professional actress were becoming a reality. I met a young Manhattan girl named Maria Neumann during a summer course at Carnegie Tech in Pittsburgh. She was a singer/songwriter like myself and we would sit in that dorm room every night, folk guitars in hand, and write songs about peace, love, and all the injustice in the world. We wanted to be the next Simon and Garfunkel or Bob Dylan.

Maria and I were singing at a party one night in the City when a man came up to us and said, "I'm a scout for Columbia Records and we're looking for new talent such as you guys." We were shocked and thought he was just trying to flirt with us. But we gave him our number, *never* expecting him to call us. One day, a few weeks later, we did get a call and he asked if we'd come down to the Columbia studios on West 57th Street to audition for recording an album. To our surprise, we walked out of that audition with a contract. Due to our affiliation with Columbia, several opportunities came our way: we got to perform at the Bitter End Cafe and Gerde's Folk City in Greenwich Village. Gerde's was a six-week performing engagement. It was exciting and we were having a blast.

Enter Joe Isaacs and Bluegrass Music

Gerde's had another band come in to do the same shows as we did every night. Frank Wakefield and the Greenbriar Boys were a four-piece bluegrass band from the South. The members were Frank Wakefield, Lloyd Hensley, Buck Parker, and Joe Isaacs. Their accents and mannerisms reminded us of the Wild West. I'd never heard a banjo in real life until that night; it was my first experience with bluegrass music and I was *green*.

Over the next few weeks I started really appreciating this raw form of expression. I'd sit and listen to this four-piece band: a guitar, a mandolin, a banjo, and an upright bass. The harmonies were tight and heartfelt. I was mesmerized. Some of the song messages were so deep and sad. They sang about hurt and poverty and true stories of love and pain. The up-tempo pieces made me want to get up and dance right on the spot. It was fun and I enjoyed all the musical variety.

This started a new chapter in my life. Joe and I were very attracted to each other. Our worlds could not have been more different. Joe was raised in eastern Kentucky. He was the baby child of seventeen children, and his father was a Pentecostal preacher. I'd never met anyone like this wild and fearless cowboy who had never met a stranger. I'm sure he'd never met anyone like me either. I'd never dated a non-Jewish boy before, much less a hillbilly!

Our relationship grew stronger during our several weeks of performing together and sharing our love of music. Joe moved to New York for a year and started a bluegrass group of his own; they performed at local bars and even recorded an album called *The Greenbriar Years*. I was excited because I got to sing harmony on a song for this album. That was an interesting adventure because I tried so hard to sing in a Southern accent, but my Bronx inflections were hard to shake. It was comical.

After Joe left the City, we dated long distance for two years and married in July of 1970. I gave up my musical career, got an office job and started a new life with my husband in Ohio. At the time Joe was playing with Larry Sparks and the Lonesome Ramblers five or six nights a week, mostly in a place called the Old Crow Bar in Middletown, about ten miles away from our house in South Lebanon.

A Change in Our Lives

One night in late December we received a phone call at 2:00 a.m. It was two days before Christmas and cold. This phone call changed our lives. Joe's brother Delmer had been killed in an automobile accident. He was twenty-seven years old, with four small children at home. During the next twenty-four hours, all of their brothers and sisters and relatives poured in from Indiana and Kentucky—we were all devastated. Several days later they had the funeral. The service ended with all of Joe's aunts and uncles standing around the casket singing:

> I will meet you in the morning at the end of the way
> On the streets of that city of gold
> Where we all can be together and be happy always
> While the years and the ages shall roll.[1]

Delmer's funeral gave me my first glimpse of Christian love and togetherness. It had a huge impact on my life. I saw something in that community of Christian people that I'd never seen before. There was a feeling of great compassion and love and honesty. It got me searching my soul.

Within a few days the entire family decided to go to church one night, before everyone went home to their different cities and states. Raised in a Jewish household, my entire being fought the idea, but my heart said I needed to go and support the family I had married into. So we went. The church was called Shawhan Road Pentecostal, and it was nothing more than a converted garage attached to someone's house. We drove down a country road, about six miles from where Joe and I lived.

About one hundred people could fit into that garage, and by the time Joe and I got there the place was packed. Delmer's widow sat at the front with their little children, and I felt so sad for her. But she was surrounded by family members, many of them sitting close and looking after the kids. The stage was empty for a moment. Then someone from the crowd got up and walked to the front and began singing a song I hadn't heard before, one about heaven.

It didn't take long before everyone joined in and sang through every verse. I didn't know the song, but the words were soothing at a very deep level. As soon as that hymn ended, someone else walked up and started singing, and the crowd joined in every time. During the singing, different people would go up front and give Delmer's widow a hug, lift the children up, and kiss their cheeks. Even in the midst of the congregation, people put their arms around one another and wept on each other's shoulders.

The singing went on for about thirty minutes and ended naturally, without an announcement or anything. After that, various folks would take turns standing up at their seat to talk about God, how good He had been to them, and what

He meant in their lives. It didn't seem out of place, even in the midst of such sadness—in fact, it made perfect sense to me, but I wasn't sure why.

I knew I wanted to be part of that community, but I didn't know what to do about it. I didn't know what to say, or how to pray. I just knelt there and cried and cried. I do believe that on that day God looked into my heart and saw my willingness, my openness to him. I didn't know what had happened, but I knew I would never be the same. I found Jesus in that little garage-church!

Joe and I had only been married a few months when this event took place. I believe God already had our destiny planned. Joe became a completely different person—he gave up playing in the bars, quit Larry Sparks's band and got a job as a logger, cutting timber and selling logs to local paper mills.

My Christian education continued during our occasional visits to Joe's family in Kentucky—his father was a sort of community pastor. Folks would come by car or horse or wagon, at all hours of the day or night, just to ask him to pray for them. Family members of those who died came to Joe's father, and he made the coffin, preached the funeral, and never charged a dime. On Friday or Saturday nights the neighbors gathered in their house for prayer meetings, their voices crying out to God long into the night.

A Part-Time Musical Career

Our musical career began unplanned and unheralded. Back in Ohio, Joe and I would get up in church at almost every service and sing a few gospel songs together. At first I didn't know any Christian songs. The pastor would ask and we'd sing "Never Grow Old," "I Found the Way," or anything out of the red-back hymnal that sounded good with the guitar, and then Joe would dig up some of the old gospel tunes that the Stanley Brothers or Bill Monroe would do, and I would try to sing harmony with him.

Learning as I went along was a challenge, but we had a lot of fun. Joe taught me all the old bluegrass favorites he grew up with. The new songs he wrote began taking on Christian themes, and sometimes he'd throw those in at church too, playing his guitar at the services on Tuesday, Saturday, and Sunday nights.

While reading the Scriptures seemed to simplify my understanding of Christ, some of the things about church complicated it. Because I knew so little about Christianity, it became easy for me to get caught up in the surface-level expectations of the church we attended. For example, there was a strict dress code, and it was pretty clear that if you didn't adhere to it you weren't living "the holiness life": women were expected not to cut their hair or wear makeup, and pants were definitely not allowed. I did my best to follow all of the rules.

I tried hard to conform to their standards, but Joe found it even more difficult, seeing that his father didn't allow musical instruments in church services. Joe loved music—it was literally part of his soul—and he would have long arguments with his father about playing music for God. Sometimes Joe would walk away from his father in frustration, giving in to that way of thinking. "I guess I'll never play that instrument again," he would say of his guitar. But he'd always pick it up again, something I was happy about.

Evenings at our church were informal gatherings, with lots of different people getting up to lead songs as they felt moved, and we loved the chance to share our music. Soon visitors approached us after the service and asked if we'd come and sing at their church. Before we knew it, we were traveling all over the area, singing at churches.

One thing led to another and soon we had a couple of bluegrass musicians join in. The first was Leroy Ramsey, an amazing mandolin player. Then we decided to record our first album as Joe Isaacs and the Calvary Mountain Boys. We found a recording studio in Hamilton, owned by a preacher named William M. Jones. The label was Pine Tree Records. We negotiated a recording fee and recorded *Live It Every Day*. I was pregnant with my firstborn, a son named Benjamin Joseph Isaacs.

The recording process crept along at an unbearable pace; we recorded onto a two-track machine, everything live to tape. Many times we'd get to the end of the song and someone would forget the words or hit a bad note and we'd have to start from scratch. Sometimes we'd work on one song for hours. Those days were long. It wasn't unusual for us to start recording at 10:00 a.m. and go until 2:00 the next morning. Throw in my pregnancy and the fact that both Joe and I were still working full-time, and some mornings I could barely pry myself out of bed.

When that process was finally finished, we took some photos to a graphic artist and had five hundred copies pressed up. I think they cost us a dollar or two each. It was an inauspicious entry into the world of Southern gospel bluegrass music, but we were proud of what we had put together.

We started traveling a lot on weekends and we'd sing at a lot of Sunday church services. Most of them were free or maybe a freewill offering. Our new albums helped—we sold them for five dollars each. We were traveling in cars then, so we packed the trunk full of albums, Joe's guitar, and Leroy's mandolin. Occasionally I'd bring my own guitar and play along.

It was fun and exciting to perform again, but this time with a purpose. Joe is a great songwriter and he was very busy writing original gospel songs for us to perform. Our house became a stopping point for local musicians, and it seemed someone was always playing music in the house. We were inspired by Southern gospel groups like the Singing Cookes, but Joe always led us toward the bluegrass sound.

People started calling from all over the Ohio Valley to book us, and soon we were busy every Sunday. People would get us to come to their church on Homecoming Day—every year they would celebrate with a covered-dish supper—and they would say, "We're going to have singing, with Joe and Lily Isaacs." We would come to Hamilton and sing with J. D. Jarvis, or meet up with Lawrence Bishop in Monroe. After a few months, we branched out into Indiana and Kentucky. It was time to purchase a van so we could carry all our luggage and two kids, since by then I also had a beautiful baby girl named Sonya Melissa.

We soon recorded another album on Pine Tree, called *Dreams of Home*, and added a few other musicians: Calvin and Mike Durham, Eldon Napier, and Troy Parker. During one of our Indiana runs, we met Vernon Bowling, Stanley Brock, and Ernie Wells of Connersville. Working with them, we became Joe Isaacs and the Sacred Bluegrass. We recorded another Pine Tree album, *Lord Light My Way*, and our popularity continued to grow.

It was amazing how our style of bluegrass gospel music just took off in the church world. Our Sunday-only bookings grew to Saturday-night gospel shows as well. Many times we were the only bluegrass band on a Southern gospel event. I guess it kind of set us apart. We were booked at some bluegrass festivals, usually the only gospel act on that roster, which made us stand out as well. We were enjoying the best of both worlds. We started recording at Dennis Hensley's Jordan Recording Studios in Covington, Kentucky.

Growing a Family Band

My last child, Rebecca Marcel, was born in 1975, and our little family of five, along with the musicians that had joined us, packed into a maxi-van with albums, instruments, and a cooler full of lunch meat and drinks. Joe built a bed in the back of the van and we put all our gear under it. We would leave on Friday after school and drive eight or ten hours somewhere to sing wherever a church invited us, and probably didn't get a dime for it but we wanted to go. We'd take turns driving, and all three of our kids would sleep in that makeshift bed. I get sentimental thinking about it now, but at the time it was hard. Very hard. I took them everywhere with me, those three kids, all of them three years old and younger. Joe worked all the time, trying to support us, and we were going to church a lot on the weekends and singing. Becky was usually right there on my hip while we sang.

During the '70s, there were not too many bluegrass gospel bands traveling the country. The Marshall Family was probably the most popular, and had a great influence on my kids. We actually got to work with David Marshall some, and he and Joe wrote several songs together. Sometime during the mid-'80s we were introduced to another great bluegrass gospel band, the Primitive Quartet from Candler, North Carolina. We soon made friends and had the opportunity to do many shows together. In the late '80s, we had a new set of musicians playing along with our family band, Tim Caudill and Randy Fox. We just went as the Sacred Bluegrass.

All three of the children got caught up in the music. There was always a banjo on the bed, a mandolin on the sofa, and a guitar in the corner of the room. The kids, as soon as they could crawl around and grab onto things, started fooling with them, plucking on the strings and smiling at the sounds. From early on, we could tell they had talent.

Ben played the bass by the time he was eight, Becky learned piano from her cousins, and Sonya was always plucking on Joe's mandolin; by the age of seven she could play really well. And, without any coaching, all three of them could harmonize. If Becky or Ben started singing lead, Sonya automatically fell into the tenor, and the other would find the third part without Joe or me showing them.

We encouraged them as much as we could, inviting them on stage with the band when we played at churches or in concerts. They had more names than we knew what to do with: the Gospel Chipmunks, or the Kosher Hillbillies, or the Briarhopper Hebrews. They sang "Someone Will Love Me in Heaven" on our *Lord Light My Way* album when they were nine, seven, and six, and they did an entire album as the Isaacs Trio a year or so later.

At some point, when musicians would move on to other jobs and leave our band, my kids just worked their way in and we became the Isaacs. At that particular time, around 1988, it was just the five of us. Becky played guitar and sang while Sonya played the mandolin and led many of the songs. Joe sang and played guitar and banjo and was also our emcee. Ben played the bass, and I was a vocalist and handled all our bookings and office management. We traveled together, lived together, and played together—it was a lot of together! But we created our own sound, and the kids grew in their knowledge of music and performance. We were very busy and loved what we were doing.

For the next seven or eight years our music just kept growing. We went from recording our own albums to having a producer, to having a label. Our venues got bigger, not in leaps and bounds, but slowly, steadily. We were playing in larger churches, farther away from home, and selling more albums.

Because we began traveling farther, and overnight, we felt the need to get something that we could sleep in and have some more space. We took a leap of faith and bought our first bus—we were comfortable doing that because Joe was such a good mechanic. We had a friend in Crossville, Tennessee, who had a 1960 GMC bus for sale. It was old but in decent shape, so we bought it for eighty-five hundred dollars. We used the money we made on weekends to pay the loan on the bus.

Soon after we bought it the transmission went out, and I have vivid memories of that old bus sprawled out in pieces on our driveway in Morrow—Joe tore the motor and transmission apart and spent many hours working on it. Ben fifteen or sixteen at the time, helped out a lot. That's where he got his schooling on being a mechanic.

The inside of the bus was a little rough, so we bought an old couch and a chair, and Joe fixed the bunks the way we needed them. We ended up with six bunks, three high on each side. The back room was a wide-open space where we put a wire from one side to the other and hung all of our clothes. Joe glued a mirror on the wall so we could do our hair. That particular bus had no toilet, so Joe put a porta-potty in the back for emergencies.

We used a cooler to store our drinks and lunch meat. The air conditioner only worked about half the time, so the windows usually stayed open. That was also the bus in which Ben learned to drive. When Joe slept, I sat on the buddy chair beside Ben while he drove. I was so worried that he would fall asleep. He kept telling me to go to bed, but I still sat there (usually falling asleep myself). The first long trip we took in that bus, after it was ready, was to somewhere in Virginia. We were so excited that we had our bus! That night we pulled off at a rest area, opened the windows, and slept in it for the first time. We thought we had finally arrived.

We went from a car to a station wagon, from the station wagon to a van, then pulled the trailer behind the van, and finally went through four buses, all in the last thirty-five years. It was a lot of blood, sweat, and tears, lots of hard work and long trips, to get from that first car to the bus we have now.

Leaving Ohio

In the '90s we would load our family and all our equipment into the bus and drive to Asheville, North Carolina, to do our recordings with Horizon Records. We headed south through Cincinnati and over the river into Kentucky. Soon the road rose and fell, running along rolling hills covered in the greenest grass. Then we'd pass into Tennessee and the mountains crept up around us.

It would take us about eight hours to get to Asheville, and it seemed like we were heading down that way more and more. As our band became known on a regional level, we started playing more shows in the South—Georgia, North Carolina, South Carolina, Florida, and Alabama. Nearly every weekend we traveled south, and when we'd pass that exit for Knoxville, we'd be about halfway to wherever we were going.

We'd been in Ohio for a long time, but many of the ties we had to Ohio were dissolving. Becky was a junior in high school and dating John Bowman (he lived in Virginia), Sonya was a senior in high school, and Ben was in his first year of college. We felt like we were ready for a change, and we wanted to move before the kids put down roots by getting married. It seemed like the right time. So we made a family decision to leave Ohio. Poor Becky—she was in her junior year and would have to finish one year in a new school. But moving to LaFollette, Tennessee, would mean she was a lot closer to John, so there was at least one positive for her.

As the kids became more accomplished musicians, they began experimenting with their own sounds and trying to play more contemporary stuff. They started finding their own musical identity, writing a lot of original material and adding new chord progressions and harmonies that were not traditional bluegrass style. I loved the creativity they exhibited, and I was proud to see them develop.

Bringing the Story Up to Date

We've had many opportunities in our forty-year career. And as life will have it, we've had major changes as well. My family grew up and all my kids developed their own styles of playing, singing, writing songs, and producing our albums. In 1998 Joe and I divorced, but my children and I continue to travel and perform. It hasn't been easy, but we make it work. We have been with several more recording labels, such as Eddie Crook Company, Crossroads, Gaither Music Group, and just recently our own label, House of Isaacs Music.

We have performed in many different genres of music. We've been a part of the Gaither Homecoming tour for more than twenty years. Bill and Gloria Gaither believed in us and certainly gave us a huge platform to work in, not to mention all the Homecoming videos we've been a part of. We appear on the Grand Ole Opry quite often. We've gotten to perform on several shows on the RFD Channel. We've toured abroad many times and gotten acquainted with wonderful people.

In 2016 we had our first Grammy nomination as a group for the album *Nature's Symphony in 432*. The category was Roots Gospel Album of the Year. Most of our recent projects have drums, piano, and electric guitar as well as mandolin, banjo, fiddle, bass and Dobro, but it has been a dream of ours to play with an orchestra. *Nature's Symphony* seemed to be the right fit, so we hired the string section of the Nashville Symphony to play on it.

I'm not sure we could be classified as a true bluegrass band anymore. We've also branched out to record and perform many positive secular songs as well. Life itself is a gift from God. A sacred song doesn't only have to address salvation but can express the heart of a human being and the joys and hardships they endure.

Ben has become one of the most popular record producers in our world of music. Sonya and Becky have become incredible songwriters. They all three possess amazing talent and have a passion for music. I wrote my autobiography, *You Don't Cry Out Loud*, and it was released in 2014. My oldest grandchild, Levi Bowman (Becky's son), recently joined our band, singing and playing guitar.

I'm not exactly sure how all of this came to be. I sometimes just sit back and reflect on my journey. I know that my destiny was sculpted by the Almighty, and I am grateful for all the opportunities we've had. It seems that my musical journey has come full circle. I guess it all started when this *green* New York City kid was introduced to a form of music called *bluegrass*.

Notes

1. "I'll Meet You in the Morning," written in 1936 by Albert E. Brumley Sr. (1905–1977), Hartford Music.

8. Buckeyes in the Briar Patch

Southwestern Ohio Bluegrass in the 1970s

JON HARTLEY FOX

ON NOVEMBER 15, 1969, the Earl Scruggs Revue performed live before half a million people at the Moratorium March to End the War in Vietnam in Washington, DC. The new band, formed by the legendary banjo player after his split with longtime partner Lester Flatt, included two of Scruggs's sons, Gary and Randy, alongside veteran bluegrass pickers Vassar Clements (fiddle) and Josh Graves (Dobro). The band's sound was a bluegrass/country/rock fusion that would prove to be very popular on college campuses over the next decade, though less well received by the bluegrass mainstream.

This appearance by the Earl Scruggs Revue was not the first convergence of bluegrass music with what was coming to be called "the counterculture," but it was surely the most momentous. It foreshadowed what would happen to bluegrass in the 1970s when a new, youngish, and non-Appalachian audience discovered the music and took it to unparalleled heights of popularity, cultural relevance, and importance. This growth was caused by new fans and players, so it's not really accurate to call it a "revival" of the music, as that implies a return to a previous standard.

Bluegrass and its cousin, old-time country music, actually experienced something akin to a *revolution* in the 1970s, one that changed virtually everything: the sound of the music, the appearance of the musicians and fans, the bars and festivals where it was heard, the radio stations broadcasting it, the media covering it, and so on. And being a revolution, there were surprises along the way.

"In the seventies," wrote Neil V. Rosenberg in *Bluegrass: A History*, "the contrast between youth and age was often stated first in terms of their hair length. This contrast suggested others, like those between drug use and drinking, or between dove and hawk positions on Vietnam. That everyone could be separated into two groups was of course unrealistic, and for that reason both sides were often surprised and encouraged by unexpected behavior on the part of representatives from the 'other side.'"[1]

Setting the Stage, Locally

On March 5, 1960, the Osborne Brothers, at the time based in Dayton, performed a concert at Antioch College in nearby Yellow Springs, becoming the first major bluegrass band to appear on a college campus. The concert also featured the Greene County Stump Jumpers (a band composed of Antioch students, including Alice Gerrard) and the Plum Creek Boys (a band composed of Oberlin College students, including Neil Rosenberg).[2]

Though the audience perceived the music of the Osborne Brothers as folk music (as opposed to country music), the concert was successful enough for the Stanley Brothers to perform at the college two months later. Other bands soon followed. *The Country Gentlemen on the Road*, the third album by that Washington, DC–based group, included cuts recorded live at Antioch.

Southwestern Ohio—Cincinnati, Dayton, Hamilton, Middletown, Springfield, and the surrounding area—had long been what Rosenberg called "one of the wellsprings of bluegrass activity,"[3] and the region played an outsized role in changes of the 1970s. A couple of things made southwestern Ohio different from other developing bluegrass scenes of the era.

First, this region already had a well-established bluegrass community. Since the early 1950s this part of the state had been home to dozens of top bluegrass musicians, including Red Allen, Carlos Brock, Hylo Brown, Noah Crase, J. D. Crowe, Jimmy Martin, Jim and Jesse McReynolds, Paul "Moon" Mullins, Bob and Sonny Osborne, Earl Taylor, Frank Wakefield, and Dave Woolum, among many others.

Second, an almost uncanny combination of factors aligned, however briefly, to develop and sustain a regional bluegrass universe of unrivaled scope and vitality. These included (1) the presence of talented bluegrass performers; (2) a plethora of homegrown record companies to document and publicize the efforts of those musicians, including Jalyn (started and operated by Jack Lynch) and Kanawha (Ken Davidson) in Dayton, King Bluegrass (Robert Trout) and Vetco (Lou Ukelson) in Cincinnati, and Pine Tree (Rev. William Jones) in Hamilton; and (3) a pair of radically different radio stations—WPFB in Middletown and WYSO in Yellow Springs—to broadcast those records to the masses.

The Allen Brothers

The premier young bluegrass band in Dayton at the dawn of the 1970s was the Allen Brothers, comprised of four sons of renowned singer/guitarist Red Allen:

Greg (banjo, lead and baritone vocals), Harley (guitar, lead and tenor vocals), Neal (mandolin, lead vocals), and Ronnie (electric bass, baritone vocals). As one might expect from sons of Red Allen, who had helped the Osborne Brothers make the high-lead vocal arrangement famous, the brothers had a tight vocal trio and an expansive repertoire that included rock and country songs as well as originals by Neal ("The Singer," "She's Country") and Harley ("Hobo Joe").

The four young brothers first performed in the late 1960s as the backing band for their father. They started working as the Allen Brothers in 1969, the band's first gig coming at the Family Room, a restaurant in North Dayton. The group worked extensively over the next few years, playing such local restaurants and clubs as Annarino's, the Clock Lounge, Club House Lounge, Gilly's, the Golden Fly, Grammer's, Sam's Bar and Grill, and T.J.'s Night Club.

The Allen Brothers began their recording career with their father on a trio of albums: *Allengrass* (Lemco, 1973), *My Old Kentucky Home* (King Bluegrass, 1973), and *Red Allen Favorites* (King Bluegrass, 1975). There was also a King Bluegrass 45 released in 1974, pairing "Roust-A-Bout" with Neal's "The Singer."

Neal Allen died suddenly in 1974 after a brief illness while the Allen Brothers were on tour in Massachusetts. The band took a short hiatus, during which Harley played with J. D. Crowe, but then Greg, Harley, and Ronnie regrouped for a second run in the late 1970s. This version of the Allen Brothers recorded three critically acclaimed albums: *Sweet Rumors* (Rounder, 1977), *Are You Feeling It Too?* (Folkways, 1980), and *Clara's Boys* (Rounder, 1982).

Harley Allen teamed with banjo picker Mike Lilly, an alumnus of Larry Sparks's Lonesome Ramblers and the Country Gentlemen, in the early 1980s as the Allen-Lilly Band, one of the best bluegrass acts Dayton ever produced. Though short-lived, the outfit (which also included mandolinist Scotti Adams) made a fine album, *Suzanne* (Folkways, 1985), and contributed several cuts to Harley Allen's solo Folkways album, *Across the Blueridge Mountains* (1983).

Harley Allen moved to Nashville in the mid-1980s to pursue recording and songwriting opportunities. He released albums on Mercury and American Originals but made his biggest impact as one of Nashville's most successful songwriters. His songs were recorded by Garth Brooks, Alan Jackson, George Jones Alison Krauss, Ricky Skaggs, and other top stars. He won a Grammy award in 2000 for singing on the soundtrack of the hit movie *O Brother, Where Art Thou?* where he, Dan Tyminski, and Pat Enright were the voices on the song "Man of Constant Sorrow." In 2005 Allen was BMI's Songwriter of the Year, and won the International Bluegrass Music Association's (IBMA's) award for Best Song, "Me and John and Paul." Harley Allen died in 2011, followed by Ronnie in 2017.

Larry Sparks and the Lonesome Ramblers

Not long after the four Allen brothers launched their band, singer and guitarist Larry Sparks, a native of Lebanon, Ohio, was ready to start a band of his own. The year was 1970, and Sparks had recently left his spot in Ralph Stanley's Clinch Mountain Boys. During three years in Stanley's band, Sparks helped make five albums, including three—*Brand New Country Songs*, *Over the Sunset Hill*, and *Hills of Home*—for King Records.

Sparks had made his recording debut in 1965 at age sixteen with a single on Jack Lynch's Dayton-based record company, Jalyn, fronting a band called the Sandy Mountain Boys. His first album after leaving Stanley was *Ramblin' Guitar* (Pine Tree, 1970), but it was with his second, *New Gospel Songs* (Pine Tree, 1971), that Sparks defined his signature sound. For his early Lonesome Ramblers band, Sparks hired mandolinist Wendy Miller, who had moved from Kentucky to southwestern Ohio five years earlier. Miller recommended that Sparks hire Dayton banjo picker Mike Lilly, another Kentucky transplant who came from a banjo-centric family. Mike's father, Bob Lilly, a fine picker and a Don Reno devotee, schooled Mike and his younger brother Keith in the fine points of the five-string. Adding bass players Neal Brackett and later Art Wydner, Sparks had just about the hottest four-piece band in bluegrass.

The Lonesome Ramblers had a lot going for them: Sparks's distinctive singing and blues-drenched lead guitar playing, impeccable trio vocal harmonies, Lilly's dazzling banjo work, strong original material, and an irresistible sense of power and drive. This was the band heard on much of *New Gospel Songs* (Pine Tree, 1971), *Bluegrass Old and New* (Old Homestead, 1972), and *Ramblin' Bluegrass* (Starday, 1973), as well as on two singles: "Blue Eyes Crying in the Rain" / "Kentucky Chimes" (Pine Tree, 1972) and "Kentucky Chimes" / "Brand New Broken Heart" (Starday, 1973). Wendy Miller and Mike Lilly also recorded on their own during this time, cutting four albums between 1973 and 1977 for Old Homestead: *New Grass Instrumentals*, *Solid Grass*, *Wendy Miller & Mike Lilly*, and *Hot 'N' Grassy*.

Larry Sparks continued to be a prolific recording artist throughout the 1970s, recording albums for County, King Bluegrass, Lesco, and Old Homestead. A longtime resident of Richmond, Indiana (about forty miles from Dayton), Sparks became a major bluegrass star in the 1980s and remains one to this day. A two-time winner of the Male Vocalist of the Year from the International Bluegrass Music Association, Sparks was inducted into the Bluegrass Hall of Fame in 2015.

The Boys from Indiana

Formed in the early 1970s, the Boys from Indiana was an intriguing blend of seasoned veterans and a couple of younger pickers that became one of the most successful and entertaining bluegrass bands of the 1970s and '80s. The core of the band was brothers Aubrey (guitar) and Jerry Holt (bass) and their uncle Harley Gabbard (Dobro), all of whom lived in southern Indiana, about fifty miles from Cincinnati. When Paul "Moon" Mullins needed an opening act for the bluegrass concerts he put on for WPFB in Middletown, he'd place a call to his friends, "them boys from Indiana." The Holts and Gabbard would drive over to play gigs with Mullins (fiddle) and Noah Crase (banjo).

Those shows prompted the formation of a real band, which began working as Paul Mullins, Noah Crase, and the Boys from Indiana. The band made its recording debut in 1973 with a gospel album on Jewel, *We Missed You in Church Last Sunday*. The second album, *Atlanta Is Burning* (1974), established the Boys from Indiana as one of the foremost new bluegrass bands on the national scene and kicked off an impressive four-year run of albums for the label, including *Bluegrass Music Is Out of Sight* (1975), *One More Bluegrass Show* (1976), and *Memories and Dreams* (1977).

While Aubrey Holt's lead singing and songwriting attracted much of the attention, it was Crase and Mullins who provided the instrumental fireworks in the early days. A member of Bill Monroe's Blue Grass Boys between 1954 and 1956 and an unsung banjo master, Crase played bars around Dayton with Red Allen, Carlos Brock, Dorsey Harvey, and Frank Wakefield in the 1950s and '60s. During those same years Mullins worked with the Stanley Brothers, was a member of the Bluegrass Playboys in Kentucky and worked with Crase and Sid Campbell in the Nu-Grass Pickers.

Mullins and Crase tired of the road and left the band at the end of the 1970s. With new members Tom Holt (mandolin), Rodney Case (banjo), and Billy Thomas (fiddle), the Boys from Indiana played on into the late 1980s, recording a handful of albums for their own Old Heritage label as well as one for Atteiram. What set the Boys from Indiana apart from their peers was the amount of new material the band introduced into the bluegrass repertoire. Aubrey Holt was one of the best and most prolific bluegrass songwriters of the era, writing roughly half of the songs the band recorded, including such favorites as "One More Bluegrass Show Tonight," "Play Hank's Song Once Again," "Shaking the Grate," and his masterpiece, "Atlanta Is Burning." The Boys from Indiana received a Distinguished Achievement Award from the IBMA in 2006.

New Bluegrass Nightspots Emerge

Bluegrass found a home in the working-class bars of southwestern Ohio. The music was loud, fast, hyped-up, and down-home, as were the bars' patrons. The region offered numerous opportunities for professional and semipro bluegrass musicians to play. You couldn't make much money at it, but you could pick and sing all night and get one hell of a musical education. The early bluegrass bars developed a rather sketchy reputation—okay if you were a regular but somewhat intimidating and perhaps even dangerous for newcomers.[4]

The decade of the 1970s was a time of tremendous growth for bluegrass, both nationally and in southwestern Ohio. That growth was fueled, at least in part, by large numbers of new devotees from outside the older bluegrass subculture. The regional bar scene evolved to reflect this change in demographics. Safer, more welcoming venues were needed for the boom to continue, and new clubs like Sam's Bar and Grill in Dayton; Aunt Maudie's Country Garden, Arnold's, King's Row, and the Village Tavern in Cincinnati; and the Crying Cowboy Saloon in Springfield set the tone—nothing fancy or elegant, but the bathrooms worked, the sound was good, the beer was cheap, and the threat of violence was practically nonexistent. These changes opened the doors for women (both as musicians and fans), hippies, non-Appalachians, college students (the drinking age at the time was eighteen), and others without whom the glories of the 1970s bluegrass world would have been impossible.

Sam's Bar and Grill, located at 9 West Fifth Street in downtown Dayton, was one of the centers of the southwestern Ohio bluegrass music scene. The nondescript bar that had originally been named Sam's Lunch Room was owned by Mike Zunis, known as "The Greek." Sam's began presenting bluegrass music in the early 1970s, featuring such regional acts as Lee Allen and the Dew Mountain Boys, Red Allen and the Allen Brothers, the Dorsey Harvey Band, the Dry Branch Fire Squad, the Falls City Ramblers, the Hagan Brothers, the Hotmud Family, the Muddy River Band, and Earl Taylor.

"Back in the seventies, Sam's was a great place to play," remembers Hotmud Family's banjo picker Rick Good. "The Hotmud Family kept a pretty regular schedule there—almost monthly—along with the Falls City Ramblers, a somewhat notorious string band from Louisville. Touring bands were always able to pick up a fill-in date and occasionally we'd double up and do a big night with two bands, which is what Hotmud did with both Red Clay [Ramblers] and Highwoods [Stringband]. I still run into people around here that remember those nights with great fondness."[5]

Aunt Maudie's Country Garden, located at 1207 Main Street in Cincinnati's Over-the-Rhine district, opened in the early 1970s and was owned by Lou Ukelson. The bar featured bluegrass music from the start, most notably Earl

Taylor, Jim McCall, and the Stoney Mountain Boys; Vernon McIntyre and the Appalachian Grass; and the Katie Laur Band. Ukelson also owned Vetco Records, which recorded those bands as well as the Hotmud Family and the Falls City Ramblers.

The Hotmud Family

The Hotmud Family is perhaps the most significant band to emerge from the vibrant scene of the 1970s in southwestern Ohio. Its blend of bluegrass and old-time country music was deeply influential, as were the powerhouse presence and singing of Suzanne Thomas. The band's music, disseminated on eight albums between 1974 and 1981, was widely heard and well received. An album review in *Bluegrass Unlimited* correctly pointed out the band's towering strength, hailing "a superb job spanning that sometimes large chasm between Appalachian old-time and bluegrass, and still maintain[ing] the traditional integrity of each."

The story of the Hotmud Family began in the late 1960s when three young musicians from Dayton—Suzanne Thomas (guitar), Rick Good (banjo), and Dave Edmundson (mandolin, fiddle)—joined forces to sing and play the old-time country music songs and tunes they loved. All three had come up through the folk scene but now wanted to dig deeper into country music of the 1920s and 1930s. They began searching out and learning from old records by such pre–World War II country artists as the Carter Family, the Delmore Brothers, Uncle Dave Macon, Mainer's Mountaineers, Jimmie Rodgers, and the Skillet Lickers.

The trio started playing around Dayton, adding bass player Tom Harley Campbell in 1974 before recording its second album. A job working with students in the Dayton Public Schools led the band to the Living Arts Center and formation of the *WYSO Country Jamboree*, a free, ninety-minute concert each Wednesday night, broadcast live on local public radio.[6] The Hotmud Family served as the hosts and house band for the first two years of the program. The band appeared regularly at Sam's Bar and Grill and probably played more free gigs for WYSO than any band in the history of the station.

During an especially productive five-year period, the Hotmud Family recorded four albums for Vetco—*Til We Meet Here Again or Above* (1974), *Stone Mountain Wobble* (1974), *Buckeyes in the Briar Patch* (1975), and *Years in the Making* (1978)—as well as two backing Fiddlin' Van Kidwell, an award-winning old-time fiddler originally from Madison County, Kentucky—*Fiddlin' Van Kidwell with the Hotmud Family* (1974) and *Midnight Ride* (1975). The band later recorded two albums for Flying Fish: *Live, as We Know It* (1979) and *Meat & Potatoes and Stuff Like That* (1981).

The Hotmud Family covered a lot of ground during its decade-and-a-half run. The band performed extensively throughout the US and Canada, playing the major festivals and clubs from its home base in Spring Valley, a tiny musician-friendly town in Greene County. The three founding members—augmented in time by fiddlers Greg Dearth, T. J. Lundy, and Tom McCreesh and bass players Tom Harley Campbell, Gary Hopkins, and Jerry Ray Weinert—played and recorded some of the freshest and most creative traditional country music of their era. Suzanne Thomas says of those days, "Our goal was simply to be 'the best band ever,' which we worked at full-time until about 1984. One of the primary tenets of the band was to learn only songs we loved. This turned out to be a really good decision."[7]

In the years after the Hotmud Family, both Edmundson and Thomas spent several (non-overlapping) years in the Dry Branch Fire Squad. Good, Hopkins, and Dearth spent a few years as the Rugcutters, an eclectic, high-energy trio. Thomas recorded an acclaimed solo album for Rounder, *Dear Friends & Gentle Hearts*, in 1999. Good spent twenty-three years as codirector of Rhythm in Shoes, a dance and music ensemble based in Dayton. He has recorded a pair of albums—*Nova Town* (1998) and *The Human Banjo Player* (2012)—and currently plays as often as he can with the Red Clay Ramblers.

In 2010 the Hotmud Family's first four albums were reissued as a two-CD set, *The Complete Vetco Recordings*. To celebrate, the band commandeered Dayton's Canal Street Tavern for an autumn weekend and three nights of reunion concerts. The original trio—Dave Edmundson, Rick Good, and Suzanne Thomas—was joined by former bandmates Tom Harley Campbell, Greg Dearth, Gary Hopkins, and Jerry Ray Weinert, along with a few hundred longtime fans.[8]

Bluegrass Radio Reaches New Audiences

From the late 1940s through the mid-1950s, bluegrass was regularly included on country music radio; records by Bill Monroe and Flatt and Scruggs were played alongside those of Ernest Tubb and Hank Williams. As radio programming moved from mostly live to mostly recorded entertainment, the major country stations in southwestern Ohio were WONE in Dayton and WCKY in Cincinnati. Beginning in the early 1950s, the regional country music crown was shared with those two stations by WPFB in Middletown.

A young DJ from Menifee County, Kentucky, named Paul "Moon" Mullins started on WPFB in 1964 and quickly became immensely popular with the station's audience. A bluegrass fiddler who had worked with the Stanley Brothers in the late 1950s, Mullins played bluegrass and country music records and spoke in a folksy, down-home manner that made his ad-libbed commercials as entertaining as the records he featured.[9]

By 1970 bluegrass had become a scarce commodity on mainstream country radio, an occasional record by the Osborne Brothers notwithstanding, so Mullins was pretty much it when it came to bluegrass on the radio in southwestern Ohio. But WPFB was not the kind of station that would easily attract a new young audience for the music. Mullins was fond of saying that the station's call letters stood for "We Play For Briars," and while that was fine for "briars" (a name given to Kentucky transplants living in Ohio), it wasn't the most welcoming invitation to those who hadn't been steeped in Appalachian culture. A new kind of bluegrass radio was needed to attract a new kind of bluegrass fan. It came from an unlikely source.

Licensed to Antioch College in Yellow Springs, a college that put the "liberal" in "liberal arts," WYSO-FM went on the air in 1958. For its first few years, WYSO was a low-power station serving mainly students and faculty on campus. By the early 1970s, WYSO had evolved into a community radio station with a bit more power, an affiliation with National Public Radio, a small paid staff, and dozens of volunteer programmers from throughout the Dayton/Springfield area.

Early in 1972, three young brothers from Yellow Springs—Jim, Dan, and Tom Duffee (then ranging in age from mid-teens to early twenties)—started a Saturday night program called simply the *Saturday Night Request Show*. The playlist included old-time artists like Mainer's Mountaineers, the Skillet Lickers, and Doc Watson as well as bluegrass bands, particularly the Stanley Brothers and Stanley-style bands. A bit of classic country music was included, as were such folksinger/songwriters as Mary McCaslin, Utah Phillips, and Jim Ringer. The Duffee brothers typified the volunteer DJs who would soon join them at the station: ardent, knowledgeable fans and avid record collectors who liked sharing their love of the music.

"I still remember that Saturday night show the Duffees did," said Rick Good, nearly fifty years later. "It was very important to my musical education, and I'm sure that's true for many others as well. They started each week's show with 'Soldier's Joy' by Gid Tanner and the Skillet Lickers. I had never heard of the Skillet Lickers. It completely opened my mind."[10]

Bluegrass and old-time country programming on WYSO expanded rapidly. By 1976 the station aired roughly twenty-five hours of bluegrass and old-time music each week. *Rise When the Rooster Crows* was the flagship program, airing from 6:00 to 9:00 a.m. Monday through Friday and 7:00 to 9:00 a.m. Saturday and Sunday. The *WYSO Country Jamboree* was a live, multi-artist concert originally broadcast from the Living Arts Center in Dayton from 7:00 to 9:00 p.m. Wednesday, and the *Request Show* continued from 6:00 to 9:00 p.m. on Saturdays. Two more eclectic live music programs, *Nightclub of the Air* and *Live Music Crawling Out Your Radio*, frequently showcased bluegrass and string band music.

The importance of WYSO to the bluegrass scene and community of southwestern Ohio during this era cannot be overstated. On a good day weather-wise, the station could be heard all the way to Columbus and Cincinnati. Before Spotify and online music, WYSO was the only place in the region to hear many lesser-known bluegrass artists. Each of the volunteer DJs had their own perspective, on-air style, record collection, and musical knowledge. No two shows were the same, and if you listened faithfully, you learned a lot about the music.

WYSO was the hub around which Dayton/Springfield's bluegrass community revolved. The station offered widespread airplay and exposure for local bands as well as a free, targeted, and effective means to promote their upcoming gigs. Festival promoters and music bar owners also utilized this free publicity. Public service announcements were a part of every WYSO program. WYSO DJs often served as festival and concert emcees; some even judged local fiddle contests.

WYSO was not the only bluegrass radio voice in southwestern Ohio. Community radio station WAIF in Cincinnati also had some bluegrass programming. For several years in the late 1970s, even Dayton's Top 40 country station, WONE, aired a weekly Sunday night bluegrass program, hosted by bluegrass musician and historian Fred Bartenstein. WMUB, at Miami University in Oxford, was home to Jan McLaughlin's *Oak Street Ramble* for twenty-five years, ending in 2006. WNKU, licensed to Northern Kentucky University in Highland Heights, Kentucky, just across the Ohio River from Cincinnati, went on the air in 1985 with a format consisting of bluegrass and folk music. WOBO, an all-volunteer station in Batavia, started broadcasting bluegrass programs around 1980.

The Hutchison Brothers and the Falls City Ramblers

Though neither band resided in southwestern Ohio, the Hutchison Brothers (based in Athens, Ohio) and the Falls City Ramblers (from Louisville, Kentucky) were a big part of the scene in Dayton, where both bands appeared regularly at Sam's Bar and Grill and received heavy radio airplay on WYSO.

The Hutchison Brothers had one of the most interesting and distinctive bands of the era. Self-described as "The Most Depressingest Man There Is Alive,"[11] and the pride of Barnesville, a tiny village in Belmont County in southeastern Ohio, John "J. D." Hutchison was among the most gifted singer/songwriters in 1970s bluegrass. His "A Year Ago Today," "Lately She Understands," "Money to Burn," "More Than All I Have to Give," "Off the Deep End," and "Silver Tongue and Gold Plated Lies" are modern classics.

J. D., his banjo-playing brother, Bob "Zeke" Hutchison, and bass player Tim Sparkman were playing in a folk-ish bluegrass trio in the mid-1970s when they were joined by a pair of musicians from the Dayton area, fiddler Greg Dearth and mandolinist Tom "Peach" Hampton. The Hutchison Brothers recorded a pair of albums for Vetco: *The Hutchison Bros.* in 1975 and *The Hutchison Bros. Band* two years later (apparently creative album titles were not a high priority).

The latter album contains some of the earliest recorded work of Tim O'Brien, then a young multi-instrumentalist from Wheeling, West Virginia, who played fiddle on three songs. O'Brien, who cofounded the band Hot Rize in the late 1970s and is now a Grammy-winning solo artist, recalled:

> Back in 1975, after playing the Telluride Bluegrass Festival for the first time, I returned home to West Virginia. And while there I met the amazing J. D. Hutchison. Here was a hip, contemporary music head, and a tobacco-chewing hillbilly who quoted Shakespeare and who just happened to channel his muse through a great traditional bluegrass band. We became fast friends and I set about imitating him.[12]

O'Brien went on to describe J. D. Hutchison as "a contemporary songwriter who found a way to write new bluegrass material that sat right in the tradition, at a time when the norm was to go into a more progressive direction. He came from the roots naturally, having parents who played and sang traditional music, and he honored that but didn't let it limit him. . . . J. D. was born with the body of a hillbilly and the brain of an artist."[13]

The Hutchison Brothers didn't record again after 1977, and the band faded away not too long after that. But the Hutchison Brothers, who played from coast to coast and made a lasting impact on countless fans, were one of the most compelling bands to arise from this fertile bluegrass ground.

Whereas the Hotmud Family toggled between old-time and bluegrass, the Falls City Ramblers ranged all over the musical map, from bluegrass to early jazz and from ragtime to hokum blues. Hailed by the *New York Times* as "an old-time band in the broadest sense of the word,"[14] the Ramblers boasted a pair of powerful (and very different) singers, mandolinist "Memphis Beck" Gentry and guitarist Jim Webb. The zany crew of musicians also included Roy Gentry (banjo, guitar); Robin Rose (Dobro, washboard, harmonica); Bob Wood (bass); and David Harvey (mandolin, fiddle), the teenage son of Dayton's legendary mandolin genius Dorsey Harvey. The Falls City Ramblers formed in 1972 and were originally based in Louisville before moving to a communal farm near China, Indiana. As Murphy Henry notes in her book *Pretty Good for a Girl*, "Their avant-garde musical attitude, hippie appearance, and eclectic material found ready acceptance in the clubs and bars in Louisville and in Dayton, Ohio, particularly among the college crowd."[15]

The Ramblers worked the road as hard as any of the bands discussed above and did so very successfully, garnering positive reviews in both the *New York Times* and the *Washington Post*, a rarity for a Midwestern bluegrass band. Jim Webb (not to be confused with the famous pop songwriter) did most of the lead vocals on the hard-driving bluegrass songs, but as the *Times* pointed out, "The focal point of the Falls City Ramblers is Memphis Beck Gentry."[16] Her singing on such numbers as Memphis Minnie's "There Ain't Nothing in Ramblin'" and Bessie Smith's "Jazzbo Brown" never failed to bring the house down.

The Falls City Ramblers recorded two albums during their decade-long run: *Ain't Nothing in Ramblin'* (1975) for Vetco and *Early Indiana Days* (1976) for the band's own Palm Tree label. Popular among fans, the Ramblers had an uneasy relationship with the bluegrass establishment. A record reviewer in *Bluegrass Unlimited* criticized them for making fun of traditional music and for treating their songs from Black traditions as "camp."[17] The band members were rightly stung by this slam from someone who had obviously never seen them perform. They may not have taken themselves all that seriously, but they were dead serious about their music. The Falls City Ramblers broke up in 1981.

Vernon McIntyre and Appalachian Grass

Vernon McIntyre Jr., who moved from Baltimore to Cincinnati around 1960, was born into a life of bluegrass. His father was a bass player and comedian who used the stage name "Boatwhistle" and performed with a number of bluegrass bands, primarily Earl Taylor and the Stoney Mountain Boys. McIntyre joined his father in the Stoney Mountain Boys at the age of fifteen, shortly after he moved to town, replacing banjo player Walter Hensley. The young musician had already played bass on a pair of albums by the Stanley Brothers for King Records. He subsequently spent brief hitches playing banjo in the bands of Jimmy Martin and James Monroe.

Jim McCall, a hard-edged singer and guitarist, was a longtime mainstay of the Cincinnati scene, best known for his association with mandolinist Earl Taylor. McCall teamed up in the early 1970s with McIntyre in the band Jim McCall, Vernon McIntyre, and Appalachian Grass, which included Katie Laur on vocals, David Cox on mandolin, and Dalen Jackson on bass. McCall and McIntyre recorded a pair of Vetco albums: *Presenting Jim McCall, Vernon McIntyre & Appalachian Grass* and *Jim McCall, Vernon McIntyre & Appalachian Grass*.

When McCall left in 1974, McIntyre moved to guitar and lead vocals and renamed the band Vernon McIntyre and Appalachian Grass. That same year, McIntyre recorded an interesting album with guitarist and singer Roy Lee Centers and mandolinist Fred Spencer (*I've Lived a Lot in My Time*, Vetco). It was one of Centers's last recordings before he was murdered in May of 1974. McIntyre and his band worked extensively throughout the tristate region, and he recorded several more albums during the decade, including one with Mike Lilly and Wendy Miller in 1977 and *A Bluegrass Singer's Life* (1978), both for the Old Homestead label.

McIntyre purchased the Famous Old Time Music Company in Cincinnati in 1981. In business since the early 1970s, the FOTMC was a performance venue and bluegrass specialty store offering instruments and music lessons. McIntyre and his wife, fiddler Kitty McIntyre, ran the operation until 2013. As of this writing, the McIntyres live near Oxford and teach music lessons at the reopened FOTMC in Millville, Ohio. Vernon McIntyre and Appalachian Grass are still a working band in the Cincinnati area.

The Katie Laur Band

The increasing number of women playing bluegrass was one of the main stories of the music in the 1970s, but female bandleaders were still few and far between. A native of Paris, Tennessee, who settled in Cincinnati in 1966, singer and guitarist Katie Laur formed her own band in 1975 after a two-year stint with Jim McCall, Vernon McIntyre, and Appalachian Grass. She said she became the leader of the band because nobody else wanted to, but likely the real reason was that she loved to sing and figured leading a band was the best way to guarantee that happening.

Laur quickly carved out a space for herself and her band—Rich Flaig (bass), Buddy Griffin (fiddle), Jeff Roberts (banjo), and Jeff Terflinger (mandolin)—with a sound that blended bluegrass with classic jazz vocalizing. Griffin (a West Virginia state fiddling champion), Roberts, and Terflinger laid down powerful, hard-driving bluegrass on such instrumentals as "New York Ramblin'," "Sweet Dixie," and "Kentucky Chimes," but the main selling point of the band was Laur's singing. She was particularly effective on older jazz/pop songs like "Ain't Misbehavin'" and solo showcases like "Lovesick Blues," "T for Texas," and "Weary Blues."

The Katie Laur Band recorded three albums for Vetco: *Good Time Girl* (1975), *Cookin' with Katie* (1977), and *M(i)sbehavin'* (1979). Laur was a bluegrass pioneer as one of the very first female bandleaders. Her work fronting an otherwise all-male band has been hugely influential and helped pave the way for such later musician/bandleaders as Dale Ann Bradley, Alison Krauss, Lynn Morris, and Rhonda Vincent, among many others. "I wanted to be able to play," Laur would later explain, "to lead a life of a merry road warrior, and, yes, I always wanted to make a statement. I just never had any idea that I was making it just by enduring."[18]

Laur has kept on enduring up to the present—singing, writing for magazines and newspapers, and, in the late 1990s, forming, and recording with the Katie Laur All Girl Bluegrass Band. From 1989 to 2017 she hosted a popular bluegrass radio program, *Music from the Hills of Home*, on WNKU-FM in Highland Heights, Kentucky. Katie Laur was awarded an Ohio Heritage Fellowship by the Ohio Arts Council in 2008.

Bill Lowe's *Kentucky Farewell* and Ron Thomason's *The Mandolin and Other Stuff*

If an individual record album can be said to capture the musical zeitgeist of a particular time and place, *Kentucky Farewell* (Ramblin', 1977) by Bill Lowe would be my pick to convey traditional country music in late-'70s Dayton. From the all-star cast of characters, to the intricate fusion of bluegrass and old-time sensibilities, to its poignant title, *Kentucky Farewell* pretty much sums up the memorable scene.

Not to be confused with the musician who worked with the Stanley Brothers, this Bill Lowe was born in 1930 in Pike County, Kentucky. He came to the town of Farmersville (near Dayton) in the mid-1970s from Los Angeles, where he had played both country music and bluegrass after a stint in the US Marines. Lowe was a guitar player and singer with a style not unlike that of his friend Doc Watson. He was a central part of the *WYSO Country Jamboree* and gladly performed dozens of benefit concerts for the station, usually with lead guitarist Dan Spires, but was always up for anything musically.

Lowe was in his mid-forties when he made *Kentucky Farewell* in 1977 and assembled his own multigenerational dream team for it, including Tom Harley Campbell, Rick Good, and Suzanne Thomas from the Hotmud Family; Greg Dearth and Tom "Peach" Hampton from the Hutchison Brothers; and Dayton mandolin legend Dorsey Harvey. A showcase for Lowe's rich baritone voice, the album deftly captures the warmth and humanity at the heart of his singing, especially on his vocal solos, including "Hang Your Head in Shame," "Man of Constant Sorrow," "Pastures of Plenty," and Lowe's theme song, "You've Been a Friend to Me." Other high points of this album were Lowe's superb, stirring duets with Suzanne Thomas ("Another Broken Heart") and "Peach" Hampton ("A Miner's Child"). Another treat is hearing the woefully under-recorded mandolinist Dorsey Harvey, who shines on "Lost Indian," "Blue Grass Stomp," and "Red Apple Rag."

Another iconic album showcasing the region's talent in the seventies is *The Mandolin and Other Stuff* (Kanawha 324) by Ron Thomason. Recorded in 1975, while Thomason was a member of Lee Allen and the Dew Mountain Boys and before he started the Dry Branch Fire Squad, this album features many of the same musicians heard on Lowe's record plus Lee Allen, Howard Aldridge, Tommy Boyd, Tom Duffee, and Dave Edmundson.

The Dry Branch Fire Squad

The Dry Branch Fire Squad is an internationally acclaimed bluegrass band but has always been first and foremost a vehicle for its founder—mandolinist, singer, and humorist Ron Thomason. A native of Russell County, Virginia, Thomason moved to Springfield, Ohio, to teach school after graduating from Ohio University. He worked in a band with Frank Wakefield and Howard Aldridge and then logged time in Ralph Stanley's Clinch Mountain Boys and Lee Allen and the Dew Mountain Boys before forming Dry Branch Fire Squad in 1976.

The Squad hit the ground running, recording three albums in 1977: *Live at the Crying Cowboy Concert Saloon*, *Spiritual Songs from Dry Branch*, and *Dry Branch Fire Squad* (the last recorded at WYSO during the Great Blizzard of 1977). From there, the band moved to Rounder, a lasting association that has produced some fifteen albums, starting with *Born to Be Lonesome* in 1979. The list includes such popular albums as *Golgotha* (1986), *Long Journey* (1991), *Just for the Record* (1993), and *Memories That Bless and Burn* (1999).

The first iteration of the band to record was Thomason (mandolin, lead guitar, lead and harmony vocals), Johnny Carpenter (bass), Bob Leach (banjo), and Chris Montgomery (guitar, lead vocals). Guitarist and singer Johnny Baker (son of Bill Monroe's longtime fiddler Kenny Baker) replaced Montgomery on the second album and stayed with the band for several years. A number of other outstanding musicians have passed through the Fire Squad over the years, including Tommy Boyd, Dave Edmundson, Bill Evans, John Hisey, Charlie Leet, Mary Jo Dickman Leet, Danny Russell, and Suzanne Thomas.

Ron Thomason moved to Colorado in 1999 and the band performs less frequently in Ohio, but the Dry Branch Fire Squad stands as one of the most successful and long-lived bluegrass bands to emerge from the fertile ground of the Miami Valley—the funniest, as well.[19]

Old-Time String Bands

Though the bluegrass sound was predominant in southwestern Ohio, there was always a strong undercurrent of old-time string-band music in the mix. This pre-bluegrass style of traditional country music was heard regularly on WYSO programs from the very beginning. The Hotmud Family started out as an old-time band and continued to prominently feature old-time music in their shows and albums.

A native of Madison County, Kentucky, and contemporary of the great fiddler Doc Roberts, Fiddlin' Van Kidwell was retired and living in the Dayton area when he hooked up with the Hotmud Family in the mid-1970s. Kidwell was a gifted fiddler with an extensive repertoire. He performed sometimes with the Hotmuds, including an appearance at the prestigious Mariposa Folk Festival in Canada in 1974. He made two albums for Vetco, backed by the Hotmud Family, in the mid-1970s: *Fiddlin' Van Kidwell* and *Midnight Ride*.

When it comes to sheer persistence and durability, nobody has flown the old-time flag quite as high as the Corndrinkers—Tom Duffee (banjo), Barb Kuhns (fiddle), Linda Scutt (fiddle), Doug Smith (guitar, Dobro), and Al Turnbull (bass). The band was formed in 1975 to play square dances at Carriage Hill, a farm, park, and historical site north of Dayton that recreates agricultural life of the late nineteenth century.

The Corndrinkers specialize in old-time country music of the 1920s and '30s, from such iconic musicians as the Carter Family and the Skillet Lickers to more obscure figures like J. P. and Annadeene Fraley and Art Galbraith. Duffee, Scutt, and Smith share the lead singing duties, but everybody gets in on the act at some point. Still active, the Corndrinkers have two albums to their credit: *The Corndrinkers* and *The Corndrinkers Still.*

Two long-running associations have helped define the Corndrinkers over the years: WYSO and the Fraley Family Mountain Music Festival held near Grayson, Kentucky. All five members of the band have been DJs on WYSO, and the band took over the hosting and house band duties on the *WYSO Country Jamboree* when the Hotmud Family stepped down.

Beginning in the late 1970s, the Corndrinkers made annual pilgrimages to the small, down-home festival that celebrated the fiddling of J. P. Fraley, the duet singing of J. P. and Annadeene Fraley, and the fiddling traditions of eastern Kentucky.

Other Noteworthy Bands

Space doesn't permit a close look at every band active during the 1970s in southwestern Ohio, but the following acts helped make the scene and deserve at least a mention.

A Dayton-based band active in the mid-1970s, **Bluegrass Special** recorded an album for King Bluegrass in 1976, *Mountains, Music and Memories.* The band—Del Holt (mandolin), Joe Karns (bass), Tony Lewis (banjo), John Lipot (guitar), and John Noftsger (guitar)—played at such local clubs as the Dry Dock Lounge and the Open Door.

Based in the town of New Lebanon (west of Dayton on US 35), the **Boys from Johnsville** were a progressive bluegrass band playing around Dayton in the late 1970s and early 1980s, especially at the Avalon Bar and New Lebanon Inn. Original members of the band were Tim Jackson (banjo), Steve Mullis (guitar), Bordley Palk (Dobro), Bob Staggs (bass), and Lonnie Staggs (mandolin). The band recorded an album for Old Homestead in 1980, *Smokin' Bluegrass.*

Not to be confused with Mike Lilly's band of the same name, **Country Grass,** based in Springfield, was formed in 1971. Country Grass played frequently on the *WYSO Country Jamboree*, at the Living Arts Center, and at festivals throughout the region. Band members included Johnny Carroll (bass), Bob Ferguson (banjo), Wayne Horsley (guitar and lead vocal), Earl Huff (Dobro), and Ted Wallace (mandolin and tenor vocal). The band recorded an album in 1978, *Don't Forget to Care.*

Founded in the mid-1970s by mandolinist and lead singer Bob Hamblin, the **Dixie Ryders** have been active in the Dayton area for forty-plus years. The band recorded an album for Old Homestead, *Bluegrass the Ryders Way* (1977), and two for Central, *Blue Grass in Orbit* (1979) and *Bluegrass Nailed Down* (1983). Other band members include Gene Bowling (lead guitar), Todd Elam (banjo), Delbert Holt (guitar, comedy), Bill Howard (banjo), and Fiddlin' Harold Staggs.

The **Hagan Brothers** weren't brothers and none of them were named Hagan, but this Spring Valley–based band was noteworthy for recording the album *Life, Liberty, Bluegrass Music* for Kanawha in 1974, and for including fiddler Greg Dearth and mandolinist Tom "Peach" Hampton, who later played with the Hutchison Brothers.

The **Dorsey Harvey Band**, based in Dayton, consisted of Fred Bartenstein (guitar), Glen "Cookie" Inman (bass), Sherrill Jennings (banjo), and, of course, Dorsey "Little David" Harvey, the enigmatic mandolin virtuoso. Originally from Irvine, Kentucky, Harvey was a contemporary of Frank Wakefield and Red Allen in Dayton during the 1950s. Harvey recorded one album, *Bluegrass Instrumentals*, in 1977 for Poca River Records, an offshoot of Ken Davidson's Kanawha label. In the liner notes, Frank Wakefield said of Harvey, "He is the best mandolin player I ever heard. Dorsey, Jesse McReynolds, and Bill Monroe are the only mandolin players I listen to."

The **Marcum Brothers**—Bill (guitar, lead and tenor vocals) and Dewey (lead guitar, banjo, lead vocals)—fronted a band called the Stanton Mountain Boys that played throughout southwestern Ohio in the 1970s. Among the musicians who worked with them were Jimmy Brewer (banjo), Dorsey Harvey (mandolin), and Herman Holt (bass). The band recorded two albums, *Modern Bluegrass* (Jalyn, 1974) and *Mountain Sound of Bluegrass* (Old Homestead, 1980).

Muddy River was another Spring Valley–based band, formed by bass player Ron Murphy, a former member of the Hagan Brothers. Quite active in the Dayton/Cincinnati area in the late 1970s and early '80s, the band also included Danny Cade (fiddle), Pam Gadd (banjo), and Ron's wife, Lora Murphy (guitar). The band recorded one album, *Roll On Muddy River* (Vetco, 1980).

One of the very few bluegrass bands of the 1970s to feature a female banjo picker, **Wheat Straw** was a Dayton band that showcased folk-ish trio harmonies and hard-driving banjo from Julie Gray (aka Julie Madru). Julie's husband, Alan Gray, played guitar and sang lead vocals, and the Grays were joined by bass player Joe Gibbs and mandolinist Miles Hathaway. Wheat Straw recorded a pair of LPs for Old Homestead: *It Ain't Hay* (1975) and *The Wheat Goes On* (1976).

The End of an Era

Times change, and some revolutions are neither won nor lost but just kind of fizzle out. Only a few of the bands profiled here lasted past the mid-1980s. Sam's Bar and Grill, Aunt Maudie's, and the rest of the bars are long gone, killed by changing tastes, the raising of the drinking age in Ohio from eighteen to twenty-one, and more vigorous enforcement of drunk-driving laws. All the record companies have long since closed their doors, and WYSO no longer offers bluegrass on a daily basis.

The decade of the 1970s was a tremendous time to be a bluegrass musician or fan in this part of the country. The music and the people were great and the memories remain. Looking back at that era from this vantage point, what stands out most are two developments that changed the look, sound, and relevance of bluegrass here and across the country. These were fundamental, transformational alterations that enabled bluegrass to make it into the twenty-first century as a vital musical form.

The first was the prominence of women on stage in bluegrass and old-time bands during the 1970s in southwestern Ohio: Pam Gadd, "Memphis Beck" Gentry, Julie Gray, Barb Kuhns, Katie Laur, Mary Jo Dickman Leet, Lora Murphy, Linda Scutt, and Suzanne Thomas, among others. That didn't seem strange, improper, or unusual. It was the way things were in that time and place, and area fans liked it that way. They didn't know that these women were groundbreaking pioneers or role models for countless little girls, but they were. And that's important.

The second was the preponderance of new folks who came to bluegrass from outside its native culture. Most hadn't been born in a ramshackle shack on a hill or a little old log cabin in the lane. They'd never been in a coal mine or a dark hollow. But they loved the music as well and as deeply as those born to it.

The "traditional" way of learning to play bluegrass was face-to-face instruction from an older relative or neighbor, and there were still young musicians here who came up that way, including the four Allen brothers, David Harvey, Mike Lilly, and Vernon McIntyre Jr. But most of the musicians discussed here—and virtually all of today's bluegrassers—learned the music from secondhand sources, primarily recordings. Many of these singers and pickers came to bluegrass through the "folk revival" of the 1950s and 1960s or through an interest in country music. Bluegrass was a choice for these musicians in southwestern Ohio, and that's important too.

The scene changed; the music endures.[20]

Notes

1. Neil V. Rosenberg, *Bluegrass: A History* (1985; Urbana: University of Illinois Press, 2005), 318.

2. Ibid., 154–55.

3. Ibid., 138.

4. On early bluegrass bars, see chapter 5, "Sing Me Back Home."

5. "The Red Clay Ramblers at Sam's Bar & Grill, Dayton, Ohio—April 12, 1979," Tommy Thompson interview from the live NPR radio broadcast," http://www.earlyblurs.com/calendars/npr_dayton1979.htm.

6. See chapter 9, "The Living Arts Center's East Dayton Roots."

7. The Hotmud Family, "The Hotmud Family, the Complete Vetco Recordings," August 25, 2010, http://www.hotmudfamily.com/?page_id=2.

8. Except as noted, the section about the Hotmud Family is adapted from "Present to the Present: the Hotmud Family on Vetco," the writer's liner notes accompanying *The Complete Vetco Recordings*, 2010. Used by permission.

9. See chapter 3, "All the Way to the Fence."

10. Rick Good, telephone interview, January 23, 2018.

11. J. D. Hutchison, "You've Found 'Lost John,'" http://www.jdhutchison.com/lost-john.html.

12. Ibid.

13. Terry Smith, "40 Years Later, Old Bluegrass Allies Come Full Circle in Legacy Project," *Athens (OH) News,* July 17, 2016, www.athensnews.com/culture/arts_and_entertainment/years-later-old-bluegrass-allies-come-full-circle-in-legacy/article_ec508b00-4c49-11e6-bac8-a717a0f87e9b.html.

14. "Ramblers Present Old-Fashioned Country Music," *New York Times*, October 1, 1977, http://www.nytimes.com/1977/10/01/archives/ramblers-present-oldfashioned-country-music.html.

15. Murphy Hicks Henry, *Pretty Good for a Girl: Women in Bluegrass* (Urbana: University of Illinois Press, 2013), 187–88.

16. "Ramblers Present," *New York Times,* October 1, 1977.

17. Henry, *Pretty Good for a Girl*, 189.

18. Ibid., 228.

19. For example, Ron Thomason always brought the house down with his shaggy-dog story about Bill Monroe. He tells of walking past Monroe's motel room, unable to resist peeking through the drapes. To his amazement, he sees that Bill has tied suspenders to both posts of the bed on which he is vigorously jumping. Launching himself into the air, Bill lands perfectly into his dress trousers and says to his guitarist, Wayne Lewis, "Like everybody else, indeed." Dry Branch Fire Squad, *Live at the Newburyport Firehouse* (Rounder Records, 2005).

20. Discographical information in this chapter came primarily from the writer's memory and record collection. Additional information came from the following online websites: *Bluegrass Discography* (www.ibiblio.org/hillwilliam/BGdiscography/?v=home) and *Discogs* (www.discogs.com). Biographical information in this chapter came primarily from the author's memory and record collection; additional information came from the online website *Cincinnati-Dayton Ohio Bluegrass Heritage*, swohiobluegrass.com.

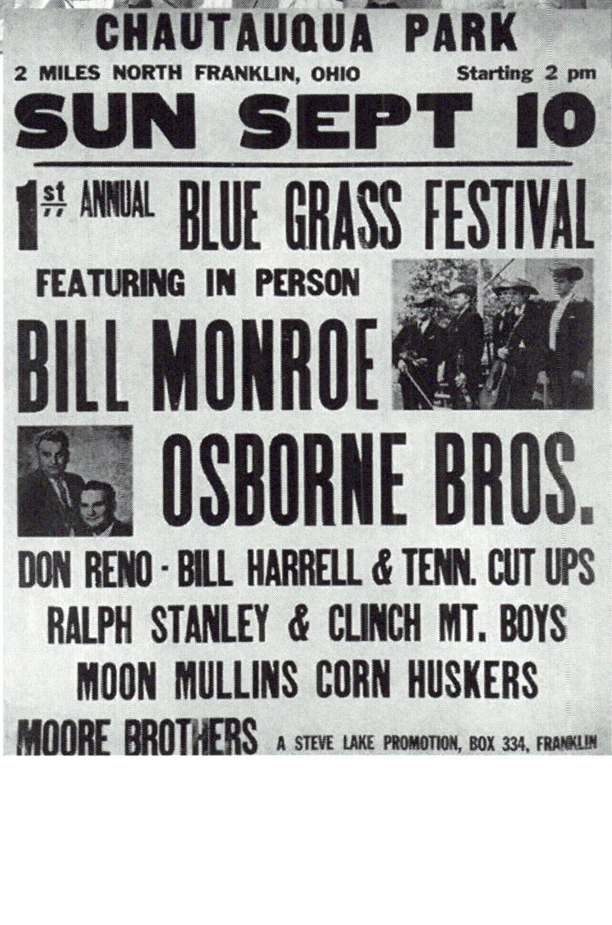

Bill Monroe and His Blue Grass Boys at the Chautauqua Park Bluegrass Festival, Franklin, Ohio, September 8, 1968; left to right, Kenny Baker, Vic Jordan (hidden), James William Monroe, Bill Monroe, Roland White (hidden). (Photo by Carl Fleischhauer; 1967 poster, Joe Mullins Private Collection)

Terrace Bar, Cincinnati, Ohio, March 1970, just before the name was changed to Aunt Maudie's Country Garden. On stage: left to right, Lowell Varney, Hylo Brown; conversing at the front table: Jim McCall and Earl Taylor. (Photo by Carl Fleischhauer)

Terrace Bar, Cincinnati, Ohio, March 1970; left to right, Earl Taylor, Vernon McIntyre Jr., Jim McCall, Vernon "Boatwhistle" McIntyre (hidden). (Photo by Carl Fleischhauer)

Mr. Spoons (Joe Jones) at Aunt Maudie's Country Garden, Cincinnati, Ohio. (Photo by Cal Kowal ©1975/76)

Katie Laur at Aunt Maudie's Country Garden, Cincinnati, Ohio, 1974. (Photo by Mimi Fuller; Fred Bartenstein Private Collection)

Vernon McIntyre Jr., proprietor of Famous Old Time Music Company, Cincinnati, 1991. (Vernon McIntyre Private Collection)

Schedule of 1981–1982 performers at Village Tavern, Cincinnati. (Mac McDivitt Private Collection)

Jalyn Records proprietor Jack Lynch, Dayton, 1978. (Photo by Bill Shepherd, *Dayton Daily News*; Mac McDivitt Private Collection)

The Hotmud Family, residents of Spring Valley (near Dayton), mixed folk, old-time, and bluegrass music. *Years in the Making* was released in 1978 on Cincinnati-based Vetco Records. (Fred Bartenstein Private Collection)

Keith Whitley and Ricky Skaggs were Kentucky high school students and members of Ralph Stanley's Clinch Mountain Boys when they made their debut recordings together on Dayton-based Jalyn Records, 1971. (Mac McDivitt Private Collection)

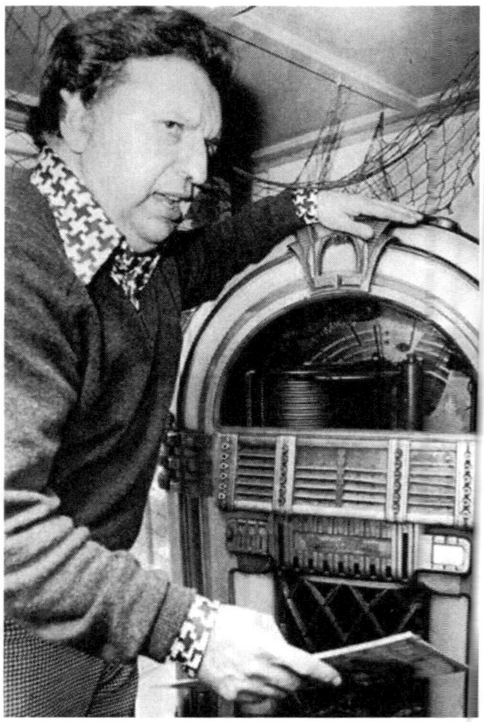

Lou Ukelson, proprietor of the Jimmie Skinner Music Center, Aunt Maudie's Country Garden, and Vetco Records, Cincinnati, 1974. (Photo by Mimi Fuller; Fred Bartenstein Private Collection)

Ken Davidson, who moved his Kanawha and Poca River labels to Dayton in the early 1970s, sells records at the Union Grove Fiddlers Convention in North Carolina, 1971. (Photo by Carl Fleischhauer; Record label image, Fred Bartenstein Private Collection)

Wilbur "Red" Lake's family-operated Lake Jewelry in Franklin, Ohio, carried the largest selection of bluegrass and country LPs, 45s, and cassettes in the Dayton/ Cincinnati area. (Steve Lake Private Collection)

Larry Sparks (right), born in Lebanon, Ohio, played with Ralph Stanley (left) from 1967 to 1969; Chautauqua Bluegrass Festival, Franklin, Ohio, 1968. (Photo by Carl Fleischhauer)

Left to right, David Cox, Larry Sparks, Joe Isaacs, and Bernice Sparks on Hamilton, Ohio–based Pine Tree Records, 1971. (Fred Bartenstein Private Collection)

Blue Grass Music
Tom's Tavern
1511 E. Fifth St.
Every
Friday & Saturday
LARRY SPARKS
and His Lonesome Ramblers

Dayton Daily News, 1973. (Mac McDivitt Private Collection)

A Kentucky migrant to Dayton, Roy Lee Centers (1944–1974) realized a dream in 1970 when Ralph Stanley hired him as his lead singer; Webster, Massachusetts, 1972. (Photo by Fred Robbins)

Ralph Stanley met his future wife, Jimmi, in 1961 at the Ken-Mill Café in Cincinnati; left to right, Tonya Carletta, Ralph, Lisa Joy, and Jimmi Stanley; Rosine, Kentucky, 1973. (Photo by Carl Fleischhauer)

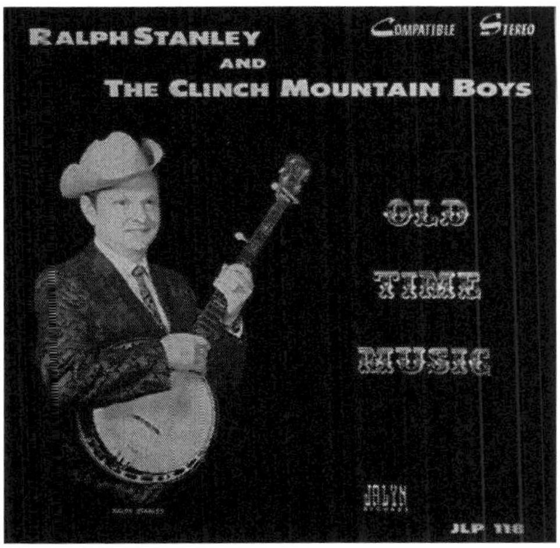

Two 1968 albums by Ralph Stanley and the Clinch Mountain Boys on the Dayton-based Jalyn label. (Fred Bartenstein Private Collection)

The Hotmud Family at a Dayton Public School performance, 1973; left to right, Dave Edmundson, Rick Good, Suzanne Thomas. (Photo by Chuck Good; Mac McDivitt Private Collection)

Audience at the Wednesday-night *Country Music Jamboree*, Living Arts Center, Dayton, broadcast live on WYSO. (Photo by Wally Nelson; Rick Good Private Collection)

Sam's Bar and Grill, 35 West Fifth Street, Dayton, a bluegrass hotspot for young audiences, 1977. (Special Collections and Archives, Wright State University, Dayton, Ohio)

Left to right, Neal, Harley, Ronnie, Red, and Greg Allen; Dayton, 1972. (Photo by Tom Teepen; Courtesy of the Country Music Hall of Fame and Museum)

The Dorsey Harvey Band, 1977; left to right, Fred Bartenstein, Glen Inman, Dorsey Harvey, Sherrill Jennings. (Photo by Karen Copher; Fred Bartenstein Private Collection)

The Mandolin and Other Stuff, Ron Thomason's 1975 debut album on Kanawha, featured guest appearances by Howard Aldridge, the Duffee brothers, Dorsey Harvey, the Hotmud Family, and others from the Dayton/Springfield bluegrass scene. (Fred Bartenstein Private Collection)

J. D. Jarvis, born in Kentucky, worked as a painting contractor in Hamilton, Ohio, while devoting his musical talents almost entirely to sacred performance and composition. Jewel LP, 1967. (Courtesy of the Archives of Appalachia, East Tennessee State University, Lewis Deneumoustier Collection, Johnson City Tennessee)

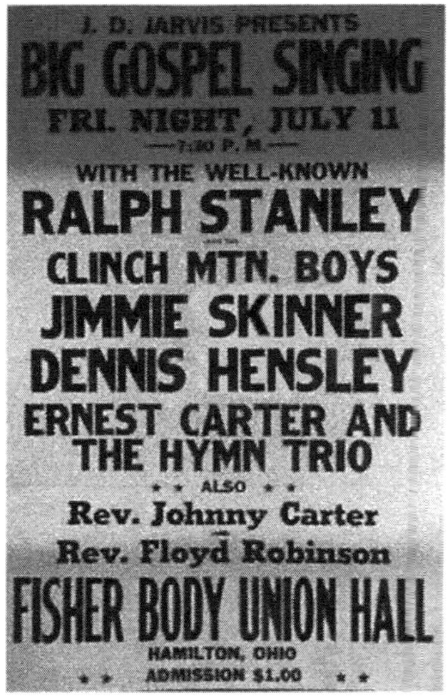

Poster for Hamilton, Ohio, gospel concert, 1968. (Mac McDivitt Private Collection)

The Jewel Recording Studio in the Cincinnati suburb of Mt. Healthy and its owner and engineer, Rusty York, 1972. (Photos by Carl Fleischhauer)

Joe Isaacs and the Sacred Bluegrass, 1982; left to right, Stanley Erock, Ben Isaacs, Mike Durham, Joe Isaacs, Troy Parker, Lily Isaacs, Rebecca Isaacs, Calvin Durham, Sonya Isaacs. (Fred Bartenstein Private Collection)

Lillimae and the Dixie Gospel-Aires, 1968; left to right, Junior Stennett, Curnie Collins, Charles Whitaker, Noah Hollon, Lillimae Haney Whitaker. (Ivan M. Tribe Private Collection)

The Boys from Indiana, 1975, Richmond, Kentucky; left to right, Noah Crase, Frank Godbey, Paul Mullins, Harley Gabbard, Jerry Holt, Aubrey Holt. (Photo by Marty Godbey; Frank Godbey Private Collection)

Left to right, Paul Mullins, Jerry Holt, Joe Mullins; early 1980s. (Photo by Leon Osborne for *Bluegrass Unlimited*; Courtesy of *Bluegrass Unlimited*; Mac McDivitt Private Collection)

The Traditional Grass, 1993; left to right, Mark Rader, Joe Mullins, Gerald Evans, Paul Mullins, Mike Clevenger. (Joe Mullins Private Collection)

For decades, starting in 1974, WYSO's *Rise When the Rooster Crows* began the day for Miami Valley residents with bluegrass and old-time music. (Art by Greg Dearth)

WMUB, at Miami University in Oxford, Ohio, broadcast Jan McLaughlin's *Oak Street Ramble* from 1981 to 2006. (Walter Havighurst Special Collections, Miami University, Oxford, Ohio)

Jim and Tom Duffee, along with their brother Dan (not pictured), hosted bluegrass/old-time country programs and performed on Antioch College's WYSO-FM, starting in the early 1970s. (WYSO Archives)

Fred Bartenstein, shown here at Dayton's WONE in 1980, also hosted bluegrass radio programs at WBZI, Xenia, and WYSO, Yellow Springs. (Photo by Susan Zurcher; Fred Bartenstein Private Collection)

Appalachian Mountain Day, later Mountain Days, was an annual celebration of Appalachian culture held at Dayton's Eastwood Park from 1986 to 2009; schedule is from the 1988 event. (Photo, UrbanOhio.com; Schedule image, Mac McDivitt Private Collection)

3rd Annual

Appalachian Mountain Day

FESTIVAL

Saturday, August 26 10 A.M. to 8 P.M.

Eastwood Park Dayton, Ohio

on Harshman Road near the Air Force Museum

$1.00 per person

Music..... Arts & Crafts..... Food

SPECIAL ATTRACTIONS

Sharon Lustre, Storyteller Dulcimer Player Knife Swap County Trees
Arts & Crafts Booths Liar's Corner Buckskinners Muzzleloaders
Children's Activities Canoe & Hay Rides Square Dancers Cloggers

SPECIAL GUEST PERFORMER GENE WATSON

BLUEGRASS STAGE *sound by Al Elam*		MAIN STAGE *sound by Darrel Marcum*	
11:00 - 11:45	Southern Nights	11:00	Dayton Ambassadors
11:45 - 12:30	Twin Valley Bluegrass	12:00	Darrel Marcum and
12:30 - 1:15	Dixie Riders		the Slick Nickel Band
1:15 - 2:00	Keith Lilly & Friends	1:00	Dayton Ambassadors
2:00 - 2:45	Southern Nights	2:00	Crystal River Band
3:00	*BREAK*	3:00	Gene Watson
4:00 - 4:45	Twin Valley Bluegrass	4:00	Darrel Marcum and
4:45 - 5:30	Dixie Riders		the Slick Nickel Band
6:00	*BREAK*	5:00	Crystal River Band
7:00 - 7:45	Keith Lilly & Friends	6:00	Gene Watson

Supported by

Our Common Heritage Miami Valley Arts Council
City of Dayton WONE *COORS*

No Bottles or Coolers, please

CALL 253-0322 FOR MORE INFORMATION

Program for the 1979 Appalachian Festival, a multiday annual event in Cincinnati begun in 1970 and continuing into the present. (Courtesy of Archives and Rare Books Library, University of Cincinnati)

Poster for the 1979 Stone Valley Bluegrass Festival, West Harrison, Indiana (Cincinnati metro), featuring numerous artists with current and former regional connections. (Mac McDivitt Private Collection)

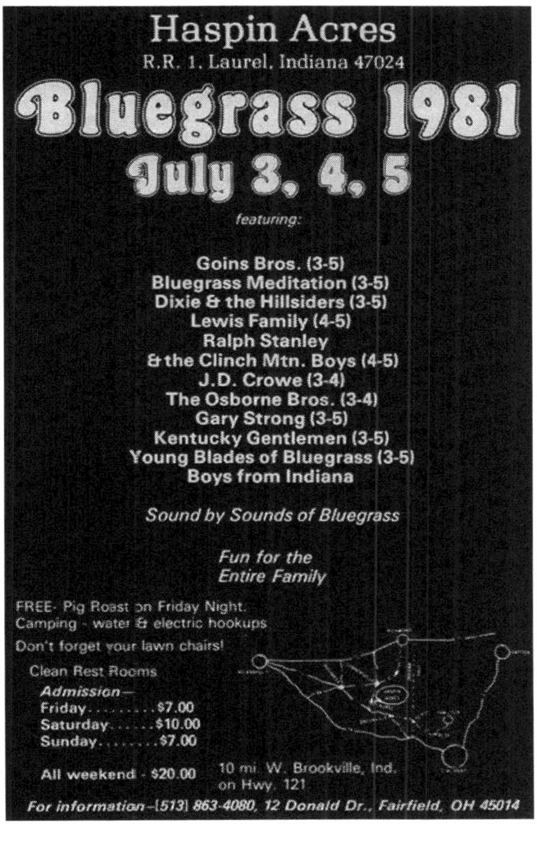

Advertisement for the 1981 Haspin Acres Bluegrass Festival in Laurel, Indiana. (Mac McDivitt Private Collection)

Left to right, Frank Wakefield, Red Spurlock, Larry Nager, and Red Allen at Cityfolk's Dayton Bluegrass Reunion, April 22, 1989. This event narrated the story of the region's rich bluegrass heritage and featured many of its legendary participants. It was held at Dayton's Memorial Hall, where Bill Monroe and His Blue Grass Boys first brought bluegrass music to the area in 1947. (Photo by Stephen Matyi for Cityfolk; Larry Nager Private Collection; Program cover image, Mac McDivitt Private Collection)

Middletown Traditions: Appalachian Ties chronicled the rich musical history of WPFB radio and southwestern Ohio, June 11–12, 1983, at Middletown's Sebald Park. (Mac McDivitt Private Collection)

9. The Living Arts Center's East Dayton Roots

RICK GOOD

IN THE 1960S AND '70S, Inner East Dayton was the bluegrass side of town. That's where many of the white factory workers made their homes—the "briarhoppers" who had left Kentucky, Tennessee, Virginia, and West Virginia to work for General Motors, National Cash Register, and other Ohio manufacturers. It was in the taverns of East Dayton that the second generation of bluegrass music thrived.

In 1967 the US Department of Health, Education, and Welfare awarded a grant of just over a million dollars to the Dayton Board of Education to fund an arts facility. Emphasizing creativity and self-expression, the Living Arts Center provided after-school instruction by a staff of professionals. The center served about four hundred students in an abandoned 1895 factory on Linden Avenue in East Dayton. It offered creative writing, dance, drama, music, and the visual arts to pupils in grades five through twelve, from the city and from other schools in Montgomery and Greene counties.

For ten years the Living Arts Center enhanced the region's cultural life, a vital source of inspiration and artistic expression. Looming over the street, a sidewalk's width from passing cars, the two-story brick structure was typical of Dayton's older industrial buildings. It had been repurposed on the inside with a seemingly endless maze of high-ceilinged studios, and on any given night one could wander the rambling halls and hear a high school jazz ensemble learning to swing, the metronomic rhythm of a piano accompanying a dance class, or the iambic pentameter of a Shakespearian soliloquy. The smell of linseed oil, palettes of paint, and darkroom chemicals filled the air, and the building vibrated with creative energy.

In 1975, well into the Living Arts Center's decade-long run, director Ernie Rock felt it was long past time to acknowledge the cultural roots of the center's

East Side neighborhood by providing programs that would engage the Appalachian population of the entire region. It was time, he rightly thought, to add some banjos and fiddles to the mix. To this end, Rock approached the Hotmud Family. Already well-known as part of the nationwide traditional music revival, the four-member band (where I played banjo) was in its fourth year, with two LPs on Cincinnati's Vetco Records and a long list of club and festival appearances. Our group had a strong local following and performed regularly on weekends at the now legendary Sam's Bar and Grill in downtown Dayton.[1] We had already reached an even younger generation during a fifteen-week stint with the Dayton Public School system, where we showcased string band music for an average of six classes a day in East Side schools. The Hotmud Family readily accepted Rock's invitation to join the Living Arts Center staff; we worked there two evenings a week for the next two years.

Every Tuesday night, Dave and Suzanne (Thomas) Edmundson, Harley Campbell, and I would host a "song swap" in one of the center's studios. Participants sat in a circle—usually about twenty aspiring musicians—and took turns playing songs and tunes from the traditional Appalachian repertoire. The song circles provided a weekly opportunity for a new generation to share in traditions that ran through the cultural fabric of the Miami Valley. We also gave one-on-one lessons to novice banjo, fiddle, mandolin, and guitar players. Scattered throughout the echoing halls and—weather permitting—outside in the parking lot, informal jam sessions with another two or three dozen local musicians offered more opportunities for people of all ages and abilities to share in the music making. For some it was a weekly trip "back home"; for others it was the beginning of a lifelong musical journey.

Kathy Anderson later became a nationally respected and well-loved square-dance caller. She recalls:

> It was a great entrée into the old-time and bluegrass scene. I was teaching at Fairview High School and my students went after school for pottery, weaving, and literature. I took pottery and t'ai chi classes there. When they opened up the Tuesday-night jam and Wednesday-night radio shows, I was delighted. I had wanted to learn banjo, so I connected with a group of women at the Tuesday song circle. Suzanne Edmundson, Becky Peapples, and Linda Scutt were my teachers in the ladies' room, the only quiet spot! Bluegrass banjo had been my goal, but I found old-time to be more my style.[2]

On Wednesday nights we took it to the stage for ninety minutes of music. Transmitted through a phone line from the Living Arts Center in Dayton to Antioch College in nearby Yellow Springs, the *Country Music Jamboree* was broadcast live over the airwaves of WYSO. In an October 1976 *Bluegrass Unlimited* article, local musician Al Turnbull captured the spirit of the weekly *Jamboree*:

Every Wednesday evening from 7:30 to 9:00 p.m., a bit of magic takes place at the Living Arts Center in Dayton, Ohio, and over the airwaves of WYSO-FM radio. Banjos, fiddles, guitars, singing, and an excited audience get together and create the *Country Music Jamboree*, one hour and thirty minutes of "live" bluegrass and old-time country music performed for a studio audience of several hundred enthusiastic folks.

The Hotmud Family and a core of volunteers, in conjunction and cooperation with the Dayton Public Schools and WYSO-FM radio, have worked long and hard to produce and develop programs each week, locate musicians to perform, coordinate the technical aspects, host the show, make everyone feel welcome and comfortable, and generally make sure that everything is running smoothly.

The net result is an exciting, informal, entertaining, educational program of good, down-home bluegrass and old-time country pickin' and singin' performed for the most part by local, amateur musicians. An occasional guest appearance by a nationally recognized group or individual has also added to the many "surprises" of the show.

The entire show is free and open to the public at the Living Arts Center, which has a seating capacity of several hundred folks (standing-room only each week has been an indication of the show's popularity) and it is broadcast live on the radio to thousands who listen regularly in the Dayton–Miami Valley area.

Old-timers who haven't played regularly for years and young people who are just learning get together and trade licks, swap tunes and stories, and provide their friends and neighbors in the audience with ninety minutes of good, solid pickin' and singin' that is hard to duplicate anywhere. There are no "commercial breaks" or paying sponsors.

Backstage, before the show, in the midst of musicians jamming, new friendships are made, acquaintances renewed, vintage instruments admired, styles compared, harmonies worked out, instruments tuned, and the order of performers is planned. Each group or performer is busily making last-minute decisions on their selection of tunes for the show.

The audiences are treated to shows featuring a variety of musicians from around the Dayton area, such as the exceptional fiddling craftsmanship of Arnold Cox, Van Kidwell, Wendell McCoy, or Harold Staggs; the intricate mandolin work of musicians such as David [Dorsey] Harvey, Ron Thomason, and Fred Hoskins; the banjo virtuosity of Bob Ferguson and Howard Brown; the amazing guitar flat-picking ability of Dan Spires; the personality, warmth, charm, and singing of Bill Lowe; the down-to-earth, easy-going, old-time pickin' and singin' style of the Duffee Brothers; the fine traditional bluegrass of Elzie and Danny Davis; the vocal and instrumental versatility of Phyllis Tipton Moyer; the special ability of Bill Stockwell to communicate the feeling of a song or story to others; plus many, many others.

The efforts of all these people have caused a rebirth of interest in bluegrass and old-time country music in the Dayton–Miami Valley area. They have found

> that some of the best bluegrass and country musicians and performers have been nearby all the time—neighbors just down the street or in the next town. Bluegrass and old-time country music has begun and renewed many lasting friendships and given us a feeling of community. The roots were always here; they needed only to be watered with encouragement and enthusiasm.

Al Turnbull's enthusiasm mirrors that of many who, more than forty years later, still cherish the memories of what now seems like a bluegrass renaissance. Jim Johnson, an accomplished fretless banjo player and a lifelong member of Dayton's traditional music scene, recalls:

> The Living Arts Center was the anchor of my introduction to bluegrass and old-time music. On Tuesday nights everyone sat in a big circle and, one by one, each person or two would play a song they'd just learned or a tune they wished to share. The next night, if you felt confident enough, you could go on stage in front of an audience and play live on WYSO radio, right up there between the professional bands. This was a very positive learning experience.
>
> I remember the great banjo player Mike Lilly riding his Harley into the building . . . walking into the men's room and watching J. D. Crowe primping his pompadour . . . hanging out in the hallway watching Dorsey Harvey tune his mandolin . . . banjo wunderkind Terry Tipton explaining to me this new "chromatic" style he was messing around with, and how I lusted after his bow-tie Mastertone. It was at the Living Arts Center that I first met some of the folks who went on to form the Corn Drinkers. Tom Duffee amazed me then with his depth of knowledge, a feeling that has matured into one of solemn respect.
>
> On Thursday nights we would journey up to a Yellow Springs jam session and play stuff we'd heard at the Living Arts Center. Then, on Friday, it was off to Sam's Bar and Grill. My lord, the bands I saw! The Allen Brothers, the Hotmud Family, the Hagan Brothers, the Falls City Ramblers, the Dry Branch Fire Squad. . . . Thinking of those '70s Dayton bands, it occurs to me how great an influence Red Allen and Ralph Stanley had on the local scene. It's a style I like to call "bargrass," something played in honky-tonks, not in hollers. With this pedigree, I should be a better banjo player than I am, but that's a whole 'nuther story.[3]

I can add to these recollections a few special memories of my own:

- Orville Gillespie of Gratis, Ohio, singing "The Dying Cowgirl," a heart-wrenching ballad I never forgot or heard again.
- Jim Morrison, a Dayton transplant from Renfro Valley, Kentucky, picking "Trouble on the Brandywine," a banjo tune that only he played until I learned it from him.
- Local songwriter Dave Gordon, not only blowing people away with his remarkable songs but also his dazzling "Watson-esque" flat-picking.

- Young Terry Tipton accompanying his dad and sister with his latest Sonny Osborne–inspired licks.
- Dorsey Harvey playing the "Blue Grass Stomp" on his stove-baked Gibson mandolin.
- Tom Duffee, Barb Kuhns, Linda Scutt, Doug Smith, and Al Turnbull—aka the Corndrinkers—starting their "forty years and still going" run.
- A rowdy trio of Scandinavian musicians who hit as many festivals as they could one summer and followed us home.
- The hyper-driven bluegrass of our visiting East Coast buddies, Bottle Hill.
- Larry Sparks commanding the stage with Mike Lilly and Wendy Miller.
- The thrill of playing banjo with Red Allen.

Federal funding ended after three years, but the Living Arts Center kept going until Dayton Public Schools budget cuts closed it in 1977. Sometimes one looks back to recognize past places and events that turn out to be more significant than previously imagined. But when it comes to my time at the Living Arts Center, I knew—just as everyone else there knew—that it was destined to become the "good old days." And indeed it was.

Notes

1. See chapter 8, "Buckeyes in the Briar Patch."
2. Personal communication from Kathy Anderson, October 29, 2019.
3. Personal communication from Jim Johnson, November 4, 2019.

10. Bluegrass Music and Urban Appalachian Identity in Cincinnati

NATHAN McGEE

IN THE MID-1980S, an Appalachian migrant named Dave Banks sat down with an interviewer for a conversation about living in Cincinnati. The discussion turned briefly to music and to Aunt Maudie's, the Cincinnati nightspot. Banks happily gave his opinion of the place: "Hardly any Appalachian folks goes in there much, 'cause, one thing, you got a two-dollar cover charge which people don't believe you have to pay just to go hear music. Another thing, they don't allow no dancin.'"[1]

For many, the popular bar represented a hallmark of Appalachian mountain traditions. Banks, however, saw the opposite: "All you have in there is your jet setters from Mount Adams that come down and think it's so groovy to hear a little bluegrass, or you get some of the college babies. . . . And you can't hear the music half the time in 'er. 'Cause they're all hootin' an' hollerin' an' then they think they gotta stomp their foot, and it's almost insultin' to ya if ya really enjoy the music."[2] When friends from Harlan County, Kentucky, came to visit, Banks sometimes suggested a trip to Maudie's only to see their disappointment. "They didn't like it at all," he recalled.

Despite these protestations—one voice among, no doubt, many similar ones—the years between 1960 and 1980 saw the words "bluegrass" and "Appalachian" become increasingly associated. Paradoxically, this was the very time in which the musical genre was growing in an urban context. A Google Ngram based on a global search of online sources discloses that popular usage of the two words rose and fell in relative consistency through these decades.[3]

Commercial bluegrass music—as historians have increasingly noted—is not of Appalachian geographic origin.[4] Yet, from its beginnings and throughout its infancy, the "high lonesome sound" became strongly associated with that American region. Despite the influence of blues, jazz, and religious traditions

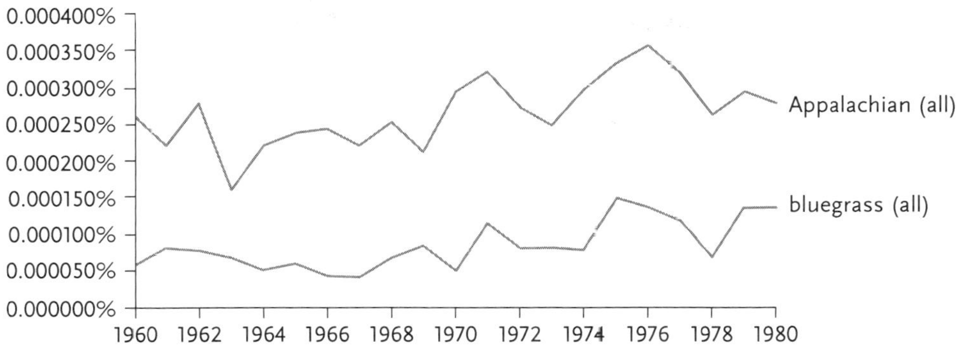

Google Ngram of "Appalachian" and "bluegrass"

from elsewhere on the evolution of bluegrass music, its Appalachian connections were stressed by musicologists who saw a direct line from British ballad singing and Appalachian fiddle tunes of the nineteenth century to the fast-driving mandolin and syncopated three-finger banjo style of modern bluegrass.

A case study of one city, Cincinnati, discloses how the intersection of a folk-music boom, Appalachian migration, and late-1960s identity politics led to a *bluegrass* phenomenon that became increasingly understood as *Appalachian*.

Appalachian "Authenticity"

American interest in Appalachia as a folk region and ideas about the authenticity of its music have existed since at least the turn of the twentieth century. Folklorists, urban reformers, and Christian missionaries each brought their own perceptions about mountain people and mountain life, and invented myths that still abound in popular understandings of Appalachia. For example, the region has been perceived as a place untouched by modernity, where "our contemporary ancestors" abide and cherish quaint archaic traditions.[5] It has also long been identified as a "strange land" full of "peculiar people," prone to the exotic feuding epitomized by the Hatfield-McCoy conflict on the Kentucky–West Virginia border. Nineteenth-century urban reformers also saw in the region's inhabitants what later generations have repeatedly found, "authenticity." This word carries much baggage, but understanding how individuals across disparate eras conceived of what it meant to be authentic is key to understanding the growth and popularity of bluegrass music.

Historian David Whisnant has noted how, in the post–World War II era, popular understandings of Southern music developed in an American "mainstream starved for rooted cultural energy and authenticity."[6] While the nation appeared to become more culturally uniform and its popular culture more regionally undifferentiated, the baby boom generation sought music that reflected something more than the capitalist trappings of the era.[7]

As Southerners moved north in the mid-twentieth century, Southern culture began to be nationalized. Fascination with Southern culture grew in parallel with the migrations. The rising popularity of Southern music was linked both to its increasing visibility and to a desire for authentic expression amid the racial, cultural, and political changes that marked the decades after World War II. Southern music—whether country, blues, or bluegrass—was and still is used to connote "simpler times" by individuals on both the political right and left.

Baby boomers who felt alienated from their roots and their country often took to activism as a means of finding their more authentic selves. Doug Rossinow, writing about the New Left in the 1960s and '70s, observed that "the search for authenticity lay at the heart" of that movement.[8] Activist causes consumed decades and led individuals of this generation in disparate directions. One such direction involved embracing the culture of Appalachia, its novelty, and its "authenticity."

The notion of Appalachia as a folk region rooted modern perceptions of bluegrass music in an "authentic" mountain past. The resilient hillbilly archetype, itself a product of the invention of "Appalachia" in the late nineteenth century, also became embedded in the popular image of bluegrass. To present an authentic image, musicians emphasized their connections to Appalachia specifically or the South more generally, drawing on the history and popular understanding of these regions. They accomplished this most often through biography: the story of their family past and bluegrass music connections made along the way.

Place of geographic origin became an important element for establishing an authentic bluegrass identity. Previous direct mountain connections had the most persuasive appeal for a musician who was a migrant or descendant of a migrant. If local musicians could trace their musical genealogy backward to the founding of the bluegrass genre, all the better. For others, claiming as one's place of origin a romantically rural-sounding Kentucky hamlet like Peewee Valley or Rabbit Hash provided greater credibility and status than rooting one's origins in Louisville or Cincinnati.

Stylistic choices, especially recreating bluegrass sounds of the past, could provide another element of authenticity to one's music. Folklorist and radio personality John Lair, who founded the *Renfro Valley Barn Dance*,[9] considered music of the urban folk revival to be inauthentic but bluegrass to be derivative of the "old-time" music he championed for decades on the radio. Lair not only neglected or denied the extent to which his programs were themselves designed to evoke a fictive past, but he also sometimes hid from his radio audience the reality behind his artists' constructed narratives.[10]

Authenticity is a moving target, defined by what one historian has termed a "folk process," in which "local community cultures give each tradition its own inflection, and its history (changing over time)."[11] As the popularity of bluegrass grew nationally during the folk revival of the 1950s and '60s, Cincinnati's Appalachian migrants and alienated urban baby boomers co-created a local bluegrass scene. These fans sought out artists, repertoire, and venues that embraced aspects of "authentic" Appalachian and hillbilly archetypes.

Earl Taylor: An "Authentic" Bluegrass Figure

Cincinnati's bluegrass tradition developed around the figure of Earl Taylor. Taylor emerged on the Cincinnati scene in the 1960s, just as the baby boom generation came of age, urban Appalachian migration peaked, and a new sense of activism arose in American cities.

Taylor's life had begun in 1930 in the small town of Rose Hill, amid the fruitful musical cradle of far southwestern Virginia that had recently produced the Carter Family. His background gave him the credibility of an authentic Appalachian. He often referred to his home region as "that last part of old Virginia," embedding his legacy in the founding era of American history.[12] Other bluegrass legends, such as the Stanley Brothers and Jim and Jesse, first cut their musical teeth in this same region. Taylor's family surrounded him with music from an early age. He had four brothers who played clawhammer banjo and a mother who nurtured his own latent talent.

As a child, Earl Taylor stumbled upon Bill Monroe, who was then playing on the radio with his brother Charlie as the Monroe Brothers. Taylor came to idolize Monroe's musical styling, particularly his mandolin playing. As with so many musicians, this interest quickly developed into an obsession. He recalled, "I'd come in at twelve o'clock of a day and swallow my lunch as fast as I could and pick [on the mandolin] just a little bit. And then [my brothers would] make me go back to the fields to keep me from picking."[13] Shortly thereafter, Taylor also took up the harmonica and found its portability to his liking.

Taylor went north, like so many people in the World War II era, and found work as a laborer before he started filling in as a musician on the radio and in live shows. At the age of seventeen Taylor moved to Michigan, following a path blazed by an acquaintance from Rose Hill. Detroit was an emerging country music haven, thanks to the thousands of migrants who populated postwar auto factories.[14] Taylor won a talent competition and earned a job with a local band there, but its western-swing style did not suit his ear.

By the late 1940s, Taylor's idol Bill Monroe had formed the Blue Grass Boys and pioneered—along with Lester Flatt and Earl Scruggs and the Stanley Brothers—the style of music that would later be known as bluegrass. Taylor recruited two musicians from Cincinnati who shared his love for the new sound and brought them to the Detroit area to form the first incarnation of his Stoney Mountain Boys. The band lasted just a short while, however, and Taylor moved east, this time to Rockville, Maryland.

In Rockville, as in other suburbs of the Washington/Baltimore metropolitan area, picking parties became common among migrant groups. At one of these gatherings, Taylor met Vernon "Boatwhistle" McIntyre, and the two began a musical partnership. Taylor reformed his Stoney Mountain Boys with all new members and joined the local musical scene as a popular group.

In 1953 the band moved to Baltimore, and Taylor recruited a fiddler he met on the street. The new band did not immediately find work. Taylor had only performed at parties and other social gatherings since his short stint in Michigan. He promised his new band that Baltimore would prove more profitable than Rockville.

When club owners rebuffed his band's efforts at nearly every turn, Taylor found a part-time job hanging drywall alongside fellow musician Charlie Waller, later of the Country Gentlemen. One afternoon the work crew sat in Waller's car on the way home from a day's labor when they happened upon some bluegrass music on the radio. The two listened for a time before Earl looked around the car and said, "What those boys need is a tenor singer and a mandolin player. I won't be in to work tomorrow." He subsequently showed up at the radio station and joined the house band.[15] Taylor's group quickly transitioned into nightly work in clubs around the city, sometimes as many as nine gigs a week.[16] This pattern lasted for approximately two years before Taylor and banjo player Sam Hutchins left Baltimore for Detroit.

Their decision to leave echoed a pattern followed by radio stars of an earlier generation. Artists would work an area until it became "played out" and then move to a new region. It is possible that Taylor was similarly motivated as he moved on to new cities, hoping for bigger paydays. The relatively small number and close network of bluegrass musicians also encouraged some of this moving about.

Just before Taylor's and Hutchins's arrival, Jimmy Martin's collaboration with the Osborne Brothers in Detroit ended, and Martin needed a band. He hired Hutchins and Taylor after a one-night audition at a club, and the two became important participants in some of Martin's most popular recordings, including "Hit Parade of Love."[17] Taylor contributed to Martin's success during this time, and the collaboration resulted in a once-removed tie to his childhood idol Bill Monroe.[18] This band lasted just a few years, however, and then Taylor and Hutchins went back East.

In Baltimore, Earl Taylor reformed his own group, this time hiring Walter Hensley to play banjo. A fellow migrant from the coal mines of Grundy, Virginia, Hensley had come to Baltimore in 1956. This new iteration of the Stoney Mountain Boys made an appearance on *Mountain Music Bluegrass Style*, an album Mike Seeger produced for Folkways. Hensley came to epitomize the fast-paced and hard-driving urban banjo style eventually associated with Baltimore. Folklorist Alan Lomax described Hensley as "intense, randy, and ironic" and commented that "there [is] true folk music in every note he plays."[19] Lomax hired this edition of the band for a 1959 multi-genre folk music concert in New York, the first appearance of bluegrass music at Carnegie Hall.

Following the Carnegie Hall performance, the band traveled around the Midwest, looking to expand their brand and find steady work. Most of their forays did not end well; brief stays in Kansas City and Chicago left them wanting for jobs. Taylor barnstormed the Atlantic states before once again settling in Baltimore.

He came to Cincinnati around 1960 and helped forge a powerful musical connection between that city and Baltimore, two hotbeds of urban bluegrass activity. In Cincinnati he and his band found a six-night-a-week job at a local watering hole, the Ken-Mill Café, just northeast of downtown.[20] Over the early part of the decade, this club became notorious for its rowdiness. Despite the negative attributes that became associated with the place, those who went there remember it fondly.

Memories of the Ken-Mill are often tied to the character of the owner, Stewart Salmons. It was rumored that he kept a loaded weapon near the cash register as a crowd-control device, operated a prostitution ring out of the club, and had done time in prison for murder.[21] John Morgan summed up his experiences at the Ken-Mill in a *Bluegrass Unlimited* article: "Drunken fights were fairly common. Usually one just had to step back and avoid any thrown bottles. Once, however, as I nobly protected a young lady from the pushing and shoving of a fight, I realized the dark object being waved near my head by one of the fighters was a revolver. I stayed away for at least a month after that."[22]

Gossip about alleged criminal activity only added to the Ken-Mill's aura of authenticity and its reputation as the best place in Cincinnati to see and hear tried-and-true bluegrass music. Similar recollections are found in articles about other early bluegrass clubs around the country.[23] The band and the owner, in short, seemed to live up—or down as the case may be—to the various stereotypes developed about Appalachians.

Taylor's band opened up opportunities for urban musicians to join him and become part of what they perceived as an authentic Appalachian experience. Numerous musicians recounted that seeing Taylor was their first exposure to *authentic* bluegrass.[24] Many later Cincinnati bluegrass legends honed their skills playing or enjoying Taylor's music. He came to represent an archetype of Appalachian character in the urban environment, often described as a "natural" musician, largely illiterate, and always in possession of a knife or a stronger implement of self-defense.

He also became notable for never changing his essential sound over the course of his rather long career. He made a living emulating his idol Bill Monroe, and, while this may have helped cement his authenticity as a musician, it did not necessarily aid his pocketbook. His obliviousness to finances shocked some of his bandmates, as did his more than occasional indifference to regular work. All of this was often chalked up to natural tendencies, to "Earl being Earl," as numerous people have remembered. This behavior magnified his aura of authenticity.

The Ken-Mill became the yardstick against which all other Cincinnati bluegrass venues were subsequently measured. The rough reputation became part of its charm; worries about guns, knives, and fights were perceived as part of the *real* Appalachian character of the venue. As the bluegrass scene shifted to the Cincinnati neighborhood of Over-the-Rhine, more musicians discovered the allure of Earl Taylor, and eventually his music intersected with interests of civic groups like the Urban Appalachian Council.

Jeff Roberts: A New-Generation Cincinnati Bluegrass Musician

A new generation of bluegrass players emerged in the 1970s.[25] Some of its members had been steeped in the music from childhood, attached to both the Appalachian migration and the urban folk revival. Cincinnati musician Jeff Roberts's life typifies this pattern. Born in the small town of Crab Orchard, Kentucky, in the Appalachian foothills, Roberts's family moved to northern Kentucky when he was a child and eventually settled in Covington. Roberts credited his roots in Crab Orchard with his musical foundation. "You go back, you visit the grandparents," he remembered, "and I think as far as the music goes, my parents had it in them."[26] Note Roberts's allusion to a natural proclivity toward a musical sound, a hallmark of its authenticity.

As an urban resident, Roberts, and others like him, did not have to travel far to seek out live performances of music that sounded to them like home. Roberts had an early band in high school and after graduating, around 197[illegible], he began envisioning his music as a serious professional career. At the Kings Row bar, near the University of Cincinnati campus, Roberts found a band—the Appalachian Grass—playing nightly gigs. He recalled, "I just *stayed* there. I wanted to know as much about the business, as much about the music and the people that played, and learning as much material as I could . . . [and] sit in with bands when they'd let me sit in and learn as much banjo as I could. I was totally consumed with the music. *Totally*. To where I didn't want to do anything else."[27]

Such visits soon paid dividends in the form of full-time jobs. In addition to King's Row, Roberts also visited Aunt Maudie's in Over-the-Rhine to see Earl Taylor. "I was going to Aunt Maudie's, listening to him play and his band, and I got to know his banjo player Jeff Campbell," Roberts said. "Jeff quit and Earl asked me if I wanted to play banjo with him, and I did."[28] For Roberts, the opportunity to play and tour with Taylor certified his status as a true bluegrass player. In 1975 Roberts noted he finally "felt like I got a *real* bluegrass gig playing the banjo with a bluegrass guy that people knew. . . . He was kind of a bluegrass legend. . . . He was a real name; that was a big step for me."[29]

Urban Appalachian Activism

In Cincinnati the search for bluegrass authenticity was connected to an Appalachian identity movement. Concurrent with the nightclub developments and individuals like Roberts joining the bluegrass sound, United Appalachian Cincinnati emerged, a forerunner to the Urban Appalachian Council. The scholars and activists involved in this group professed to speak for the Appalachian population in the city and sought to develop a positive identity for the migrant group. Historian Bruce Tucker notes that from the beginning, "these activists claimed a public identity for urban Appalachians and the power to tell other Cincinnatians who they were and what they needed."[30] As was typical in the Cold War era, new advocates and activists searched for cultural and political affirmation within America's "melting pot" of cultures.[31] For urban Appalachians, this often meant embracing a renewed interest in their home region and its people.[32]

In addition to exposing the general population to the culture and needs of Appalachians, activists in the group worked to teach Appalachians about themselves. Their efforts were similar to those of many other groups immersed in identity politics of the era. To a great degree, activists piggybacked on mainstream culture's existing perceptions about the people with whom they worked. These urban reformers were inventing "Appalachian" identity and ethnicity in the city, helping to explain an increased use of the term as the decade progressed. They created something not wholly new by borrowing from comfortable notions about the Appalachian people and a softened image that was rooted in early twentieth-century romantic literature.

Appalachian people who had moved to urban centers in the years after World War II often intended to move out of decaying urban cores and assimilate into middle-class culture. While many of them were successful in doing so, generations of urban reformers observed and addressed problems of continued poverty and poor education in the urban core.

In Cincinnati a nascent advocacy group emerged out of the Mayor's Friendly Relations Commission, which was renamed the Cincinnati Human Relations Commission in 1965. It steadily grew in size in the 1960s and '70s. Reformers within the group worked with others to provide services to the urban Appalachian population in the city. They established a new model for Appalachian advocacy that corrected the "culture of poverty" approach that had dominated sociological and political thinking of previous decades.

These new advocates—often younger, college-educated, and migrants themselves—occasionally embraced New Left cultural ideals, especially the notion of identity politics. As a result, they tried to establish a new positive sense of "Appalachian-ness" as a means of pulling urban migrants out of poverty. They often participated in the folk music scene as well, reflecting the general overlap of music and activism that was emerging in this period.

Urban Appalachian aid efforts proved strongest and most organized in Cincinnati, though the movement occurred elsewhere with varying success. In Cincinnati a coalition of disparate groups pursued the same approaches: developing positive identity for Appalachian culture through self-affirmation, and cultural outreach showcasing positive aspects of Appalachians.

Mike Maloney, a migrant who came to Cincinnati from Breathitt County, Kentucky, to study at Mount St. Mary's of the West, involved himself in these efforts from nearly the beginning of his time in the city. Later, as a student at Xavier University, Maloney worked for various War on Poverty initiatives in addition to pursuing a degree in education. He recalled that, around 1966, "I got a part-time job as a community organizer in Walnut Hills [the neighborhood home of the Ken-Mill]. They wanted an Appalachian on the staff because there was still some Appalachians living in Walnut Hills at the time."[33]

Maloney's move into activism occurred concurrently with other local initiatives. Ernie Mynatt, another migrant from Harlan County, Kentucky, began teaching in the Over-the-Rhine neighborhood in 1960. Maloney referred to him as the "patriarch and founder of the movement." Much of what developed in later years came through Mynatt's connections to influential people.[34]

In Cincinnati, Mynatt met Stuart Faber, whose father established the Appalachian Fund to aid migrants working in his Formica plant. Faber assumed control of the fund in 1956, and the group sought leaders to help organize the city's large Appalachian population. Mynatt fit that need. Faber noted how Mynatt "sensitized many people to the culture and unique problems of Appalachian people" and used an approach that avoided stigmatizing Appalachian cultural traits.[35]

Mynatt practiced his outreach through evangelism. He walked the streets of the neighborhood, developing name recognition and personal relationships with the local population. Eventually, residents began to approach him to talk about issues in their homes and lives. Faber recalled the listening techniques practiced by Mynatt as revolutionary for the time, far removed from the top-down assimilation attempts of prior years.[36] In 1964 Mynatt established the Main Street Bible Center in Over-the-Rhine. It attempted to mimic the storefront churches that migrants had established on the city's streets. Workers in the center did proselytize and attempt to convert residents, but also recognized the need for additional social services and immersed themselves in that work as well.

The center took an ecumenical approach to social work. Maloney remembered, "Ernie got most of his volunteer troops from seminarians, ex-seminarians, nuns, ex-nuns. One of his key volunteers was Quaker, so there [were] others involved. And there were Lutherans doing GED work and that sort of thing."[37] Mynatt remembered the center, which lasted until 1972, as the beginning of consolidated efforts to help Appalachians in the area.

Mynatt went on to organize and found a program called Hub Services, based in Over-the-Rhine, that provided a more secular approach to aid. Maloney recalled that "it was a multi-service agency funded with anti-poverty funds, and Ernie recruited me to be the outreach director of that program."[38] This was the first step for Maloney in becoming one of Mynatt's main "lieutenants," as he puts it.[39] Hub Services became a one-stop for all social service needs of Appalachian people and other neighborhood residents. This strategy echoed other attempts to coordinate the many War on Poverty programs that proliferated throughout the decade.

Maloney recognized a need for outreach programs and organizations tailored to the specific life challenges Appalachians were facing during migration and resettlement. He recalled his experience with the civil rights movement as a major impetus for recognizing how a positive sense of "consciousness" among Appalachians would be different from that of the Black Power movement:

> As a community organizer working with both blacks and [white] Appalachians, it eventually became clear that we needed to do some special work with Appalachians. As one of my black friends put it, "Mike, you can't tag along on the civil rights movement. You need to do some work with your own people." And that fit my experience, 'cause I would take white Appalachians to black rallies, and [they would respond], "What is going on here?!" This was the period of riots and turmoil in inner-city America, and our folks just didn't know what to make of that. You just couldn't get them to the second meeting.[40]

Migrants to the city were losing touch with their roots, and, rather than helping them assimilate, that loss was thought to contribute to issues of crime, poverty, and inadequate education in Appalachian sections of the city. Leaders of organizations like the Appalachian Identity Center (AIC) sought ways to provide renewed contact with those roots, build self-esteem, and aid broader assimilation. The AIC emphasized aspects of Appalachian character that city residents and the population at large would find palatable and familiar. This was the inverse of older methods that encouraged members of minority cultures to abandon their heritage in order to achieve greater public acceptance.[41]

In the early 1970s the loosely organized United Appalachian Cincinnati led a multipronged approach toward teaching both the larger city and Appalachians about the Appalachian population. In March they opened the Appalachian Identity Center in the same Over-the-Rhine neighborhood as the Main Street Bible Center. Founder Ernie Mynatt hoped for an improved version of some of his previous approaches. From the beginning, AIC emphasized a positive vision of Appalachian character. "Other approaches in working with Appalachian youth have largely failed," Mynatt wrote. "It is time to try something new. The culture of the Southern mountaineer has a lot to offer. Renewed contact with it should be a part of the emergence of Appalachians into urban society as strong, free, and open individuals."[42]

The Intersection of Music and Advocacy

As Appalachian leaders searched for ways to promote a positive Appalachian identity, they reached into the past—sometimes a romanticized past—to present an appealing image. Music helped to drive the popular reconsideration of Appalachia. It operated as the single most visible, positive form of Appalachian culture in the contemporary lives of urban residents.

In the spring of 1970, the city of Cincinnati hosted its first Appalachian Festival, an event that subsequently became an annual spring tradition. The festivals reflected activists' new vision of Appalachian identity, far removed from local attitudes of the 1950s and early '60s when Appalachian character was typically viewed as needing redemption. Positive cultural traits were showcased in these folk festivals, although they sometimes bordered on caricature. In 1971 the Appalachian Festival moved to Cincinnati's historic Music Hall, where a two-day arts and crafts festival accompanied daily live music.[43] This festival served as the culmination of an Appalachian Week in Cincinnati that included programs focusing on the positive culture of mountain people. Earl Taylor and the Stoney Mountain Boys headlined, along with Grand Ole Opry star Roy Acuff.[44] Musicians also held sessions and workshops demonstrating traditional styles and songs.

Mainstream interest in Appalachian folk culture easily connected to the bluegrass revival that was already on display for urban residents in hip venues far different from the rough bars where an earlier generation of urban migrants had brought their music to Cincinnati. The Appalachian Festival developed during the time that a bluegrass festival scene was growing nationally.[45] The Cincinnati festival did not rely solely on bluegrass, but music increasingly became part of its appeal, and the equating of bluegrass and Appalachian culture was magnified as a result. The Cincinnati Appalachian Festival made the bluegrass and cultural connection explicit when the 1979 festival adopted as its motto "Our History Is Our Music."[46]

All of these efforts combined to present an idealized image of urban Appalachians. They pushed the image of bluegrass music back in time, envisioning pastoral origins far removed from seedy clubs where two decades earlier the music had thrived. Now bluegrass musicians performed alongside basket weavers, quilt makers, and craftspeople in gingham dresses and other traditional garb. This version of the Appalachian story was quite different from the downtrodden, shoeless, violent, and backward image the city had heard about in earlier years. The new image for Cincinnati's Appalachians intersected with the interest of some advocates in a political as well as a cultural movement.

Mike Henson, the Heritage Room, and Katie Laur

Mike Henson first engaged in Appalachian advocacy during the late 1960s. He came to Cincinnati, from a family with roots in the Deep South, to study at Xavier University. Like many in that decade, he was attracted to Appalachian work because of the politics of the era and his own search for identity:

> I got into Appalachian volunteer stuff, and it spoke to me, and I realized those are my roots too. It wasn't mountains, but this was what I could relate to. My mother was an Irish Catholic from Massachusetts; she was very proud of her [roots], but my dad, I had to dig to find that side of myself.
>
> I first came [to Over-the-Rhine] in 1968 and it was teeming [with people]. A lot more people occupying a lot more buildings. . . . It was all just straight-up-to-the-sky families. Most of them were white Appalachian, from East Kentucky and West Virginia, and a lot of displaced coal miners, and a lot of musicians. So one of the things I was doing at that time was trying to find musicians.[47]

Henson's interest in both the neighborhood and bluegrass music stemmed partly from a more general interest in folk music and culture. "My grandpa was a musician," he said. "He sang the pre-bluegrass stuff. He was my idol growing up." Henson quickly immersed himself in the musical scene of Over-the-Rhine: "Sometimes sittin' out there on Orchard Street, I'd just bring my guitar out on the front . . . stoop and a neighbor would show up with his fiddle. And this guy, you know, back in his younger days had played on the radio down home with bands, and we'd pick for an hour."[48]

Henson focused on culture and music as he took on greater roles as a community activist.[49] In 1973 the Appalachian Committee within the Cincinnati

Human Rights Commission submitted a proposal for an Appalachian Heritage Room. The Heritage Room became another tangible embodiment of identifying and spreading the message about positive Appalachian traits. The proposal placed this room inside the Washington Park School in Over-the-Rhine, at the time a 70 percent Appalachian white neighborhood. Despite a high poverty rate, leaders within the Appalachian Committee believed that "the people of the neighborhood [had] many strengths" and that "develop[ing] a sense of community" within the population would be the first step in enabling those strengths.[50] The proposal emphasized a cultural approach to helping the resident population reach higher levels of achievement at both the school and in the city generally. The stated goal of the project was "to foster the mutual respect and understanding of the different cultural backgrounds at [the school]: Appalachian, Southern migrant, and urban patterns of culture."[51]

The Heritage Room made efforts to bring in authentic examples of cultural activities by working with popular musicians and other artists in the city. "We did a lot of jamming at the Heritage Room," Henson recalled. "It was kind of a mix between folkies [and] bluegrass. So there [was] this kind of anonymous level of people that they'd just show up. You just never knew."[52] The Heritage Room proved effective in drawing some interest by the Appalachian community and the population at large, but it did so by suggesting familiar notions of what it meant to be an authentic Appalachian. The room also attracted people whose interest was solely in the music. The University of Cincinnati Bluegrass Club attempted to establish a relationship there, and regional bluegrass acts often participated in programs.[53]

UAC advocates maintained that "the thread that holds all this diverse programming together is *cultural affirmation*. We provide the physical base for cultural celebration. But we also stand by with a constant message of pride and respect, a sense that whatever we do at the Heritage Room comes not from a misplaced charity but from a shared sense of pride in who we are, where we have come from, and a conviction that we can move forward from there."[54]

The Heritage Room provided one form of outreach; others took Appalachian culture directly to the people. The locally popular Katie Laur Band used connections to Appalachian organizations to stay busy during slower months of the festival off-season. Laur recalled, "One of the first things [our band] did was to get a government grant to play in the Cincinnati Appalachian district schools. I went to the Urban Appalachian Council . . . and we thought it desperately needed to be done in Cincinnati. We got the grant and hooked up with the PTAs to sponsor us."[55]

Laur and company were somewhat surprised by the lack of knowledge among children in local schools about their own Appalachian cultural background and used the grant to expose students to it: "We explained the history of the instruments and were big on letting the kids touch them, and then we did little programs. We did mostly old-time and Appalachian things like 'Pawn You My Gold Watch and Chain,' 'You Are My Flower,' 'Froggy Went a Courtin',' and 'Wreck of the Old '97,' and always 'Banks of the Ohio.' The program lasted a few months in the winter and then we started doing PTA programs with the whole band, and that helped us financially through the winter."[56]

With UAC and other organizations, such musical activities served as a cultural introduction as well as providing enrichment for students and families in the schools.

* * *

Through much of the 1970s, conceptions of what it meant to be an authentic Appalachian and what authentic Appalachian culture looked like gradually coalesced around music. Essential notions about culture dovetailed with essential notions about bluegrass, helping to cement Earl Taylor as a quintessential figure.

Although many city residents, and bluegrass fans everywhere, had long associated the music's sound with the Appalachia mountains, the growth and prosperity of bluegrass had largely occurred outside that region. Cincinnati's Appalachian community advocates, capitalizing on the music's popularity, worked hard to form urban Appalachian identity by driving the sound back up the mountains and into the past, in doing so inadvertently deemphasizing the music's rich urban evolution.

Many years later, when she was asked about her personal concept of identity, Cincinnati resident Lucy Peterson—a neighbor of the same Mr. Banks who disliked Aunt Maudie's—said, "'Appalachian.' What in the hell is 'apple'? I could never say it no how."[57]

Lucy Peterson, and perhaps others like her, may not have been able to define or even pronounce "Appalachia." But by the end of the 1970s there was little doubt that it *sounded* something like bluegrass music.

Notes

1. Dave Banks interview with John R. Williams in "Appalachian Migrants in Cincinnati, Ohio: The Role of Folklore in the Reinforcement of Ethnic Identity," PhD diss., Indiana University, 1985, 180.

2. Ibid., 181.

3. The Google Ngram graph tracks written language word usage in works collected by Google's digital book project.

4. Bill C. Malone, *Bill Clifton: America's Bluegrass Ambassador to the World* (Urbana: University of Illinois Press, 2016), 17. "The belief in the presumed 'Appalachian origins' of country music . . . has been endlessly appealing to Americans, and hillbillies themselves . . . have been seduced by the notion that their music came not from the often

sordid commercial interchange between rural and urban America but from a pristine, tradition-oriented, and semi-isolated way of life."

5. William Goodell Frost, "Our Contemporary Ancestors in the Southern Mountains," reprinted from *Atlantic Monthly*, March 1899, https://www.theatlantic.com/magazine/archive/1899/03/our-contemporary-ancestors-southern-mountains/581332/.

6. David Whisnant, *All That Is Native and Fine: The Politics of Culture in an American Region* (Chapel Hill: University of North Carolina Press, 2009), 7.

7. Country music historians have noted a similar process.

8. Doug Rossinow, *Politics of Authenticity: Liberalism, Christianity, and the New Left in America* (New York: Columbia University Press, 1998), 4.

9. See chapter 3, "All the Way to the Fence."

10. See Michael Ann Williams, *Staging Tradition* (Urbana: University of Illinois Press, 2006), for more on the manufactured Lair image. This debate overall is borne out in numerous works on country music history, in particular Richard A. Peterson, *Creating Country Music* (Chicago: University of Chicago Press, 1997). Others deal with the common language trope of "real" country music, distinguishing it from the more "manufactured" Nashville approach. For an ethnography of the process in action, see Aaron A. Fox, *Real Country: Music and Language in Working-Class Culture* (Durham, NC: Duke University Press, 2004).

11. Daniel J. Walkowitz, *City Folk: English Country Dance and the Politics of the Folk in Modern America* (New York: New York University Press, 2010), 4.

12. Gary Bushorn, interview with the author, February 17, 2014, Cincinnati, Ohio.

13. Tom Ewing, "Earl Taylor: One of the Bluegrass Greats," *Bluegrass Unlimited*, September 1976, 10.

14. For more on individual country music performers in Detroit, see Craig Maki and Keith Cady, *Detroit Country Music: Mountaineers, Cowboys, and Rockabillies* (Ann Arbor: University of Michigan Press, 2013).

15. Bushorn interview.

16. This work pattern would not have been uncommon for bands relying on club and bar venues for employment. Typically they would play every night of the week and afternoon or matinee shows on the weekends as well.

17. Neil V. Rosenberg, "Jimmy Martin: You Don't Know My Mind," in *The Bluegrass Reader*, ed. Thomas Goldsmith (Urbana: University of Illinois Press, 2004), 60.

18. Jimmy Martin played guitar and sang with Bill Monroe in the late 1940s and early 1950s. For more on Martin's career, see Tom Piazza, *True Adventures with the King of Bluegrass: Jimmy Martin* (Nashville: Vanderbilt University Press, 2009).

19. Liner notes to *Alan Lomax Presents Folk Songs from the Blue Grass*, Earl Taylor and the Stoney Mountain Boys (United Artists, 1959).

20. Band members also likely found a kindred spirit in the club owner, Stewart Salmons, who came to Cincinnati from West Virginia after World War II. See chapter 5, "Sing Me Back Home," for more on the Ken-Mill Café.

21. Wayne Clyburn, interview with the author, November 9, 2013, Union, Kentucky. The rumor is nonetheless telling about the overall nature of Salmons and the club in general as a cultural artifact of its time and place.

22. John P. Morgan, "Walter Hensley," *Bluegrass Unlimited*, March 1972, 19.

23. For other examples, see Tim Newby, *Bluegrass in Baltimore: The Hard Drivin' Sound and Its Legacy* (Jefferson, NC: McFarland, 2015).

24. Harry Sparks, interview with the author, March 5, 2014, Covington, Kentucky; emphasis mine.

25. See chapter 8, "Buckeyes in the Briar Patch."

26. Jeff Roberts, interview with the author, October 23, 2013, Park Hills, Kentucky.

27. Ibid.

28. Ibid.

29. Ibid.

30. Bruce E. Tucker, "Toward a New Ethnicity: Urban Appalachian Ethnic Consciousness in Cincinnati, 1950–87," in *Ethnic Diversity and Civic Identity: Patterns of Conflict and Cohesion in Cincinnati since 1820*, ed. Henry D. Shapiro and Jonathan D. Sarna (Urbana: University of Illinois Press, 1992), 235.

31. For an exploration of these ideas, see Bruce Schulman, *The Seventies: The Great Shift in American Culture, Society, and Politics* (New York: Free Press, 2001); and Douglas C. Rossinow, *The Politics of Authenticity* (New York: Columbia University Press, 1998).

32. See Ron Eller, *Uneven Ground: Appalachia since 1945* (Lexington: University Press of Kentucky, 2008), for a concise and general exploration of the postwar renewed interest in Appalachia. Of particular note is the Ford Foundation survey of the region in 1962, the growth of Appalachian studies organizations at regional universities, the creation of the Appalachian Regional Commission (ARC), the development of the Appalachian Volunteers (AVs), and a general renewed interest in what Eller terms "poverty knowledge."

33. Mike Maloney, interview with the author, April 23, 2013, Cincinnati, Ohio.

34. Ibid.

35. Thomas E. Wagner and Phillip J. Obermiller, *Valuing Our Past, Creating Our Future: The Founding of the Urban Appalachian Council* (Berea, KY: Berea College Press, 1999), 10.

36. This acceptance was not far removed from liberation theology, which developed nearly concurrently with this outreach in Cincinnati's urban core. The focus on outreach to the poor is especially relevant.

37. Maloney interview.

38. Ibid.

39. Ibid.

40. Wagner and Obermiller, *Valuing Our Past*, 33. Maloney highlighted the movement toward self-actualization in both populations, but his memory likely softened some of the racial animosity inherent in the tension between white Southern migrants (and white city residents more generally) and Black urban residents.

41. There was, of course, some irony in advocacy groups working to find authentic connections to mountain heritage while at the same time manufacturing and fostering a more acceptable version of that heritage.

42. Letter from Ernie Mynatt to Jeanne Powell, undated, folder 11, Archives and Rare Books, Blegen Library, Urban Appalachian Council Records, University of Cincinnati, Cincinnati, Ohio (hereafter, ARB, UAC).

43. A craft village was a key part of John Lair's Renfro Valley, Kentucky, complex, though Lair borrowed some of this from other popular notions about Appalachian authenticity. The equation of Appalachian people with handcrafted goods dates to at least the late nineteenth century and the Industrial Revolution. See Henry Shapiro, *Appalachia on Our Mind: The Southern Mountains and Mountaineers in the American Consciousness, 1870–1890* (Chapel Hill: University of North Carolina Press, 1978).

44. Program of Events, Appalachian Handcraft Exhibition, 1971, folder 14, ARB, UAC.

45. By the mid-1970s bluegrass festivals had become staples in nearly every state across the country and, by the end of the decade, even reached abroad into Japan, Canada, and Western Europe. These events, held mostly in bucolic rural settings, often embraced the rural Appalachian roots of the music as a key aspect of their appeal to audiences. The Appalachian Festival in Cincinnati mirrored a general shift in the way bluegrass music was being promoted and sold.

46. 1979 Appalachian Festival Program, UAC Collection, ARB, folder 18.

47. Mike Henson, interview with the author, December 13, 2013, Cincinnati, Ohio.

48. Ibid.

49. In addition, he wrote fictional works based on his experiences living and working in Over-the-Rhine during this time, drawing examples from the real-life people of the neighborhood. One family, headed by Roscoe Morgan, had a profound influence. "I started out as a folkie," he recalled, "and after I met Roscoe I wanted to play [bluegrass]." The Morgan family provided impetus for other cultural outreach efforts promoted by Cincinnati's Appalachian activists.

50. "Heritage Room Project Proposal: Washington Park Elementary School," box 12, folder 20, Southern Appalachian Archives (SAA), Hutchins Library, Berea College, UAC Collection. In particular, the group found the middle-class focus of typical public school curriculum lacking for the educational needs of the poor Appalachian population in the area. The authors recognized how "children who are subjected to name-calling (e.g., 'hillbilly') and ridicule have a lower self-concept." This in turn contributed to high dropout rates among the Appalachian population and a self-fulfilling prophecy of low achievement.

51. Heritage Room Project Proposal.

52. Henson interview.

53. Cultural Task Group Meeting Minutes, UAC, February 18, 1974, UAC Collection, ARB, folder 8.

54. Cultural Heritage Project Proposal—Heritage Room, October 21, 1976, SAA, UAC Files, box 12, folder 22; emphasis mine.

55. Dodie Murphy, "On the Banks of the Ohio with Katie Laur," *Pickin'* 4, no. 8, September 1977, 38.

56. Ibid.

57. Dave Banks, interview with John R. Williams, in "Appalachian Migrants in Cincinnati, Ohio: The Role of Folklore in the Reinforcement of Ethnic Identity," PhD diss., Indiana University, 1985, 207.

11. Distinctive Qualities of Southwestern Ohio Bluegrass

BEN KRAKAUER

Sounds of Dislocation

The mid-century advent of bluegrass music took place just in time to serve the needs of displaced Appalachian workers in southwestern Ohio. Like so many other genres of twentieth-century American popular music, bluegrass was an outgrowth of mass economic migration. Bill Monroe first assembled the bluegrass sound as an amalgamation of the influences of his Kentucky youth with those of his economic exile in the industrial Midwest. Monroe's eclectic sound, at once nostalgically in dialogue with the past while aggressively careening into the future, resonated with audiences throughout the country, especially those who found themselves similarly removed from their rural roots.

Many have noted the machine-like qualities of bluegrass music, including its fast tempos, its bright metallic tones, the highly choreographed stage movements of five performers weaving around a single microphone, and the complexities of its interlocking parts.[1] The vocal blend of the original Blue Grass Boys contained a particular tension that added to this mechanized drama. Robert Cantwell's description of bluegrass singing evokes a piece of machinery frantically churning at the verge of self-destruction: "Bluegrass harmonies are not choral; bluegrass harmony seeks to oppose, not to join, voices, not to blend but to fuse them. Everywhere there is friction or stridency, a kind of electrostatically charged field."[2] In addition, the instrumental layers fit together in an interlocking fashion, from the polarized boom-chick created between the bass and the guitar or mandolin strums to the additive rhythms of the banjo, which stack three-note sequences of eighth notes against the 4/4 and 3/4 time signatures.

This latter feature was refined by Earl Scruggs, who synthesized a variety of preexisting banjo styles into the now ubiquitous "Scruggs style" of picking.

Indeed, many bluegrass historians and participants mark the beginning of the bluegrass genre with Scruggs's joining Monroe's band. To music fans in the 1940s, Scruggs's approach to the instrument was a radically innovative and exciting sound and provided a key aspect of the high-tempo, competitive drama that played out between banjo, mandolin, and fiddle instrumental lines.

In the homes and barrooms of mid-century southwestern Ohio, bluegrass music resonated deeply with Appalachian economic migrants. It gestured toward the musical, religious, and moral traditions of their rural homes but also responded to the unrelenting pressures and intensities of their contemporary industrialized lives. When the rock and roll craze hit in the 1950s, bluegrass music was less than a decade old and was still a form of contemporary popular music that served the needs of a generation of young Appalachian workers finding their place in a rapidly changing world.

When these workers took to the barrooms in the evenings, their entertainment was a serious business. Like other migrant laborers before and after them, they were working hard to support themselves and to send money back to their families. A night in the barroom involved pleasure, expense, and the threat of unpredictable violence.[3] The musicians who played at these bars provided an important service and had to be very effective in doing so. They had to entertain, help the patrons release their tensions and anxieties, and provide a musical product that could compete with the other bands and jukeboxes in town.

In this southwestern Ohio context, a unique flavor of bluegrass music developed that matched the tension and intensity of workers' lives, delivering a tightly executed, high-pitched, and emotionally forceful blend that resonated with experiences of urban dislocation and factory life. As much as this style referenced the rural past, it also embraced technical innovations and idiosyncratic virtuosity, creating novel additions to the stylistic blueprint established by Monroe, Flatt and Scruggs, and the Stanley Brothers.

This chapter addresses five major musical contributions of artists who spent significant portions of their careers performing and recording in southwestern Ohio. First, I look at the legacy of Scruggs-style banjo playing as interpreted by banjo, mandolin, and guitar players working in the region. Second, I draw attention to a decentralization of the fiddle as an iconic ensemble instrument. Third, I discuss the prominence of the bluegrass vocal trio in southwestern Ohio, highlighting its connections to contemporary popular music and its continued prevalence in the bluegrass mainstream of future decades. Fourth, I discuss individual innovators of the region who set a precedent for the progressive bluegrass, "newgrass," "Dawg" music, and mainstream contemporary bluegrass of future generations. Finally, I discuss two prominent southwestern Ohio frontwomen who helped pave the way for women bandleaders in bluegrass.

The Legacy of Scruggs-Style Banjo in Southwestern Ohio

Of all bluegrass instrumental techniques, the most distinct, the most foundational to the genre, and the most widely emulated is Scruggs-style banjo playing. An early example is on Bill Monroe and His Blue Grass Boys' 1947 recording of "Will You Be Loving Another Man?" Scruggs's solo (1:29–1:44) features three-note sequences of eighth notes, which create dotted quarter-note rhythms on each of the separate strings he plucks while also outlining the melody. In the opening two measures, for example, Scruggs emphasizes phased, dotted-quarter rhythms on the second and fifth string (the third and first scale degrees, respectively). An important aspect of the technique is the evenly spaced staccato articulation of the notes.

It seems almost superfluous to describe Scruggs's technique in words, as it is so well known to bluegrass music listeners. Indeed, most bluegrass banjo players—including those in southwestern Ohio—draw heavily from Scruggs's technique, musical vocabulary, and rhythmic articulation. One thing that is striking about bluegrass in southwestern Ohio is the extent to which other instrumentalists, besides banjo players, adopted this musical approach.[4]

The brothers Jim and Jesse McReynolds, performers at the time at Middletown's *WPFB Jamboree*, first recorded in Cincinnati with Larry Roll as the Virginia Trio. On their 1951 recording of "I Like the Old Time Way," Jesse McReynolds uses a crosspicking technique to closely replicate the Scruggs-style sound on the mandolin. Through playing three-note sequences of eighth notes on separate strings in 4/4, he creates phased dotted-quarter-note rhythms on separate pairs of strings while also outlining the song's melody. Like Scruggs, he plays an evenly articulated passage of staccato notes that occupies the high range of the ensemble texture. On the 1952 Jim and Jesse recording "Are You Missing Me?" McReynolds's crosspicked mandolin solo (0:41–0:58) features an even more elaborate arpeggiation of chord and color tones across three pairs of strings, featuring the same even and staccato articulation and bright tone.[5]

Scruggs-style banjo playing in the southwestern Ohio region in many instances resembled Jesse McReynolds's high, clear mandolin sound. Scruggs's banjo tone, while certainly bright and metallic, also had a mid-range depth.[6] Many Ohio players favored an extremely taut banjo tone that accentuated high-frequency overtones, lending the instrument a more aggressive attack and putting it closer to the sonic range of Jesse McReynolds's mandolin. A great example of this tone can be heard in the 1954 Dave Woolum recording of "Single Girl, Married Girl," featuring Noah Crase on banjo. Crase's loud, bright metallic sound launches the performance with an incredible intensity and stays prominently audible in the mix behind the vocals, even after the banjo volume drops down. Another great example is the 1956 Jimmy Martin recording of "You'll Be a Lost Ball" with Sam "Porky" Hutchins on banjo. As Martin sings the first verse (0:37–0:51), Hutchins's up-the-neck banjo backup cuts through with crystal clarity, adding intensity to the sound without competing with Martin's volume or vocal range. A contrasting example of a similar effect is on the 1955 Hylo Brown recording "I'll Be Broken Hearted." In this down-tempo song, Jackie Phelps's banjo is clearly audible throughout due to its bright, piercing tone, a tonal quality it shares with the fiddle and mandolin on this recording.

I initially speculated that the preference for a bright metallic banjo tone may have been inspired by Jesse McReynolds's crosspicking mandolin rendition of Scruggs-style banjo. In talking with several people familiar with the music of southwestern Ohio, however, I didn't find any who supported that idea.[7] Instead, they attributed this tonal preference to the acoustic conditions of taverns where early artists performed. Playing over the noise of glasses, conversation, and barroom fights in a packed room with substandard amplification equipment would likely have encouraged musicians to adopt bright and piercing tones that would cut through the ambient din.[8] Indeed, an ensemble where all of the instrumentalists and vocalists could produce such cutting, distinctly audible sounds would have been very impressive in such an environment.

Not all banjo players in southwestern Ohio favored the taut, bright banjo tone. Both Sonny Osborne and J. D. Crowe produced a more resonant banjo tone and adapted a range of blues, honky-tonk, and rockabilly guitar vocabulary to the instrument. Osborne even played a six-string banjo in the 1970s and today continues to endorse a set of banjo strings that produce a mellower, fuller banjo tone because of the heavier gauge on the first and fifth strings.[9] Sonny Osborne's other stylistic contributions to bluegrass banjo playing are discussed below.

Several guitar players from the region also adapted the Scruggs-style sound to their instrument. Bill Napier and George Shuffler, using right-hand techniques similar to those of Jesse McReynolds, recorded crosspicked guitar solos on various Stanley Brothers recordings for King Records, despite Ralph and Carter Stanley's initial distaste for the sound.[10] Many of Shuffler's guitar leads were on gospel songs in 3/4 time, and in many of these recordings his crosspicked guitar replaces the banjo altogether. Such arrangements are in keeping with the bluegrass tradition of gospel songs without banjo but maintain the Scruggs-style rhythmic component by adapting it for guitar. On a later recording from the region, by Jack Lynch and the Miami Valley Boys (1968), Fred Spencer takes a spectacular crosspicked guitar lead on "Wildwood Flower" that is far more in the Scruggs vein than Maybelle Carter's influential lead-guitar arrangement of that song.

A Diminished Role for the Fiddle

The bright, even, staccato articulations of Scruggs-style banjo, as adapted by banjo, mandolin, and guitar players, strongly informed the instrumental approach to bluegrass in the southwestern Ohio region. The powerful, percussive sound generated by this approach certainly lends itself to the title of this book, *Industrial Strength Bluegrass*.

Although there were some good fiddlers in southwestern Ohio (notably Paul "Moon" Mullins), the bluegrass of the Cincinnati/Dayton area relied far less on the fiddle than was the case in other regional hotbeds for early bluegrass. Many bands and recordings in southwestern Ohio dispensed with the fiddle altogether. Fred Bartenstein has observed that bands without fiddles subsequently dominated East Coast and West Coast bluegrass of the 1960s and 1970s but that the idea of eliminating a once-essential instrument seems to have originated in the Cincinnati/Dayton scene of the early 1950s.[11]

In the early bluegrass music of Bill Monroe's Blue Grass Boys and the Stanley Brothers, the fiddle contributed lyrical phrasing, swing vocabulary, and old-time fiddle references. Monroe was often quoted as saying the fiddle was the central instrument in his music.[12] In a striking departure, the characteristic ensemble sound of southwestern Ohio is dominated by percussive, plucked-stringed instruments that overshadow the fiddle.[13]

Rosenberg provides an additional explanation for why the fiddle was not a prominent instrument in this region: "When bar owners would pay for only three musicians, the instruments abandoned were the bass, its rhythm taken by the guitar's bass strings, and the fiddle, its lead voice taken by the mandolin, which could also provide the percussive 'chop' that delineated the rhythmic structure of the music."[14] In personal correspondence Fred Bartenstein shared another perspective: "In pondering the diminution of the fiddle's role in southwestern Ohio, I note that it is the least 'mechanical' of the bluegrass instruments in both performance style and construction. People who work all day amid the clank and whir of punch presses, drills, and assembly lines might well be inspired by those mechanical rhythms and, consciously or unconsciously, reflect them in their arrangements and playing styles."[15]

The Vocal Trio in Southwestern Ohio

Another important contribution of southwestern Ohio bluegrass, also noted by Rosenberg, is the predominance of the vocal trio.[16] Bill Monroe, the Stanley Brothers, and Flatt and Scruggs did perform vocal trios but more often featured duets.[17] Recordings by artists whose careers began in southwestern Ohio—the

Osborne Brothers, Red Allen, Jim and Jesse, and Jimmy Martin—all featured powerful bluegrass trios that set the standard for future decades of bluegrass harmony vocals. The trio continued as the dominant vocal arrangement in progressive bluegrass and newgrass of the 1970s, neo-traditional bluegrass of the 1980s, and mainstream "mashgrass" of the 1990s, and it remains important today.[18]

The Virginia Trio's 1951 recording of the bluegrass gospel "God Put a Rainbow in the Clouds" features their characteristically sweet three-part singing style in one of the early southwestern Ohio bluegrass recordings. Jim McReynolds's mellifluous tenor voice, in particular, imparts a softer touch to their trio than those of earlier bluegrass recordings. Jim and Jesse's 1953 recording of "A Memory of You" features a similarly sweet vocal trio on a more straight-ahead bluegrass song. Their voices create an incredibly smooth vocal blend, coming across almost as one voice, with the baritone full and present and with the tenor nicely balanced rather than overshadowing the lower parts.

A contrasting vocal trio is featured on Jimmy Martin's 1956 "Hit Parade of Love." Here, the baritone is low in the mix, behind Martin's charismatic lead and Earl Taylor's piercing, powerful tenor. The intensity and timbrally differentiated sound of this vocal trio matches the aggressive, trebly, and slightly raucous energy of the instrumental ensemble, with its driving banjo and mandolin and Martin's assertive guitar runs. It is easy to imagine this exciting sound energizing a crowded after-hours barroom.

The vocal trios recorded by the Osborne Brothers and Red Allen between 1956 and 1958 split the difference between these two approaches. Their 1958 recording of "It Hurts to Know" features trio singing through both verse and chorus and includes a combination of elements discussed above: all three vocalists sing with powerful and cutting vocal timbres, but Bobby Osborne's tenor is balanced in a way that doesn't overshadow the other parts. This powerful but cohesive blend exemplifies an aesthetic found through much of the Osbornes' catalog, simultaneously in tune with the ethos of hardcore bluegrass and that of contemporary honky-tonk and rhythm and blues.

A pop aesthetic is also present in the Osborne Brothers and Red Allen's iconic 1957 recording of "Once More." The innovative vocal arrangement of this song places the lead in the highest voice.[19] High-lead vocal arrangements were very common in rhythm and blues music during the 1950s, and the arrangement of "Once More" gave the record a contemporary flavor. The pop aesthetic is reinforced by the use of heavy reverb, snare drum, and sentimental suspensions in the rubato ending. Both the song's arrangement and its production markedly separate it from the old-timey flavor of earlier bluegrass recordings.

One thing that sharply differentiates "Once More" from rhythm and blues, however, in addition to its instrumentation, is the hard nasal vowel sounds of the aahs during the chorus. Unlike the warmly resonant oohs and aahs of rhythm and blues, the distinctive vocal timbre in "Once More" aligns it with working-class white dialects featured in bluegrass and honky-tonk recordings of the time. This somewhat abrasive quality is also reflected in the trebly timbres of the banjo, the scraping attack of the mandolin tremolo, and the brassy resophonic guitar fills.

The Osborne Brothers' signature vocal trio style echoes pedal-steel guitar techniques introduced by Bud Isaacs on Webb Pierce's "Slowly" (1954), where two notes in a chord are held while another changes. Their other connections to then-contemporary country and western, rhythm and blues, and rock and roll anticipated the cross-genre excursions of newgrass and progressive bluegrass bands of the 1970s.[20] In addition, the Osbornes' recordings anticipated the adoption of contemporary country vocal timbres and production by mainstream bluegrass acts since the 1990s who, not incidentally, typically sing vocal trios.

Southwestern Ohio Banjo Innovations

Bluegrass musicians working in southwestern Ohio further set the stage for newgrass, progressive bluegrass, and contemporary mainstream bluegrass through their innovations of instrumental techniques. One of the most iconic innovations of the 1960s that influenced newgrass was the "melodic" style simultaneously developed by Bill Keith and Bobby Thompson. This technique enabled five-string banjo players to play linear melodic lines while keeping multiple strings simultaneously resonating, thus maintaining a ringing tone. According to Steve Arkin, Bill Keith got the idea for his version of the style by listening to southwestern Ohio–based banjo player Noah Crase's instrumental "Noah's Breakdown," recorded by Dave Woolum and Noah Crase in 1957.[21]

Crase plays several "melodic-style" passages in this recording. In the intro he plays a standard four-note Scruggs lick but then shifts the left-hand position to create a chromatic passage of the sort more commonly played on the banjo in 1970s newgrass contexts. Later, in the B part of the tune, he plays a passage alternating open first and fifth strings with other strings fretted at the fifth and seventh frets. This particular approach to fingering, which combines open strings with others fretted higher on the neck, is one of the most commonly used in melodic-style banjo; it allowed Keith to play fiddle tunes note-for-note on the banjo with a ringing, resonating tone.[22] Crase rarely gets credit for the development of this style.

One of the most celebrated and innovative musicians from the region is Sonny Osborne. Osborne produced a full and resonant banjo sound and adapted a diverse blues and honky-tonk vocabulary to the banjo.[23] He is also notable for use of the six-string banjo, eclectic original compositions, and double-banjo arrangements that appeared on many Osborne Brothers recordings.[24] In addition,

Osborne's approach to Scruggs-style playing has widely influenced subsequent generations of bluegrass banjo players.

One aspect of Sonny Osborne's style that is rarely emulated in mainstream bluegrass circles, however, is his eclectic and idiosyncratic spontaneity. Like Frank Wakefield on mandolin, some of Osborne's conspicuous banjo fills and licks function as commentary and punch line, rewarding the attention of listeners and occasionally drawing laughs.[25] The novel and humorous aspects of his musicianship were likely rewarded in the barrooms of southwestern Ohio, where these elements differentiated him from other instrumentalists. His eclecticism and experimental forays inspired budding newgrass banjo players in the 1960s and '70s.[26]

Modern Mandolin Styles Pioneered in Dayton

Just as Noah Crase paved the way for the melodic banjo style in newgrass, Bobby Osborne, Frank Wakefield, and Dorsey Harvey—all residents of Dayton in the early 1950s—established essential techniques for later generations of mandolin players. On the Osborne Brothers and Red Allen's 1956 recording of "My Aching Heart," Bobby Osborne plays a mandolin solo featuring linear passages of eighth notes where each note is a different pitch. This approach is closer to the virtuosic fiddle style of Kenny Baker, whom Osborne greatly admired, than to earlier bluegrass mandolin players. Osborne's approach to mandolin playing, with its linear eighth-note passages, not only influenced 1970s newgrass musicians but is still the norm in the bluegrass mainstream, as exemplified by Adam Steffey, Sam Bush, and others.

Another influential and innovative Ohio mandolin player was Frank Wakefield. His composition "New Camptown Races" first appeared in 1957 in a recording with Marvin Cobb. "New Camptown Races" features a greater variety of chords than previous bluegrass instrumentals, including the dominant II chord and the minor vi chord, and even modulates to a new tonal center at the beginning of the B part. Wakefield released another version of "New Camptown Races" with Red Allen in 1964, produced by future Dawg music pioneer David Grisman. Whereas the 1957 version modulates from B-flat major to G major in the B part, the 1964 version modulates to G minor. Interestingly, in both recordings Wakefield takes a solo where he plays the opposite tonality from the rest of the band, playing minor over the major chord in 1957 (0:15–0:17) and major over the minor chord in 1964 (1:29–1:32). This flamboyant inverted aesthetic is reflected in his jocular stage banter and appears on other musical recordings as well, such as his and Red Allen's 1963 recording of "Little Birdie." Here, Wakefield plays most of his solo (1:09–1:24) using a D modal pentatonic scale (D E G A C) over the D major tonality of the song.[27] Wakefield uses this same modal pentatonic scale over a more "appropriate" tonality in his 1964 recording of "Little Maggie" with Red Allen. Wakefield's "Little Maggie" solo is also striking for its structure, which emphasizes the fourth intervals found throughout the pentatonic scale. Elsewhere, however, Wakefield plays very much in the vein of Bill Monroe, including his 1957 intro to "New Camptown Races," which is a paraphrase of the solo mandolin introduction to Monroe's 1955 "Roanoke." With both his reverence for Bill Monroe and his comically flamboyant musical gestures, Wakefield anticipated some of the aesthetics of the 1970s experimental bluegrass of New York City.[28]

A lesser-known Ohio mandolin innovator was Dorsey Harvey, who, like Wakefield, employed an eclectic approach that drew heavily from Bill Monroe's mandolin sound. Harvey and Wakefield spent much time together developing alternatives to the Monroe technique.[29] Harvey's 1977 LP included "Teco Teco," a bluegrass-ified interpretation of Zequinha de Abreu's composition "Tico-Tico no Fubá." Harvey's record came out the same year as the David Grisman Quintet's debut album of Dawg music, with both records drawing inspiration from Brazilian mandolin sources.[30]

As previously discussed, Jesse McReynolds's innovative mandolin crosspicking approach was premiered in his Ohio recordings. Unlike Bobby Osborne's mandolin playing, which many have emulated, and Frank Wakefield's playing, which cast a huge influence on the innovations of David Grisman, McReynolds's playing is widely admired but rarely accurately replicated, due to his challenging and idiosyncratic right-hand technique.[31]

King Records, a Catalyst for Flat-Picked Lead Guitar

Syd Nathan, the founder and owner of King Records, was an early proponent of bluegrass lead guitar and encouraged the flat-picking of Don Reno, Bill Napier, and George Shuffler.[32] All three heavily influenced Doc Watson and Clarence White, who in turn set the standard for later bluegrass lead guitarists.[33] George Shuffler played a particularly striking role in many Stanley Brothers recordings, at times emulating the banjo with his crosspicked lead (as on 1962's "Harbor of Love") and at other times replicating a mandolin tremolo intro (as on 1962's "When He Reached Down His Hand for Me"). On Moore and Napier's 1966 "Don't Wait Too Long," Bill Napier produced a full and sweet guitar tone with slightly swung phrasing, much like Doc Watson in subsequent years.

Larry Sparks is a later influential flat-picking guitarist whose early recordings with Ralph Stanley were also on the King label. Sparks grew up in the 1950s and early '60s, exposed to the rich array of bluegrass, country, rhythm and blues, and rock and roll on the region's radio stations. These varied influences are reflected in his lead and rhythm playing, which parallel in many ways approaches that Clarence White was popularizing in California. They also show up in his performance kinesthetics, including the "gyrating body motions" that Gary Reid notes in his profile of Sparks for the Bluegrass Music Hall of Fame and Museum.[34] Sparks's stunning lead guitar is featured on his 1967 recording of "It's Never Too Late"; his solo (1:36–1:54) included a variety of gorgeous suspensions and chord inversions, all phrased with an impeccable blues-oriented timing.

In addition to their innovative lead guitar playing, many of the Ohio guitarists were exceptionally strong rhythm players. Examples include Jimmy Martin on the 1956 "Hit Parade of Love," Red Allen on Allen and Wakefield's 1963 "Beautiful Blue Eyes," and Jim McCall on his 1967 "Ain't Nobody Gonna Miss Me When I'm Gone" with Earl Taylor.[35]

Women in Southwestern Ohio Bluegrass

Murphy Henry, Liza Sapir Flood, Jordan Laney, and others have written and spoken about the erasure of women in canonical bluegrass histories.[36] While male musicians from southwestern Ohio received the majority of professional opportunities and historical renown, there were a number of important women bluegrass musicians active in the region.

Lillimae Whitaker and Katie Laur are particularly notable as frontwomen of their respective groups, Lillimae and the Dixie Gospel-Aires and the Katie Laur Band.[37] A strong example of Lillimae's warm and powerful tenor voice is on the Dixie Gospel-Aires's 1971 recording of "I'm Going to Make Heaven My Home," where she helps to create a relaxed, Stanley-esque harmony blend without any of the strain often created by male tenor singers. In contrast to Lillimae's traditional sound, Katie Laur's 1975 debut album, *Good Time Girl*, features an eclectic variety of songs, with outstanding singing and playing throughout. Laur's vocals on "You Are My Flower" particularly stand out with a lyricism and light vibrato unusual in bluegrass. "Driving Back to Tennessee," from the same album, has a classic 1970s newgrass sound, featuring a flat seventh chord and a modulation to the relative minor. This album, along with Laur's other work, was part of a wave through the 1970s and 1980s that established a more prominent place for women in bluegrass, often at the helm of newgrass and progressive bands.

* * *

Bluegrass in mid-century southwestern Ohio was born out of economic displacement. It served the needs of migrants who existed at a crossroads between an industrial present and the unrecoverable rural past.[38] While the music referenced sounds, values, and narratives of their Appalachian origins, it was also a clear articulation of their current hardscrabble lives. Forged in urban experience, the virtuosic distinctiveness of this region's music yielded notable and lasting innovations in modern bluegrass.

Notes

1. Bluegrass as machine-like was a recurring theme in personal correspondence with Fred Bartenstein, Ira Gitlin, Joe Mullins, Ron Thomason, and others. It is also featured prominently in Rachel Liebling's 1992 film, *High Lonesome: The Story of Bluegrass*.

2. Robert Cantwell, *Bluegrass Breakdown: The Making of the Old Southern Sound* (Urbana: University of Illinois Press, 1984), 212. Elsewhere, Cantwell writes, "Bluegrass singing . . . is at the very least venturesome; at most it is ardent, daring, angry, reckless, desperate, or wild. . . . It seems sometimes almost as if the powerfully expansive sound might blow the singer's head apart" (76).

3. See chapter 5, "Sing Me Back Home."

4. Flatt and Scruggs's resonator guitar player, Josh Graves, notably adopted this technique for his instrument. Unlike the mandolin and guitar players discussed here, Graves was aided by his use of an open tuning and a three-finger picking technique.

5. One thing that differentiates McReynolds's technique and rhythmic micro-phrasing from subsequent generations of mandolin crosspickers is his unusual down-down-up and up-up-down right-hand picking patterns.

6. For an example of the mid-range depth of Scruggs's tone, listen to Flatt and Scruggs's 1950 "I'll Never Shed Another Tear."

7. Thanks to Fred Bartenstein, Ron Thomason, and Joe Mullins, in particular, for sharing their memories and insight.

8. Jon Weisberger, "Earl Taylor and Jim McCall," in *The Bluegrass Reader*, ed. Thomas Goldsmith (Urbana: University of Illinois Press, 2004), 127.

9. The Sonny Osborne Signature Set of banjo strings by GHS is marketed as "Medium Light," although the first and fifth strings are heavier than those of a medium set.

10. Jon Hartley Fox, *King of the Queen City: The Story of King Records* (Urbana: University of Illinois Press, 2009), 137.

11. Fred Bartenstein email, December 16, 2019. Fiddles did return to most bluegrass bands in later decades.

12. For example, "I've used fiddle music in my music, you know, 'cause I think the fiddle is the king instrument in string music. I've used that fiddle all the way, with banjo, mandolin, guitar, and bass—it gives me what I want in the way of instruments in bluegrass." From Charles Wolfe, "Bluegrass Touches—An Interview with Bill Monroe," originally published in the *Nashville Banner*, July 30, 1975, and included in Tom Ewing, ed., *The Bill Monroe Reader* (Urbana: University of Illinois Press, 2000), 80.

13. In Joe Isaacs's 1969 recording of "Why Have You Left Me?" guest fiddler Richard Greene, in an apparent nod to the percussive strings aesthetic, emulates the unisons and half-step dissonances of mandolin double stop and the chromatic up-the-neck banjo backup during his solo (0:34–0:49).

14. This was before Richard Greene's advent of the fiddle "chop." See Laura Risk, "The Chop: The Diffusion of an Instrumental Technique across North Atlantic Fiddling Traditions," in *Ethnomusicology* 57, no. 3 (2013): 428–54.

15. Fred Bartenstein email, October 2, 2019.

16. For the influence of the Osbornes' trio singing on the Country Gentlemen in the

DC area, see Neil V. Rosenberg, *Bluegrass: A History* (1985; Urbana: University of Illinois Press, 2005), 159–60.

17. Fred Bartenstein email, October 2, 2019.

18. "Mashgrass" is a term that has become increasingly common to describe the crisply orchestrated, compressed, and highly produced sound associated with 1990s recordings by bands like the Lonesome River Band, IIIrd Tyme Out, and Mountain Heart. A characteristic feature of the style is downbeat strums at key structural points by the guitar, often syncing with emphases by the banjo.

19. See chapters 2 and 5. See also Rosenberg, *Bluegrass: A History*, 155–56.

20. Mexican and Tejano genres were also reflected in Sonny Osborne's 1970 banjo instrumental "Siempre."

21. Steve Arkin, "Banjo Playing: Reno, Thompson, Scruggs, Keith Style and Beyond," *Pickin'* 1, October 1974, 12–17.

22. Ibid.

23. For an example of this blues and honky-tonk vocabulary, listen to Osborne's backup playing on the 1957 recording of "Two Lonely Hearts" by the Osborne Brothers and Red Allen.

24. For an example of an original Sonny Osborne composition featuring six-string banjo, see the Osborne Brothers' 1974 "Side Saddle." For examples of double banjo, see the 1956 recordings of "Ho Honey Ho" and "Ruby, Are You Mad?" by the Osborne Brothers and Red Allen, and the MGM album *Bluegrass Instrumentals* (1962) by the Osborne Brothers.

25. This is similar to the aesthetic of the experimental bluegrass of 1970s New York City. In a telephone interview on November 4, 2015, bassist Roger Mason said that in the New York band Breakfast Special, "every solo is a sophisticated joke with a punch line." See Benjamin Krakauer, "A 'Traditional' Music Scene and its Fringes: Experimental Bluegrass of 1970s New York City," *American Music* 36, no. 2 (2018): 174.

26. Marty Cutler, telephone interview, October 28, 2019. Cutler said that he and Tony Trischka were particularly inspired by Osborne's collaboration with jazz vibraphonist Gary Burton on Burton's 1967 album *Tennessee Firebird*. It is easy to see the title track from that album as a precursor to many of Cutler's and Trischka's bold musical endeavors in the following decades.

27. Thanks to Jody Stecher for bringing this solo to my attention.

28. See Krakauer, "'Traditional' Music Scene," 163–93.

29. In "Listen Here—Frank Wakefield" by Glenn Weiser, *Metroland*, November 11, 2010, Wakefield quotes Bill Monroe's advice: "Boy, now you play my own style about as good as me. Now what you got to do is play your own style."

30. David Grisman reissued Jacob do Bandolim's recordings of Brazilian choro music for mandolin on his Acoustic Disc label in 1991 and 1994. The David Grisman Quintet recorded "Tico Tico" in 1995.

31. Some of the few, notable practitioners of McReynolds's crosspicking style are Jordan Ramsey, Tristan Scroggins, Luke Shamblin, Herschel Sizemore, and Andy Statman.

32. Fox, *King of the Queen City*, 135.

33. Fred Bartenstein email, September 28, 2019. Earlier lead guitarists in bluegrass—

notably Earl Scruggs, Charlie Cline, and Joe Stuart—all played in a three-finger rather than flat-picking style.

34. Bluegrass Music Hall of Fame and Museum, "Hall of Fame Inductees," Larry Sparks, https://www.bluegrasshall.org/inductees/larry-sparks.

35. Another example of strong rhythm guitar playing, recorded by Earl Taylor and the Stoney Mountain Boys just before they moved to Ohio, is their 1959 "They're at Rest Together." Sam "Porky" Hutchins's guitar playing and Walter Hensley's outstanding banjo playing meld together exceptionally well, rising and falling together between vocal phrases and raising the volume and excitement level during the banjo solo (0:35–0:53). Hutchins's guitar playing similarly complements Hensley's melody-centered and minimalist banjo solo (1:07–1:23) on "Short Life of Trouble" from the same recording.

36. See Murphy Henry, *Pretty Good for a Girl: Women in Bluegrass* (Urbana: University of Illinois Press, 2013). Liza Sapir Flood and Jordan Laney both presented papers that addressed different dimensions of this issue at a bluegrass roundtable at the 2019 Society for Ethnomusicology annual meeting (at which the author was a co-participant). See also Liza Sapir Flood, "Instrument in Tow: Bringing Musical Skills to the Field," in *Ethnomusicology* 61 (2017): 486–505; and Liza Sapir Flood, "'Now We'll Have the Women Play': Class and Gender in Amateur Country Music Performance," PhD diss., University of Virginia, 2017.

37. On Lillimae and the Dixie Gospel-Aires, see chapter 6, "Using My Bible for a Roadmap." On the Katie Laur Band, see chapter 8, "Buckeyes in the Briar Patch."

38. Contextualizing the sounds of mid-century southwestern Ohio bluegrass leaves us with the question of how *contemporary* bluegrass articulates the needs and identities of listeners in post-revival twenty-first-century settings. To what extent does bluegrass continue to serve the needs of the present, and to what extent does it do so through evocations of the past? As southwestern Ohio remains a site of ongoing migration and economic change, the bluegrass in the region will no doubt reflect these conditions.

APPENDIX A
Recommended Southwestern Ohio Bluegrass Recordings

Compiled by Mac McDivitt, with assistance from Fred Bartenstein and Joe Mullins

1948	Jimmie Skinner	"Doin' My Time"
1950	Lonesome Pine Fiddlers (with Bobby Osborne and Larry Richardson)	"Pain in My Heart"
1951	Joe "Cannonball" Lewis	"Before I Met You"
1951	Jimmy Martin & Bob Osborne	"Blue Eyed Darling"
1951	Lou & Sonny Osborne	"New Freedom Bell"
1951	Virginia Trio (Jim & Jesse McReynolds and Larry Roll)	"On the Jericho Road"
1951	Smokey Ward (with Jim & Jesse McReynolds and Fairley Holden)	"Dog Bite Yo' Hide" / "Doin' My Time"
1952	Jim & Jesse	"Are You Missing Me?"
1953	Sonny Osborne	"Sunny Mountain Chimes"
1954	Red Allen	"Paul and Silas"
1954	Hylo Brown	"Lost to a Stranger"
1954	Jimmy Martin & the Osborne Bros.	"Twenty-Twenty Vision"
1954	Dave Woolum & Noah Crase	"Single Girl, Married Girl"
1956	Country Pardners	"Another Old Dog in the Race"
1956	Jimmy Martin	"Hit Parade of Love"
1956	Osborne Brothers & Red Allen	"Ruby, Are You Mad?"
1956	Glenn & Vivian Watson	"I Don't Believe You've Met My Baby"
1957	Osborne Brothers & Red Allen	"Once More"

1957	Frank Wakefield & Marvin Cobb	"New Camptown Races"
1957	Dave Woolum & Noah Crase	"Noah's Breakdown"
1959	Osborne Brothers	"Sweethearts Again"
1959	Red Heads (Red Allen, Red Spurlock, Frank Wakefield)	"Love and Wealth"
1961	John & Frances Reedy	"Oh Death"
1962	Bluegrass Playboys (Paul Mullins, lead vocal)	"Katie Daly"
1962	Jay Johnson & Earl Taylor	"Crazy Blues on My Mind"
1964	Jack Lynch & the Lee Brothers	"Will You Miss Me?"
1964	Osborne Brothers	"Pathway of Teardrops"
1965	Jim McCall & Benny Birchfield	"Haunted House"
1966	Erwin Keith (Larry Sparks, lead guitar)	"Between the Lines"
1966	Paul Mullins & the Backwoods Boys	"How I Miss My Darling Mother"
1966	Red Spurlock & the Powell Brothers	"Loneliness"
1967	J. D. Jarvis	"Take Your Shoes Off, Moses"
1967	Kentuckians (New Boston, OH)	"The Mountains Are Calling"
1967	Valley Ramblers	"Can't You Hear Me Calling?"
1968	Kentucky Mountain Boys (Red Allen, lead vocal)	"You're Not Easy to Forget"
1968	Earl Taylor & Jim McCall	"Ain't Nobody Gonna Miss Me When I'm Gone"
1969	Gene Higgins	"My Daddy Don't Come Home"
1969	Ralph Stanley (Larry Sparks, lead vocal; Jimmi Stanley, cowriter)	"I Only Exist"
1970	Larry Sparks	"Ramblin' Guitar"
1972	Allen Brothers (Neal Allen, lead vocal)	"She's Country"
1973	Allen Brothers (Harley Allen, lead vocal)	"Singer"
1973	Jim McCall & Vernon McIntyre	"Rock Salt and Nails"
1974	Boys from Indiana	"Atlanta Is Burning"
1975	Hotmud Family (Suzanne Thomas, lead vocal)	"Teardrops Falling in the Snow"
1975	Katie Laur	"T for Texas"
1975	Larry Sparks	"A Face in the Crowd"
1975	Ron Thomason	"Gotta Quit Kickin' My Dog Around"
1976	Allen Brothers (Harley Allen, lead vocal)	"Wildwood Flower Blues"

1976	Boys from Indiana	"West Virginia Rain"
1976	Bill Lowe	"You've Been a Friend of Mine"
1977	Dorsey Harvey (David Harvey, second mandolin)	"Lead Out"
1977	Katie Laur	"It Rains Just the Same in Missouri"
1978	Country Grass	"The Fields Have Turned Brown"
1978	Larry Sparks	"John Deere Tractor"
1979	Dave Evans	"Highway 52"
1980	Jewell Mountain Grass (Clarence Kelly, lead vocal)	"Mountain Laurel"
1980	Mike Lilly (John Cox, lead vocal)	"Somebody Loves You, Darling"
1980	Marcum Brothers	"Who Will Sing for Me?"
1980	Wilson Brothers	"Lonesome Old Home"
1980	Wilson Brothers	"The Stanleys Will Sing Again"
1981	Dave Evans	"One Loaf of Bread"
1986	Larry Sparks	"Blue Virginia Blues"

APPENDIX B

For Further Reading

Appalachia and Appalachian Migration

Berry, Chad. *Southern Migrants, Northern Exiles*. Urbana: University of Illinois Press, 2000.

Berry, Chad, Phillip J. Obermiller, and Shaunna L. Scott, eds. *Studying Appalachian Studies: Making the Path by Walking*. Urbana: University of Illinois Press, 2015.

Eller, Ron. *Miners, Millhands, and Mountaineers: Industrialization of the Appalachian South, 1880–1930*. Knoxville: University of Tennessee Press, 1982.

———. *Uneven Ground: Appalachia since 1945*. Lexington: University Press of Kentucky, 2008.

Gregory, James N. *American Exodus: The Dust Bowl Migration and Okie Culture in California*. Oxford: Oxford University Press, 1991.

———. *The Southern Diaspora: How the Great Migrations of Black and White Southerners Transformed America*. Chapel Hill: University of North Carolina Press, 2005.

Kirby, Jack Temple. *Rural Worlds Lost: The American South, 1920–1960*. Baton Rouge: Louisiana State University Press, 1987.

Obermiller, Phillip J., and Thomas E. Wagner, eds. *African American Miners and Migrants: The Eastern Kentucky Social Club*. Urbana: University of Illinois Press, 2004.

Obermiller, Phillip J., Thomas E. Wagner, and E. Bruce Tucker, eds. *Appalachian Odyssey: Historical Perspectives on the Great Migration*. Westport, CT: Praeger, 2000.

Shapiro, Henry. *Appalachia on Our Mind: The Southern Mountains and Mountaineers in the American Consciousness, 1870–1890*. Chapel Hill: University of North Carolina Press, 1978.

Straw, Richard A., and H. Tyler Blethen, eds. *High Mountains Rising: Appalachia in Time and Place*. Urbana: University of Illinois Press, 2004.

Whisnant, David. *All That Is Native and Fine: The Politics of Culture in an American Region*. Chapel Hill: University of North Carolina Press, 2009.

Williams, John Alexander. *Appalachia: A History*. Chapel Hill: University of North Carolina Press, 2002.

Williams, Michael Ann. *Staging Tradition: John Lair and Sarah Gertrude Knott*. Urbana: University of Illinois Press, 2006.

The Southwestern Ohio Region

Banks, Dave. "Appalachian Migrants in Cincinnati, Ohio: The Role of Folklore in the Reinforcement of Ethnic Identity." PhD diss., Indiana University, 1985.

Bartenstein, Fred, and Patricia N. Edwards. *A Report on Appalachians in Dayton, Ohio*. Cincinnati: Ohio Urban Appalachian Awareness Project, 1978.

Shapiro, Henry D., and Jonathan D. Sarna, eds. *Ethnic Diversity and Civic Identity: Patterns of Conflict and Cohesion in Cincinnati since 1820*. Urbana: University of Illinois Press, 1992.

Urban Appalachian Council. *Perceptions of Home: The Urban Appalachian Spirit*. Cincinnati: Urban Appalachian Council, 1996.

Wagner, Thomas E., and Phillip J. Obermiller. *Valuing Our Past, Creating Our Future: The Founding of the Urban Appalachian Council*. Berea, KY: Berea College Press, 1999.

Williams, John R. "Appalachian Migrants in Cincinnati, Ohio: The Role of Folklore in the Reinforcement of Ethnic Identity." PhD diss., Indiana University, 1985.

Bluegrass, Country, and Gospel Music and Musicians

Bartenstein, Fred. "Bluegrass Vocals." Unpublished paper. *Bartenstein & Bluegrass*, 2010. http://www.fredbartenstein.com/bgvocals.html.

———. "Noah Crase: It's Not Easy Done." *Bluegrass Unlimited*, June 1985, 48–51; and July 1985, 23–28.

———, ed. *Roots Music in America: Collected Writings of Joe Wilson*. Knoxville: University of Tennessee Press, 2017.

Bartenstein, Fred, Gary Reid, et al. *The Bluegrass Hall of Fame: Inductee Biographies 1991–2014*. Louisville, KY: Holland Brown Books, 2014.

Bear Family Records. Liner notes to compilation box sets of recordings by Hylo Brown, Flatt and Scruggs, Jim and Jesse, Jimmy Martin, Bill Monroe, the Osborne Brothers, and Jimmie Skinner.

Bill Monroe: Father of Bluegrass Music. Gebhardt, Steve, and Larry Nager, writers and coproducers. 1999; MVDvisual, 2008, DVD.

Bluegrass Music Hall of Fame and Museum Oral History Project. Video oral histories of Carlos Brock, Noah Crase, J. D. Crowe, Josh Graves, Walter Hensley, Aubrey Holt, Jerry Holt, Tom Holt, Katie Laur, Jimmy Martin, Jim McCall, Jesse McReynolds, Paul Mullins, Bobby Osborne, Sonny Osborne, Earl Scruggs, George Shuffler, Larry Sparks, Art Stamper, Ralph Stanley, Billy Thomas, and Frank Wakefield. Louie B. Nunn Center for Oral History, University of Kentucky, Lexington (some available online); all can be viewed at Bluegrass Music Hall of Fame and Museum, Owensboro, KY.

Cantwell, Robert. *Bluegrass Breakdown: The Making of the Old Southern Sound*. New York: Da Capo Press, 1992 (originally Urbana: University of Illinois Press, 1984).

Claypool, James C. *Images of America: Kentucky's Bluegrass Music*. Charleston, SC: Arcadia Publishing, 2009.

Daniel, Wayne. "Making a Joyful Noise unto the Lord The Gospel Roots of Bluegrass." In *Bluegrass and Old Time Country Music: Buried Roots of Early Days*. Special edition of *International Country Music Journal* (Winter 2016): 47–56. Nashville: Brackish Publishing, 2016.

Davidson, Donald. *The Big Ballad Jamboree: A Novel*. Afterword by Curtis W. Ellison and William Pratt. Jackson: University Press of Mississippi, 1996.

Delmore, Alton. *Truth Is Stranger Than Publicity*. Nashville: Country Music Foundation Press, 1995.

Ellison, Curtis W. "Circuit Rider of the Past: Ralph Stanley & the Appalachian Diaspora." *International Country Music Journal* (2016): 143–62. Nashville: Brackish Publishing, 2016.

———. *Country Music Culture: From Hard Times to Heaven*. Jackson: University Press of Mississippi, 1995.

Ely, Macel, II. *Ain't No Grave: The Life and Legacy of Brother Claude Ely*. Atlanta: Dust to Digital Records, 2010.

Ewing, Tom. *Bill Monroe: The Life and Music of the Blue Grass Man*. Urbana: University of Illinois Press, 2018.

———. *The Bill Monroe Reader*. Urbana: University of Illinois Press, 2000.

———. "Earl Taylor: One of the Bluegrass Greats." *Bluegrass Unlimited*, September 1976: 10–14.

Fleischhauer, Carl, and Neil V. Rosenberg. *Bluegrass Odyssey: A Documentary in Pictures and Words*. Urbana: University of Illinois Press, 2001.

Fox, Aaron A. *Real Country: Music and Language in Working-Class Culture*. Durham, NC: Duke University Press, 2004.

Godbey, Marty. *Crowe on the Banjo: The Music Life of J. D. Crowe*. Urbana: University of Illinois Press, 2011.

Goldsmith, Thomas, ed. *The Bluegrass Reader*. Urbana: University of Illinois Press, 2004.

———. *Earl Scruggs and Foggy Mountain Breakdown: The Making of an American Classic*. Urbana: University of Illinois Press, 2019.

Graves, Josh. *Bluegrass Bluesman: A Memoir*. Ed. Fred Bartenstein. Urbana: University of Illinois Press, 2012.

Gusto Records. Liner notes (mostly written by Gary Reid) to compilation box sets of recordings by Reno and Smiley, the Stanley Brothers, *The Best of King and Starday Bluegrass*.

Henry, Murphy Hicks. *Pretty Good for a Girl: Women in Bluegrass*. Urbana: University of Illinois Press, 2013.

High Lonesome—The Story of Bluegrass Music. Rachel Liebling, writer and director. 1994; Newton, NJ, Shanachie Entertainment, 1999, DVD.

Isaacs, Lily. *You Don't Cry Out Loud: The Lily Isaacs Story*. Green Forest, AR: New Leaf Press, 2014.

Johnson, David W. *Lonesome Melodies: The Lives and Music of the Stanley Brothers*. Jackson: University Press of Mississippi, 2013.

Jones, Louis M. "Grandpa," and Charles K. Wolfe. *Everybody's Grandpa: Fifty Years behind the Mike*. Knoxville: University of Tennessee Press, 1984.

Jones, Loyal. *Country Music Humorists and Comedians*. Urbana: University of Illinois Press, 2008.

Kehrberg, Kevin Donald. "I'll Fly Away: The Music and Career of Albert E. Brumley." PhD diss., University of Kentucky, 2010.

Laur, Katie. "Letter from Home: Long Time Gone." *Cincinnati Magazine,* April 2012. https://www.cincinnatimagazine.com/letter-from-katie/letter-from-katie-long-time-gone1/.

Leach, Robert. "Carlos Brock." *Bluegrass Unlimited*, April 2000, 70–76.

———. "Mike Lilly." *Bluegrass Unlimited*, November 1986, 36–39.

Lomax, Alan. "Bluegrass Underground: Folk Music with Overdrive." *Esquire*, October 1959, 108.

Lornell, Kip. *Capital Bluegrass: Hillbilly Music Meets Washington, DC*. New York: Oxford University Press, 2020.

Maki, Craig, and Keith Cady. *Detroit Country Music: Mountaineers, Cowboys, and Rockabillies*. Ann Arbor: University of Michigan Press, 2013.

Malone, Bill C., and Tracey E. W. Laird. *Country Music USA*. 1968; Austin: University of Texas Press, 2018.

McDivitt, Mac, and Fred Bartenstein, eds. *Cincinnati-Dayton Ohio Bluegrass Heritage: Bluegrass Music, Musicians, Artists, Clubs, Organizations of the Miami Valley in Ohio*. swohiobluegrass.com.

McGee, Nathan. "Sounds Like Home: Bluegrass Music and Appalachian Migration in American Cities, 1945–1980." PhD diss., University of Cincinnati, 2016.

McNeil, W. K., ed. *Encyclopedia of American Gospel Music*. New York: Routledge, 2005.

Murphy, Dodie. "On the Banks of the Ohio with Katie Laur." *Pickin'*, September 1977, 36–40.

Newby, Tim. *Bluegrass in Baltimore: The Hard Drivin' Sound and Its Legacy*. Jefferson, NC: McFarland, 2015.

Nowlin, Bill. *The Early Days of Bluegrass*. Cambridge, MA: Rounder Books, 2019.

Peterson, Richard A. *Creating Country Music: Fabricating Authenticity*. Chicago: University of Chicago Press, 1997.

Piazza, Tom. *True Adventures with the King of Bluegrass: Jimmy Martin*. Nashville: Vanderbilt University Press, 2009.

Rebel Records. Liner notes to compilation box sets of recordings by Ralph Stanley and *35 Years of the Best in Bluegrass*.

Reid, Gary B. *The Music of the Stanley Brothers*. Urbana: University of Illinois Press, 2015.

Rooney, James. *Bossmen: Bill Monroe and Muddy Waters*. New York: Dial Press, 1971.

Rosenberg, Neil V. *Bluegrass: A History*. 1985; Urbana: University of Illinois Press, 2005.

———. *Bluegrass Generation: A Memoir*. Urbana: University of Illinois Press, 2018.

———, ed. *Transforming Tradition: Folk Music Revivals Examined*. Urbana: University of Illinois Press, 1993.

Rosenberg, Neil V., and Charles K. Wolfe. *The Music of Bill Monroe*. Urbana: University of Illinois Press, 2007.

"Rusty York, Bluegrass Meets Rockabilly." *Rockabilly Hall of Fame*. http://www.rockabillyhall.com/RustyYork1.html.
Satterlee, Dennis. "Keep on Going: The Unknown Red Allen Recording." *Bluegrass Unlimited*, June 2016, 42–43.
———. *Teardrops in My Eyes: The Music of Harley "Red" Allen*. Kensington, MD: Plucked String Foundation, 2007.
Skaggs, Ricky, with Eddie Dean. *Kentucky Traveler: My Life in Music*. New York: HarperCollins, 2013.
Smith, Richard D. *Bluegrass: An Informal Guide*. Chicago: a cappella books/Chicago Review Press, 1995.
———. *Can't You Hear Me Callin': The Life of Bill Monroe, Father of Bluegrass*. Boston: Little, Brown, 2000.
Stanley, Ralph, with Eddie Dean. *Man of Constant Sorrow: My Life and Times*. New York: Gotham Books, 2009.
Stern, Richard C. "Bluegrass Gospel: The Music of Exiles." In *International Country Music Journal*, ed. Don Cusic, 51–76. Nashville: Brackish Publishing, 2013.
Stimeling, Travis D., ed. *The Country Music Reader*. New York: Oxford University Press, 2014.
———. *The Oxford Handbook of Country Music*. New York: Oxford University Press, 2017.
Tribe, Ivan M. *Folk Music in Overdrive: A Primer of Traditional Country and Bluegrass Artists*. Knoxville: University of Tennessee Press, 2018.
Walkowitz, Daniel J. *City Folk: English Country Dance and the Politics of the Folk in Modern America*. New York: New York University Press, 2010.
Willis, Barry R. *America's Music: Bluegrass*. Franktown, CO: Pine Valley Music, 1989.
Wolfe, Charles K. *Classic Country: Legends of Country Music*. New York: Routledge, 2001.
———. "The Hotmud Family: An Interview," *Pickin'*, November 1976, 6–8.
Wright, John. *Traveling the Highway Home: Ralph Stanley and the World of Traditional Bluegrass Music*. Urbana: University of Illinois Press, 1993.

Radio and Television

Friedman, Jim. *Images of America: Cincinnati Television*. Charleston, SC: Arcadia Publishing, 2007.
Godbey, Frank, and Marty Godbey. "Paul Mullins: Musician, Disc Jockey, and Bluegrass Influence." *Bluegrass Unlimited*, December 1975, 20–25.
Martini, Michael A. *Images of America: Cincinnati Radio*. Charleston, SC: Arcadia Publishing, 2011.
Mosser, Kurt. "Fred Bartenstein: The Right Place at the Right Time." *Bluegrass Unlimited*, May 1999, 26–34.
Perry, Dick. *Not Just a Sound: The Story of WLW*. Englewood Cliffs, NJ: Prentice Hall, 1971.
Stamper, Pete. *It All Happened in Renfro Valley*. Lexington: University Press of Kentucky, 1999.
Stuart, Chris. "Fred Bartenstein: Bringing Us All Together." *Bluegrass Unlimited*, February 2006, 30–34.

Record Companies, Recording Studios, and Record Stores

Broven, John. *Record Makers and Breakers: Voices of the Independent Rock 'n' Roll Pioneers*. Urbana: University of Illinois Press, 2010.

Burkhardt, Carl. Liner notes to *The Early Recordings of Jim and Jesse McReynolds with Larry Roll*. Gateway Records, 1978.

DeClark, Dan. "45 RPM Records of the Ohio River Valley." http://www.45rpmrecords.com.

Escott, Colin. Booklet notes to *Rusty* [York] *Rocks*. Bear Family Records, 2004.

Fox, Jon Hartley. *King of the Queen City: The Story of King Records*. 2009; Urbana: University of Illinois Press, 2014.

Gibson, Nathan D., with Don Pierce. *The Starday Story: The House That Country Music Built*. Jackson: University Press of Mississippi, 2011.

Kennedy, Rick, and Randy McNutt. *Little Labels—Big Sound*. Bloomington: Indiana University Press, 1999.

McNutt, Randy. *King Records of Cincinnati*. Charleston, SC: Arcadia Publishing, 2009.

———. *Too Hot to Handle: An Illustrated Encyclopedia of American Recording Studios of the Twentieth Century*. Hamilton, OH: HHP Books, 2001.

Millard, Andre. *America on Record: A History of Recorded Sound*. Cambridge: Cambridge University Press, 1995.

Powers, Brian F. X. *A King Records Scrapbook*. Cincinnati: Terra Incognita Press, 2008.

———. "Herzog Recording Studios—E. T. Herzog Recording Co." https://myspace.com/herzogrecordingstudios/photos.

Reid, Gary B. *The Best of King and Starday Bluegrass*. Nashville: King Records Box Set, 2004.

Tribe, Ivan. "Jimmie Skinner: Country Singer, Bluegrass Composer, Record Retailer." *Bluegrass Unlimited*, March 1977, 34–37.

Companion Album

Various Artists. *Industrial Strength Bluegrass: Southwestern Ohio's Musical Legacy*. Smithsonian Folkways, SFW 40238. March 2021, CD.

Contributors

FRED BARTENSTEIN is a native of Virginia and a Social Studies graduate of Harvard College. An adjunct instructor in the University of Dayton's Department of Music, he teaches courses on the history of country and bluegrass music. His many roles in those fields have included magazine editor, broadcaster, musician, festival emcee, talent director, and scholar. In his previous professional life, he managed his own organizational consulting firm, the Foundation for Appalachian Ohio, Books & Co., the Dayton Foundation, and the Victoria Theatre Association. He is coauthor of *The Bluegrass Hall of Fame* (Holland Brown, 2014) and editor of *Josh Graves: Bluegrass Bluesman* (University of Illinois Press, 2012), *Roots Music in America: Collected Writings of Joe Wilson* (University of Tennessee Press, 2017), and *Lucky Joe's Namesake: The Extraordinary Life and Observations of Joe Wilson* (University of Tennessee Press, 2017).

CURTIS W. ELLISON is Emeritus Professor of History and American Studies, Miami University. A North Alabama native and a graduate of the University of Alabama and University of Minnesota, he taught American Studies, African American Literature, Interdisciplinary Studies, University History, and Appalachian Cultures and Music at Miami University. His administrative roles included head of Miami Regionals Appalachian Studies, director of the Michael J. Colligan History Project, director of the William Holmes McGuffey Museum, dean of Interdisciplinary Studies, interim dean of Education and Allied Professions, and interim dean of Fine Arts. He published *Miami University, 1809–2009: Bicentennial Perspectives* (ed., Ohio University Press, 2009), *Country Music Culture: From Hard Times to Heaven* (University Press of Mississippi, 1996), Donald Davidson's *The Big Ballad Jamboree* (coeditor, University Press of Mississippi, 1996), two studies of nineteenth-century African American writers (coauthor, G. K. Hall), and has edited many local history works.

JON HARTLEY FOX is a Dayton, Ohio, native who resides in Grass Valley, California. He has written about music and the arts for more than forty years and won two writing awards for album annotation from the International Bluegrass Music Association. He wrote, produced, and narrated "King of the Queen City: The Story of King Records," a series of sixty-minute documentaries for National Public Radio in the 1980s, and is the author of *King of the Queen City: The Story of King Records* (University of Illinois Press, 2009, 2014). His King Records book was awarded a 2010 Certificate of Merit by the Association for Recorded Sound Collections (ARSC) for Best Research in Record Labels.

RICK GOOD is a founding member of the Hotmud Family and a twenty-four-year veteran of Rhythm in Shoes. With a half-century career as a musician, actor, writer, educator, and advocate for America's musical roots, he is respected for his driving banjo, swinging guitar, heartfelt singing, and crafty songwriting. The Ohio Arts Council presented him with the 2010 Ohio Heritage Fellowship in honor of lifelong achievements that have had a lasting positive impact on the excellence, vitality, and public appreciation of folk and traditional arts in Ohio.

LILY ISAACS was born in Germany to Polish Jewish Holocaust survivors, grew up in the Bronx, studied theater in New York, performed off Broadway, and recorded a Columbia folk album in 1968. She became a Christian in 1971 following a death in the family. Soon after, she and Kentucky-born bluegrass artist Joe Isaacs began singing gospel music. The Isaacs are an award-winning family group who blend tight family harmony with acoustic instrumentation influenced by bluegrass, rhythm-and-blues, folk, country, contemporary, acoustic, and Southern gospel traditions. They perform at the Grand Ole Opry, Gaither Homecoming concerts, and abroad, and have received several Grammy nominations.

BEN KRAKAUER is a banjo player, composer, and ethnomusicologist who writes about South Asian music and bluegrass and performs original music at the intersection of bluegrass and jazz. He has published articles in *Ethnomusicology*, *Asian Music*, and *American Music*; recorded for Acoustic Disc, CMH Records, and the Fiddle Masters series; and toured with David Grisman. His 2019 debut solo album, *Heart Lake*, includes twelve original compositions with playful, interactive, and distinctive textures. He holds a PhD in ethnomusicology from the University of Texas at Austin and is Professor of Music at Warren Wilson College.

RUSSELL "MAC" McDIVITT was born in Preble County, Ohio, and has lived in the Dayton area his entire life. A graduate of Miami University, he worked for the Internal Revenue Service for over three decades. He was a part-time disc jockey at WCTM and WCTM-FM in Eaton, Ohio, and later a frequent guest on the WYSO *Country Ramble* in Yellow Springs. For most of his life he has followed and collected country and bluegrass music of southwestern Ohio. He helps preserve that music as principal author of the online regional encyclopedia *Cincinnati-Dayton Ohio Bluegrass Heritage: Bluegrass Music, Musicians, Artists, Clubs, Organizations of the Miami Valley in Ohio*. In 2015 that site profiled 342 individuals and 252 organizations at swohiobluegrass.com.

NATHAN McGEE is a member of the faculty at the International School on the Rhine, Neuss, Germany. A Cincinnati native who holds a 2016 doctorate in American History from the University of Cincinnati, his dissertation, "Sounds Like Home: Bluegrass Music and Appalachian Migration in American Cities, 1945–1980," explores the critical role of bluegrass music in forming urban Appalachian community identity in cities such as Baltimore, Washington, Dayton, and Cincinnati. He has been a member of Cincinnati's Over-the-Rhine Museum Board, a historical tour guide for Queen City History, and held the University of Cincinnati History Department's Zane Miller Fellowship for Research in American Cities.

DANIEL MULLINS is an American Studies graduate of Cedarville University and works in many areas of the bluegrass community. His journalism appears in *Bluegrass Unlimited*, *Singing News Magazine*, *Bluegrass Today*, and *The Bluegrass Situation*. In 2016 he received the Best Liner Notes award from the International Bluegrass Music Association for contributions to the Traditional Grass album *The Blues Are Still the Blues* and has been a multiple nominee for International Bluegrass Music Association Print Media Person of the Year. He hosts *The Daniel Mullins Midday Music Spectacular* weekdays on the Real Roots Radio network.

JOE MULLINS has been a southwestern Ohio banjo artist and broadcaster for more than three decades. He owns the Real Roots Radio network and heads the award-winning band Joe Mullins and the Radio Ramblers, who regularly guest on the Grand Ole Opry, the National Folk Festival, and Bluegrass Underground. A founding member of the Traditional Grass, he earned IBMA Song of the Year and Recorded Event of the Year awards with the group Longview, and has received IBMA awards for Entertainer of the Year, Instrumental Recording of the Year, Album of the Year, Gospel Song of the Year, and Broadcaster of the Year. He hosts a syndicated radio show and is past board chair and president of the International Bluegrass Music Association.

LARRY NAGER wrote *Memphis Beat: The Lives and Times of America's Musical Crossroads* (St. Martin's Press, 1998), wrote and coproduced the documentary *Bill Monroe: Father of Bluegrass Music* (1999), and was music editor for *The Memphis Commercial Appeal*. In 2017 he was writer and musical director for *Havana Time Machine*, a PBS Great Performances production filmed in Cuba. While music editor for the *Cincinnati Post* and the *Cincinnati Enquirer*, he played from 1974 to 1991 with Ohio Heritage Fellows Tony Ellis and Katie Laur as well as Dayton bluegrass greats Red Allen and the Allen-Lilly Band. He plays on Smithsonian Folkways' *Classic Bluegrass Vol. 1* and has performed at the Kennedy Center and the Library of Congress.

PHILLIP J. OBERMILLER is a member of the Cincinnati Urban Appalachian Community Coalition, a visiting scholar in the School of Planning at the University of Cincinnati, and a research fellow at the University of Kentucky Appalachian Center. A former president of the Appalachian Studies Association, he has published twenty book chapters and numerous articles. He coedited *Appalachian Odyssey: Historical Perspectives on the Great Migration* (Praeger, 2000) and coauthored *African American Miners and Migrants: The Eastern Kentucky Social Club* (University of Illinois Press, 2004) and *Studying Appalachian Studies: Making the Path by Walking* (University of Illinois Press, 2015), which won the Weatherford Award for the best book on Appalachia published that year.

BOBBY OSBORNE is a vocalist and mandolin artist. A native of Hyden, Kentucky, he grew up near Dayton, Ohio, cofounded the Osborne Brothers, leads the Rocky Top X-Press, and has been a member of the Grand Ole Opry for more than fifty years. The Osborne Brothers' numerous awards include Country Music Association Vocal Group of the Year, *Music City News* Number One Bluegrass Group for eight years, SPBGMA Male Vocalist of the Year, IBMA Instrumental Album of the Year and Recorded Event of the Year, and Uncle Dave Macon Days Heritage Award. A member of the Kentucky Music Hall of Fame, he is a two-time member of the International Bluegrass Hall of Fame, with the Osborne Brothers and with the Lonesome Pine Fiddlers.

NEIL V. ROSENBERG is Professor Emeritus, Department of Folklore, Memorial University of Newfoundland. From 1968 to 2004 he taught vernacular music traditions, interactions of popular music with local and regional music traditions, and processes of cultural revival. A performing musician since childhood, he employs skills and experiences in bluegrass, country, folk, jazz, classical, and experimental music. His *Bluegrass: A History* (University of Illinois Press, 1985) was reprinted as a Twentieth Anniversary Edition in 2005. Other works, all published by the University of Illinois Press, include *Transforming Tradition* (ed., 1993), *Bluegrass Odyssey: A Documentary in Pictures and Words* (2001) with photographer Carl Fleischhauer, *The Music of Bill Monroe* (2007) with Charles K. Wolfe, and *Bluegrass Generation: A Memoir* (2018). In 1981 he originated the column "Thirty Years Ago This Month" that ran for twelve years in *Bluegrass Unlimited*, and he has written numerous liner notes. A Fellow of the American Folklore Society, he received the Marius Barbeau Medal for lifetime achievement from the Folklore Studies Association of Canada and is the only Canadian member of the Bluegrass Music Hall of Fame.

Index

Page numbers in *italics* refer to photographs; letter following page number indicates page of photo section.

MUSIC IN AMERICAN LIFE

Only a Miner: Studies in Recorded Coal-Mining Songs *Archie Green*
Great Day Coming: Folk Music and the American Left *R. Serge Denisoff*
John Philip Sousa: A Descriptive Catalog of His Works *Paul E. Bierley*
The Hell-Bound Train: A Cowboy Songbook *Glenn Ohrlin*
Oh, Didn't He Ramble: The Life Story of Lee Collins, as Told to Mary Collins *Edited by Frank J. Gillis and John W. Miner*
American Labor Songs of the Nineteenth Century *Philip S. Foner*
Stars of Country Music: Uncle Dave Macon to Johnny Rodriguez *Edited by Bill C. Malone and Judith McCulloh*
Git Along, Little Dogies: Songs and Songmakers of the American West *John I. White*
A Texas-Mexican *Cancionero*: Folksongs of the Lower Border *Américo Paredes*
San Antonio Rose: The Life and Music of Bob Wills *Charles R. Townsend*
Early Downhome Blues: A Musical and Cultural Analysis *Jeff Todd Titon*
An Ives Celebration: Papers and Panels of the Charles Ives Centennial Festival-Conference *Edited by H. Wiley Hitchcock and Vivian Perlis*
Sinful Tunes and Spirituals: Black Folk Music to the Civil War *Dena J. Epstein*
Joe Scott, the Woodsman-Songmaker *Edward D. Ives*
Jimmie Rodgers: The Life and Times of America's Blue Yodeler *Nolan Porterfield*
Early American Music Engraving and Printing: A History of Music Publishing in America from 1787 to 1825, with Commentary on Earlier and Later Practices *Richard J. Wolfe*
Sing a Sad Song: The Life of Hank Williams *Roger M. Williams*
Long Steel Rail: The Railroad in American Folksong *Norm Cohen*
Resources of American Music History: A Directory of Source Materials from Colonial Times to World War II *D. W. Krummel, Jean Geil, Doris J. Dyen, and Deane L. Root*
Tenement Songs: The Popular Music of the Jewish Immigrants *Mark Slobin*
Ozark Folksongs *Vance Randolph; edited and abridged by Norm Cohen*
Oscar Sonneck and American Music *Edited by William Lichtenwanger*
Bluegrass Breakdown: The Making of the Old Southern Sound *Robert Cantwell*
Bluegrass: A History *Neil V. Rosenberg*
Music at the White House: A History of the American Spirit *Elise K. Kirk*
Red River Blues: The Blues Tradition in the Southeast *Bruce Bastin*
Good Friends and Bad Enemies: Robert Winslow Gordon and the Study of American Folksong *Debora Kodish*
Fiddlin' Georgia Crazy: Fiddlin' John Carson, His Real World, and the World of His Songs *Gene Wiggins*
America's Music: From the Pilgrims to the Present (rev. 3d ed.) *Gilbert Chase*
Secular Music in Colonial Annapolis: The Tuesday Club, 1745–56 *John Barry Talley*
Bibliographical Handbook of American Music *D. W. Krummel*
Goin' to Kansas City *Nathan W. Pearson Jr.*
"Susanna," "Jeanie," and "The Old Folks at Home": The Songs of Stephen C. Foster from His Time to Ours (2d ed.) *William W. Austin*

Songprints: The Musical Experience of Five Shoshone Women *Judith Vander*
"Happy in the Service of the Lord": Afro-American Gospel Quartets in Memphis *Kip Lornell*
Paul Hindemith in the United States *Luther Noss*
"My Song Is My Weapon": People's Songs, American Communism, and the Politics of Culture, 1930–50 *Robbie Lieberman*
Chosen Voices: The Story of the American Cantorate *Mark Slobin*
Theodore Thomas: America's Conductor and Builder of Orchestras, 1835–1905 *Ezra Schabas*
"The Whorehouse Bells Were Ringing" and Other Songs Cowboys Sing *Collected and Edited by Guy Logsdon*
Crazeology: The Autobiography of a Chicago Jazzman *Bud Freeman, as Told to Robert Wolf*
Discoursing Sweet Music: Brass Bands and Community Life in Turn-of-the-Century Pennsylvania *Kenneth Kreitner*
Mormonism and Music: A History *Michael Hicks*
Voices of the Jazz Age: Profiles of Eight Vintage Jazzmen *Chip Deffaa*
Pickin' on Peachtree: A History of Country Music in Atlanta, Georgia *Wayne W. Daniel*
Bitter Music: Collected Journals, Essays, Introductions, and Librettos *Harry Partch; edited by Thomas McGeary*
Ethnic Music on Records: A Discography of Ethnic Recordings Produced in the United States, 1893 to 1942 *Richard K. Spottswood*
Downhome Blues Lyrics: An Anthology from the Post–World War II Era *Jeff Todd Titon*
Ellington: The Early Years *Mark Tucker*
Chicago Soul *Robert Pruter*
That Half-Barbaric Twang: The Banjo in American Popular Culture *Karen Linn*
Hot Man: The Life of Art Hodes *Art Hodes and Chadwick Hansen*
The Erotic Muse: American Bawdy Songs (2d ed.) *Ed Cray*
Barrio Rhythm: Mexican American Music in Los Angeles *Steven Loza*
The Creation of Jazz: Music, Race, and Culture in Urban America *Burton W. Peretti*
Charles Martin Loeffler: A Life Apart in Music *Ellen Knight*
Club Date Musicians: Playing the New York Party Circuit *Bruce A. MacLeod*
Opera on the Road: Traveling Opera Troupes in the United States, 1825–60 *Katherine K. Preston*
The Stonemans: An Appalachian Family and the Music That Shaped Their Lives *Ivan M. Tribe*
Transforming Tradition: Folk Music Revivals Examined *Edited by Neil V. Rosenberg*
The Crooked Stovepipe: Athapaskan Fiddle Music and Square Dancing in Northeast Alaska and Northwest Canada *Craig Mishler*
Traveling the High Way Home: Ralph Stanley and the World of Traditional Bluegrass Music *John Wright*
Carl Ruggles: Composer, Painter, and Storyteller *Marilyn Ziffrin*

Never without a Song: The Years and Songs of Jennie Devlin, 1865–1952 *Katharine D. Newman*

The Hank Snow Story *Hank Snow, with Jack Ownbey and Bob Burris*

Milton Brown and the Founding of Western Swing *Cary Ginell, with special assistance from Roy Lee Brown*

Santiago de Murcia's "Códice Saldívar No. 4": A Treasury of Secular Guitar Music from Baroque Mexico *Craig H. Russell*

The Sound of the Dove: Singing in Appalachian Primitive Baptist Churches *Beverly Bush Patterson*

Heartland Excursions: Ethnomusicological Reflections on Schools of Music *Bruno Nettl*

Doowop: The Chicago Scene *Robert Pruter*

Blue Rhythms: Six Lives in Rhythm and Blues *Chip Deffaa*

Shoshone Ghost Dance Religion: Poetry Songs and Great Basin Context *Judith Vander*

Go Cat Go! Rockabilly Music and Its Makers *Craig Morrison*

'Twas Only an Irishman's Dream: The Image of Ireland and the Irish in American Popular Song Lyrics, 1800–1920 *William H. A. Williams*

Democracy at the Opera: Music, Theater, and Culture in New York City, 1815–60 *Karen Ahlquist*

Fred Waring and the Pennsylvanians *Virginia Waring*

Woody, Cisco, and Me: Seamen Three in the Merchant Marine *Jim Longhi*

Behind the Burnt Cork Mask: Early Blackface Minstrelsy and Antebellum American Popular Culture *William J. Mahar*

Going to Cincinnati: A History of the Blues in the Queen City *Steven C. Tracy*

Pistol Packin' Mama: Aunt Molly Jackson and the Politics of Folksong *Shelly Romalis*

Sixties Rock: Garage, Psychedelic, and Other Satisfactions *Michael Hicks*

The Late Great Johnny Ace and the Transition from R&B to Rock 'n' Roll *James M. Salem*

Tito Puente and the Making of Latin Music *Steven Loza*

Juilliard: A History *Andrea Olmstead*

Understanding Charles Seeger, Pioneer in American Musicology *Edited by Bell Yung and Helen Rees*

Mountains of Music: West Virginia Traditional Music from *Goldenseal* *Edited by John Lilly*

Alice Tully: An Intimate Portrait *Albert Fuller*

A Blues Life *Henry Townsend, as told to Bill Greensmith*

Long Steel Rail: The Railroad in American Folksong (2d ed.) *Norm Cohen*

The Golden Age of Gospel *Text by Horace Clarence Boyer; photography by Lloyd Yearwood*

Aaron Copland: The Life and Work of an Uncommon Man *Howard Pollack*

Louis Moreau Gottschalk *S. Frederick Starr*

Race, Rock, and Elvis *Michael T. Bertrand*

Theremin: Ether Music and Espionage *Albert Glinsky*
Poetry and Violence: The Ballad Tradition of Mexico's Costa Chica *John H. McDowell*
The Bill Monroe Reader *Edited by Tom Ewing*
Music in Lubavitcher Life *Ellen Koskoff*
Zarzuela: Spanish Operetta, American Stage *Janet L. Sturman*
Bluegrass Odyssey: A Documentary in Pictures and Words, 1966–86 *Carl Fleischhauer and Neil V. Rosenberg*
That Old-Time Rock & Roll: A Chronicle of an Era, 1954–63 *Richard Aquila*
Labor's Troubadour *Joe Glazer*
American Opera *Elise K. Kirk*
Don't Get above Your Raisin': Country Music and the Southern Working Class *Bill C. Malone*
John Alden Carpenter: A Chicago Composer *Howard Pollack*
Heartbeat of the People: Music and Dance of the Northern Pow-wow *Tara Browner*
My Lord, What a Morning: An Autobiography *Marian Anderson*
Marian Anderson: A Singer's Journey *Allan Keiler*
Charles Ives Remembered: An Oral History *Vivian Perlis*
Henry Cowell, Bohemian *Michael Hicks*
Rap Music and Street Consciousness *Cheryl L. Keyes*
Louis Prima *Garry Boulard*
Marian McPartland's Jazz World: All in Good Time *Marian McPartland*
Robert Johnson: Lost and Found *Barry Lee Pearson and Bill McCulloch*
Bound for America: Three British Composers *Nicholas Temperley*
Lost Sounds: Blacks and the Birth of the Recording Industry, 1890–1919 *Tim Brooks*
Burn, Baby! BURN! The Autobiography of Magnificent Montague *Magnificent Montague with Bob Baker*
Way Up North in Dixie: A Black Family's Claim to the Confederate Anthem *Howard L. Sacks and Judith Rose Sacks*
The Bluegrass Reader *Edited by Thomas Goldsmith*
Colin McPhee: Composer in Two Worlds *Carol J. Oja*
Robert Johnson, Mythmaking, and Contemporary American Culture *Patricia R. Schroeder*
Composing a World: Lou Harrison, Musical Wayfarer *Leta E. Miller and Fredric Lieberman*
Fritz Reiner, Maestro and Martinet *Kenneth Morgan*
That Toddlin' Town: Chicago's White Dance Bands and Orchestras, 1900–1950 *Charles A. Sengstock Jr.*
Dewey and Elvis: The Life and Times of a Rock 'n' Roll Deejay *Louis Cantor*
Come Hither to Go Yonder: Playing Bluegrass with Bill Monroe *Bob Black*
Chicago Blues: Portraits and Stories *David Whiteis*
The Incredible Band of John Philip Sousa *Paul E. Bierley*
"Maximum Clarity" and Other Writings on Music *Ben Johnston, edited by Bob Gilmore*

Staging Tradition: John Lair and Sarah Gertrude Knott *Michael Ann Williams*
Homegrown Music: Discovering Bluegrass *Stephanie P. Ledgin*
Tales of a Theatrical Guru *Danny Newman*
The Music of Bill Monroe *Neil V. Rosenberg and Charles K. Wolfe*
Pressing On: The Roni Stoneman Story *Roni Stoneman, as told to Ellen Wright*
Together Let Us Sweetly Live *Jonathan C. David, with photographs by Richard Holloway*
Live Fast, Love Hard: The Faron Young Story *Diane Diekman*
Air Castle of the South: WSM Radio and the Making of Music City *Craig P. Havighurst*
Traveling Home: Sacred Harp Singing and American Pluralism *Kiri Miller*
Where Did Our Love Go? The Rise and Fall of the Motown Sound *Nelson George*
Lonesome Cowgirls and Honky-Tonk Angels: The Women of Barn Dance Radio *Kristine M. McCusker*
California Polyphony: Ethnic Voices, Musical Crossroads *Mina Yang*
The Never-Ending Revival: Rounder Records and the Folk Alliance *Michael F. Scully*
Sing It Pretty: A Memoir *Bess Lomax Hawes*
Working Girl Blues: The Life and Music of Hazel Dickens *Hazel Dickens and Bill C. Malone*
Charles Ives Reconsidered *Gayle Sherwood Magee*
The Hayloft Gang: The Story of the National Barn Dance *Edited by Chad Berry*
Country Music Humorists and Comedians *Loyal Jones*
Record Makers and Breakers: Voices of the Independent Rock 'n' Roll Pioneers *John Broven*
Music of the First Nations: Tradition and Innovation in Native North America *Edited by Tara Browner*
Cafe Society: The Wrong Place for the Right People *Barney Josephson, with Terry Trilling-Josephson*
George Gershwin: An Intimate Portrait *Walter Rimler*
Life Flows On in Endless Song: Folk Songs and American History *Robert V. Wells*
I Feel a Song Coming On: The Life of Jimmy McHugh *Alyn Shipton*
King of the Queen City: The Story of King Records *Jon Hartley Fox*
Long Lost Blues: Popular Blues in America, 1850–1920 *Peter C. Muir*
Hard Luck Blues: Roots Music Photographs from the Great Depression *Rich Remsberg*
Restless Giant: The Life and Times of Jean Aberbach and Hill and Range Songs *Bar Biszick-Lockwood*
Champagne Charlie and Pretty Jemima: Variety Theater in the Nineteenth Century *Gillian M. Rodger*
Sacred Steel: Inside an African American Steel Guitar Tradition *Robert L. Stone*
Gone to the Country: The New Lost City Ramblers and the Folk Music Revival *Ray Allen*
The Makers of the Sacred Harp *David Warren Steel with Richard H. Hulan*

Woody Guthrie, American Radical *Will Kaufman*
George Szell: A Life of Music *Michael Charry*
Bean Blossom: The Brown County Jamboree and Bill Monroe's Bluegrass Festivals *Thomas A. Adler*
Crowe on the Banjo: The Music Life of J. D. Crowe *Marty Godbey*
Twentieth Century Drifter: The Life of Marty Robbins *Diane Diekman*
Henry Mancini: Reinventing Film Music *John Caps*
The Beautiful Music All Around Us: Field Recordings and the American Experience *Stephen Wade*
Then Sings My Soul: The Culture of Southern Gospel Music *Douglas Harrison*
The Accordion in the Americas: Klezmer, Polka, Tango, Zydeco, and More! *Edited by Helena Simonett*
Bluegrass Bluesman: A Memoir *Josh Graves, edited by Fred Bartenstein*
One Woman in a Hundred: Edna Phillips and the Philadelphia Orchestra *Mary Sue Welsh*
The Great Orchestrator: Arthur Judson and American Arts Management *James M. Doering*
Charles Ives in the Mirror: American Histories of an Iconic Composer *David C. Paul*
Southern Soul-Blues *David Whiteis*
Sweet Air: Modernism, Regionalism, and American Popular Song *Edward P. Comentale*
Pretty Good for a Girl: Women in Bluegrass *Murphy Hicks Henry*
Sweet Dreams: The World of Patsy Cline *Warren R. Hofstra*
William Sidney Mount and the Creolization of American Culture *Christopher J. Smith*
Bird: The Life and Music of Charlie Parker *Chuck Haddix*
Making the March King: John Philip Sousa's Washington Years, 1854–1893 *Patrick Warfield*
In It for the Long Run *Jim Rooney*
Pioneers of the Blues Revival *Steve Cushing*
Roots of the Revival: American and British Folk Music in the 1950s *Ronald D. Cohen and Rachel Clare Donaldson*
Blues All Day Long: The Jimmy Rogers Story *Wayne Everett Goins*
Yankee Twang: Country and Western Music in New England *Clifford R. Murphy*
The Music of the Stanley Brothers *Gary B. Reid*
Hawaiian Music in Motion: Mariners, Missionaries, and Minstrels *James Revell Carr*
Sounds of the New Deal: The Federal Music Project in the West *Peter Gough*
The Mormon Tabernacle Choir: A Biography *Michael Hicks*
The Man That Got Away: The Life and Songs of Harold Arlen *Walter Rimler*
A City Called Heaven: Chicago and the Birth of Gospel Music *Robert M. Marovich*
Blues Unlimited: Essential Interviews from the Original Blues Magazine *Edited by Bill Greensmith, Mike Rowe, and Mark Camarigg*

Hoedowns, Reels, and Frolics: Roots and Branches of Southern Appalachian Dance *Phil Jamison*
Fannie Bloomfield-Zeisler: The Life and Times of a Piano Virtuoso *Beth Abelson Macleod*
Cybersonic Arts: Adventures in American New Music *Gordon Mumma, edited with commentary by Michelle Fillion*
The Magic of Beverly Sills *Nancy Guy*
Waiting for Buddy Guy *Alan Harper*
Harry T. Burleigh: From the Spiritual to the Harlem Renaissance *Jean E. Snyder*
Music in the Age of Anxiety: American Music in the Fifties *James Wierzbicki*
Jazzing: New York City's Unseen Scene *Thomas H. Greenland*
A Cole Porter Companion *Edited by Don M. Randel, Matthew Shaftel, and Susan Forscher Weiss*
Foggy Mountain Troubadour: The Life and Music of Curly Seckler *Penny Parsons*
Blue Rhythm Fantasy: Big Band Jazz Arranging in the Swing Era *John Wriggle*
Bill Clifton: America's Bluegrass Ambassador to the World *Bill C. Malone*
Chinatown Opera Theater in North America *Nancy Yunhwa Rao*
The Elocutionists: Women, Music, and the Spoken Word *Marian Wilson Kimber*
May Irwin: Singing, Shouting, and the Shadow of Minstrelsy *Sharon Ammen*
Peggy Seeger: A Life of Music, Love, and Politics *Jean R. Freedman*
Charles Ives's *Concord*: Essays after a Sonata *Kyle Gann*
Don't Give Your Heart to a Rambler: My Life with Jimmy Martin, the King of Bluegrass *Barbara Martin Stephens*
Libby Larsen: Composing an American Life *Denise Von Glahn*
George Szell's Reign: Behind the Scenes with the Cleveland Orchestra *Marcia Hansen Kraus*
Just One of the Boys: Female-to-Male Cross-Dressing on the American Variety Stage *Gillian M. Rodger*
Spirituals and the Birth of a Black Entertainment Industry *Sandra Jean Graham*
Right to the Juke Joint: A Personal History of American Music *Patrick B. Mullen*
Bluegrass Generation: A Memoir *Neil V. Rosenberg*
Pioneers of the Blues Revival, Expanded Second Edition *Steve Cushing*
Banjo Roots and Branches *Edited by Robert Winans*
Bill Monroe: The Life and Music of the Blue Grass Man *Tom Ewing*
Dixie Dewdrop: The Uncle Dave Macon Story *Michael D. Doubler*
Los Romeros: Royal Family of the Spanish Guitar *Walter Aaron Clark*
Transforming Women's Education: Liberal Arts and Music in Female Seminaries *Jewel A. Smith*
Rethinking American Music *Edited by Tara Browner and Thomas L. Riis*
Leonard Bernstein and the Language of Jazz *Katherine Baber*
Dancing Revolution: Bodies, Space, and Sound in American Cultural History *Christopher J. Smith*
Peggy Glanville-Hicks: Composer and Critic *Suzanne Robinson*
Mormons, Musical Theater, and Belonging in America *Jake Johnson*

Blues Legacy: Tradition and Innovation in Chicago *David Whiteis*
Blues Before Sunrise 2: Interviews from the Chicago Scene *Steve Cushing*
The Cashaway Psalmody: Transatlantic Religion and Music in Colonial Carolina *Stephen A. Marini*
Earl Scruggs and Foggy Mountain Breakdown: The Making of an American Classic *Thomas Goldsmith*
A Guru's Journey: Pandit Chitresh Das and Indian Classical Dance in Diaspora *Sarah Morelli*
Unsettled Scores: Politics, Hollywood, and the Film Music of Aaron Copland and Hanns Eisler *Sally Bick*
Hillbilly Maidens, Okies, and Cowgirls: Women's Country Music, 1930–1960 *Stephanie Vander Wel*
Always the Queen: The Denise LaSalle Story *Denise LaSalle with David Whiteis*
Artful Noise: Percussion Literature in the Twentieth Century *Thomas Siwe*
The Heart of a Woman: The Life and Music of Florence B. Price *Rae Linda Brown, edited by Guthrie P. Ramsey Jr.*
When Sunday Comes: Gospel Music in the Soul and Hip-Hop Eras *Claudrena N. Harold*
The Lady Swings: Memoirs of a Jazz Drummer *Dottie Dodgion and Wayne Enstice*
Industrial Strength Bluegrass: Southwestern Ohio's Musical Legacy *Edited by Fred Bartenstein and Curtis W. Ellison*

The University of Illinois Press
is a founding member of the
Association of University Presses.

University of Illinois Press
1325 South Oak Street
Champaign, IL 61820-6903
www.press.uillinois.edu